"The evidence before us shows that:
Increasing numbers of people, mainly young, in all classes of society are experimenting with this drug, and substantial numbers use it regularly for social pleasure.
There is no evidence that this activity is causing violent crime or aggressive anti-social behavior, or is producing in otherwise normal people conditions of dependence or psychosis requiring medical treatments.
The experience of many other countries is that once it is established, Cannabis smoking tends to spread. In some parts of Western Society where interest in mood-altering drugs is growing, there are indications that it may become a functional equivalent to alcohol."

Report by the Advisory Committee on
Drug Dependence — Great Britain, 1968.

The connoisseur's handbook of marijuana

The Connoisseur's Handbook of marijuana

by William Daniel Drake Jr

Straight Arrow Books

The Book Division of Rolling Stone

Library of Congress Catalog Card Number: 70-158516
ISBN 0/87932/005/2 (cloth); 0/87932/021/4 (paperbound)

Hardcover Edition
0 9 8 7 6 5 4 3 2

Paperback Edition
0987

Straight Arrow Books
625 Third Street
San Francisco, California 94107

Published & distributed in association with the Book & Film Division of the **Agrarian Reform Company, Box 2447, Eugene, Oregon 97402**

Printed in the U.S.A.
Production: Planned Production

Distributed by Simon and Schuster

Simon and Schuster order no: 02005 (cloth); 02021 (paperbound)

Cover design: Mike Salisbury

Cultivation drawings: Terry Rutledge

Now they have a wild hemp in their country, like flax, except that the hemp grows taller & stouter by far. It grows wild and it is also sown by the Scythians, and from it the people of Thrace even make clothes . . . The Scythians, then, take the seed of this hemp, and creeping under the felt covering of the tent they throw the seed on the stones glowing with heat from the fire, and there it smoulders & makes such a steam as no vapour-bath in Greece could surpass, and the steam makes the Scythians howl for joy. This serves them for a bath, for they never wash their bodies in water. Their women make a paste by grinding the wood of cypress & cedar and the frankincense tree with rough stones and pouring on water; with this they plaster their whole bodies & their faces and it has the two-fold effect of giving them a lasting perfume and, when the paste is removed after a day, it leaves them clean & sleek-skinned.

Herodotus

FEDERAL NARCOTIC DRUG AND MARIHUANA LAWS

MARIHUANA

I. IMPORTATION

A. Under 21 U.S.C. 176a, it is unlawful to import or bring into the United States any marihuana contrary to law—knowingly and with intent to defraud the United States. Alternatively, it is unlawful to smuggle or clandestinely introduce into the United States any marihuana which should have been invoiced—knowingly and with intent to defraud the United States.

1. Section 176a also prohibits receiving, concealing, buying, selling, or in any manner facilitating the transportation, concealment or sale of such marihuana after it has been imported or brought in—knowing that it was imported or brought into the United States contrary to law.

2. Conspiring to accomplish any of the proscribed acts is also an offense.

3. The Section sets up a permissive inference of guilt based solely on unexplained possession of marihuana.

4. The penalty for a first offense under Section 176a is not less than five nor more than twenty years' imprisonment. In addition, the offender may be fined not more than $20,000. For a second or subsequent offense, the offender will be imprisoned for not less than ten nor more than forty years and, in addition, may be fined not more than $20,000.

B. 21 U.S.C. 184a makes it an offense for anyone to bring on board, or have in his possession or control on board any vessel of the United States which is engaged in a foreign voyage, any mari-

Contents

(After Mal)

The connoisseur's handbook of marijuana

Hymn to all Magic and Medicinal Plants

The plants that are Brown, and those that are White;
The Red ones and the Speckled ones;
The Sable and the Black plants;
All do we invoke.

May they protect this Man from disease sent by gods
The herbs whose Father is the sky
Whose mother is the earth
Whose root is the ocean.

The waters and the heavenly plants are foremost;
They drive out from every limb thy disease.
The consequence of sin.

The plants that spread forth, those that are lush,
Those that have a single sheath, those that creep along
Do I address:
I call in thy behalf the plants that have shoots,
Those that have stalks, those that divide their branches,
Those that are derived from all the gods:
The strong plants that furnish life to Man.

With the might that is yours, ye mighty ones,
With the power and strength that is yours,
With these do ye, O Plants
Rescue this Man from disease consequent upon sin.

I now prepare a remedy.

The plants — givala the quickening
Na-gha-risha of no harm
Givanti which lives brightly
And the Arundhati which removes disease
Full of blossoms, rich in honey
Do I call these to exempt this Man from injury.

Hither shall come the intelligent plants
Who understand my speech.
May we bring this Man into safety out of misery.

They that are the food of fire,
The offspring of the waters
That grow ever renewing themselves
The strong plants, bearers of a thousand names,
The healing plants shall be brought hither.

The plants, whose womb is the Avaka
Whose essence are the waters
Shall with their sharp horns thrust aside evil.

The plants which release,
Which exempt from weariness are strong.
They destroy poisons, they destroy the disease Balasa
And ward off witchcraft.
May they come hither.

Those plants which may be purchased
That are potent, rightfully praised
Shall protect in this village horse, man, cattle.

Honied are the roots of these herbs
Honied their tops
Honied their middles
Honied their leaves
Honied their blossoms
They share in honey,
They are the food of immortality.
May they yield ghee, and food,
And cattle chief of all

Many in number and in kind
The plants here upon the earth:
May they, furnished with a thousand leaves,
Release us from death and misery.

Tiger-like is the amulet made of herbs
A savior, a protector against hostile schemes:
May it drive off far away from us all disease.

As if at the roar of the lion they start with fright;
As if at the roar of fire they tremble before the plants —
The diseases of cattle and men are driven out —
Let them pass into swiftly flowing streams.

The plants release us from fire.
Spreading over the earth ye go
Whose king is the tree.

The plants descended from Angiras
That grow upon the mountains and in the plains
Shall be for us rich in milk, auspicious,
A comfort to the heart.

The herbs which I know
And those which I perceive with sight;
The unknown, yet those which we recognize
And perceive to be charged with power —
All plants collectively note my words
That we may bring this Man out of misfortune.

The Asvattha and the darbha among plants;
King Soma, ambrosia and the oblation:

Rice and barley, the two healing, immortal
children of heaven
Ye Arise! It is thundering and crashing
Ye plants. Parganya of the rain
Is favoring you, O children of the cloud,
With his seed.

The strength of this ambrosia do we give this
Man to drink.
I prepare a remedy
That He may live a hundred years.

The boar knows, the ichneumon knows
     the healing plant.
Those that the serpents know, I call hither
     for help.
The plants which the eagles and falcons know
Which the birds and flamingos know,
Which all winged creatures know
Which all wild animals know
I call hither for help.

As many as the oxen,
As many as the goats and sheep feed upon,
So many plants when prepared shall furnish
     thee protection.
As many plants as the physicians know
That contain a remedy
So many, endowed with a healing quality
Do I apply to thee.

Those that have flowers
Those that have blossoms
Those that bear fruit
As if from the same mother they shall yield milk
To exempt this Man from injury.

We speak to the five kingdoms of five fathoms
And, too, from a depth of ten fathoms.
Moreover, you shall be saved from the chains
     of Yama,
And from every sin against the gods.

Preface

Good old Cannabis Sativa: icon for the faithful, a windfall for the glib, a bonus for under-employed experts, a thrill for the naive, a whipping-boy for the ambitious, a tool for mystic explorers, a tantalizing mystery for scientists, a cash crop for peasants; hassles, joy, shouting, tranquility, apoplexy, fear, rebellion all wash over Western man in the presence of the little green weed. It is variously the four horsemen of the apocalypse, the seven deadly sins embodied; it is The Answer, The Question, the search & resolution of the Grail, and the Godhead. It is a focus of the extremes of Western man.

Long before the more salubrious properties of Cannabis were known in the West, the plant was causing trouble. Few other plants gave Linneaus & his disciples such fits. Cannabis refused to fall neatly into place in any of their schemes. It's reproductive mode belonged to one category, its structural features to another. It shared other features with many plants, but was brother & sister to none. Those early developers of natural schemes were very neat people, and Cannabis refused to yield to their visions of an aseptic nature, leading them eventually to an 'Oh what the hell, let's call it a nettle' approach. Let posterity worry about the niceties; they were old & tired and wanted to lie back and admire their now-perfect systems.

Some literature of the Cannabis from several countries

For several generations these systems maintained their balance and the world moved along nicely. Since hemp was an important but not controversial economic plant, no one felt obligated to look further into its true nature. Then it was discovered (while some secretly smiled) that you could *smoke* the damn thing. And get high. No longer was the world to sit by while Cannabis Sativa L. — a moderate plant, a virtuous plant, a being dedicated to fibre production — flourished in the fields of Europe and America. An Asiatic varlet was at hand, producing no fibre, flouting its luxurious leaves, and turning low life people on!

14

After much shouting & recrimination the botanists sallied forth to the fields, spurred by the conviction that no plant which was such a stalwart of commerce could possibly make people feel good too. Soon their findings were announced. There was not one hemp plant; there were two: Cannabis Sativa, rope & fibre producer, and Cannabis Indica, the killer weed. Thus, the hemp industry was allowed a continued prosperity, and the Cannabinomaniacs of the Western world could be pinned to the wall by moralizers who were now provided with the additional thrill of dealings with the exotic.

What Cannabis does not do is documented in the writings of investigators who have abstained from political or moral judgments — and perhaps is best investigated from these negative observations. Cannabis is not a sedative — it imposes few barriers to the normal conscious processes and what barriers arise are largely idiosyncratic. It is not a narcotic — it produces no physiological or biochemical dependency, even at the most remote cellular level. It is not a tranquilizer — the human who smokes or eats Cannabis is under no chemical compulsion to slow down and doze. It is not a stimulant, for there are few traceable increased metabolic or mental measures which are invariably provoked by the ingestion of Cannabis. It is not hallucinogenic, for despite the common visual and auditory experiences of Cannabis users there is no basis for any cause & effect statement about a chemical imperative to hallucinate.

The image of Cannabis projected on man's mind seems to be a clarified reflection of that mind itself. Western culture is so accustomed to searching for causes & effects that we normally accept an implied separation of cause from effect, and work principally to discover the linkage. Most of our drugs are treated this way — in order to produce a predictable effect, we select the appropriate causal agent. In the instance of Cannabis it seems that we are confronted, through the uniqueness of the plant, with an aberration, in our view, within the natural order. Cannabis, despite its apparent effects, cannot be labelled a cause. If we were not so inextricably tied to our science and logic, perhaps we could investigate more fully the nature of Cannabis, looking there for the rational as well as mystical properties of this unique plant.

It seems that one of the basic difficulties in learning about Cannabis stems from a fundamental flaw in our world view. We are taught from our first encounters with nature that there are two kingdoms — the plant and the animal. Our science learning is structured so — we have separate charts, separate books, separate disciplines and separate visions of a bipartate nature. Occasionally, for entertainment, our instructors will present us with what they view as an aberration in one or the other kingdom — a plant that eats insects, a microscopic critter with elementary chlorophyll—but by & large we learn that never the twain shall meet. If we look more closely at this world view, another assumption becomes clear — the animals, no matter how uncomplicated and vacuous, are on top of the hierarchy and the plants are on the bottom. We, of course, perch upon the pointy apex, rotating slowly no doubt.

It is a gross error on our part to fail to recognize that the natural order is not based so much on the ability of one group to exploit another as it is on the proposition that organisms interact and that the availability of one group for the purposes of another is only part of the intricate natural structure. To impute a blanket superiority to the animal kingdom is to warp the premises upon which nature rests.

Technological man is not only the creator of his own world visions, he is also the inheritor of fables and myths of his past. It is deeply significant that these legacies of his primitive past, a past where man had not yet consciously separated himself from nature, portray plants as living, sensate, perceiving & active creatures.

Early in this century, little known natural philospher, A H France, wrote 'Germs of Mind in Plants.' This book, full of love for the natural order and committed to Nietzsche's proposition that science gives us 'only a world analysis and description and not an explanation,' proposed a foundation for an understanding of the natural world which has been shamefully forgotten in our times:

The narcissus, hyacinth, laurel & cypress retain their human fate and stand as enchanted mortals, in the sunny forest of the gods. For the Germans, also, forest & meadow are filled with loving if silent brothers, and their gentle queen, Balder's wife Nanna, comes down to us every year in the gentle pomp of fairyland. In India this dim outline becomes a philosophy, in which all nature meets us as a mirror, saying 'This is you'. Wherever we dig down into these old sources we meet with the same stream: the deepest conviction of a bygone race, whether it be in the wonderful didactic poem of Empedocles:

> For I was once perhaps as boy or girl
> Dust, mayhap, or bird and fish . . .

that in playful mixture of poetry & fundamental wisdom speaks of that mystic phase: evolution long ago began the unveiling of man; whether it be in the mystic sayings of the Middle Ages, or the wonderful herbs that talked on Christmas eve; or the mandrake that gave a heart-breaking cry when pulled from the earth.

In the folk-songs of the Russians & Norwegians, the plants are living, feeling fellow-creatures, and even with us, in spite of our long separation from nature, there still remains a remnant of the old feeling, that plants are animate creatures, which our poets, at least, will not permit us to forget.

We have become separated from nature. This sentence may appear to many somewhat startling and yet it is certainly true, the long & interesting story of this separation began with Aristotle and ended with blind faith in literalism & the illusion of authority. The chance statement of Aristotle in his book on animals, that the plants have souls but no sensation, was accepted as inspired by the unfortunate trend of thought in the Middle Ages, which ceased to believe in the evidence of the eyes when it differed from the written word, until Linnaeus, who stood wholly on the shoulders of the Middle Ages, raised it to the position of a dogma. This man, who had such a mania for registration that he classified even his friends into categories & subdivisions, maintained, through his great authority, even into our youth, a dead scheme of life drawn out of scholasticism, that has gained him the name of the *Verus Botanicus*, the true botantist. Wherever he went, the laughing brook died, the glory of the flowers withered, and the grace & joy of our meadows was transformed into withered corpses, which this 'true botanist' collected into the folios of his herbarium, and whose crushed & discolored bodies he described in a thousand minute Latin terms. This was called

15

scientific botany, and the more mummies such a register of the dead could bury in his museum the greater botanist he was held to be. The learning of these endless descriptions was one of the terrors of our school life. The blooming meadows and the storied woods disappeared during the botanical hour into a dusty herbarium, into a dreary catalogue of Greek and Latin labels. It became the hour for the practice of a tiresome dialectic, filled with discussions about the number of stamens, the shape of the leaves, about over, amidst & underplaced bunches of fruit, all of which we learned only to forget.

When this was completed, we stood disenchanted and estranged from nature. So it came about that in the broadest circles of culture, that the secret but universal judgment was that botany was unspeakably dry, a pedantic cram, a sort of intellectual gymnastics. Respect for the teacher prevented us from saying this openly, but if one was a true lover of natural science, botanical books were generally the last for which one reached.

This meant the renunciation of one of the greatest of pleasures. The most beautiful part of nature was thereby lost. But during the last decade something wholly different from that which the good old Linnaeus treasured is appearing in botanical works, and this 'true botany' is already dying out. It is beginning to be realized that the forms of plants are but skeletons, beautiful to be sure, pleasing and of manifold, playful forms, but which are after all only the covering of the true kernel, the life of the plant. This last, however, is filled with hitherto unseen, unobserved marvels of nature.

How did we arrive at this knowledge? In order to understand this we must turn back once more to those 'catalogues'. The botanists had almost completed the inventory of nature. It cost many a tiresome quarrel, and often dangerous expeditions, to find 'new' and undescribed species. But this did not frighten them. It is a strange leaf in human history on which is written the story of these tireless, undaunted, wandering botanists, who struggled through wastes, climbed unexplored mountains, searched among hostile unknown people, went hungry, thirsty, often perished, and endured —all this in the hope of bringing home a dozen hitherto undescribed vegetables. But it is evident that not all could do this. Because there were really so few new herbs to discover, men at last began to look closely at the old ones. So it came about that the 'true botanists' began to content themselves with a half dozen specimens. Among the hundreds of herbs that he had pressed at home there

was always one that had a hair more or less than the description called for, one of those trifling changes, from which nature develops new forms of life, and soon a host of 'joyful discoveries' were made in the herbariums.

But such work gave a new insight into life. Form is but the track left by life. As the bodies were dissected, the plants investigated in their natural conditions, and their development observed, new characteristics were constantly discovered which could be used for the differentiation of new divisions, and therefore these were even more eagerly sought for. These characteristics, however, were expressions of vital laws, and so finally many a botanist, to his great surprise, discovered that the plants, these lifeless and helpless things, that even in death were so striking and attractive, really had a part in the great battle of life, and quietly, modestly, but nonetheless surely, through slight movements & curves, defended themselves against enemies & misfortune. It was discovered that they lived in an oft dramatic battle, that they were tireless in the display of new expedients, in artifices & adjustments, to obtain eve ywhere in the first triumph of life over 'dead matter,' each in its own way with individuality; that they had long ago found a way to utilize the rest of nature, and had created a thousand relations between themselves and this concealed yet so powerful life, and had formed connections for reciprocal advantage & support through its creatures, the beetles, flies, bees, butterflies, snails & birds.

The flower-strewn meadow, every scanty pasture, even the great silent forest, all are a murmuring symphony of the most marvelous and beautiful life-phenomena. It is only the good botanist who does not hear it, because he has driven the spirits of nature out of his herbarium, and therefor they do not exist.

So it was that in an unexpected manner the old popular wisdom began once more to receive respect.

Out of fables and songs and sayings
this kernel of truth came forth:
there is something in the plants
like unto that which we find in
our own breast

When this was finally observed there was no end to astonishment. For the most part the revolution in perspective which France perceived has petered out under the pressures of our technological age. We seem to have lost the thread of thought that people like France grasped briefly during the interregnum between the domination of men's spirits by the institutional forces of the Middle Ages and the domination of their minds by the technological revolution. It is because of this lost thread of thought, I believe, that we are so far from comprehending the significance of the natural drugs to ourselves.

Yet there are people in the wings of our civilizations who may be working on strands of this thread of thought, and their work may give us some hope of understanding. This work is not directed toward any common goal, and in fact it is probably artificial to piece together their findings. Still, let us consider the following:

Students of science, casual readers of newspapers, people interested in the arcane mysteries and many others are aware of the experiments which have been done with plants over the past several decades which point to their intelligent & selective capacities. Plants which respond to voice, to action, to thought on the part of humans have been indentified and are under constant study.

In many parts of the world there is an awareness that many more aspects of human life than are commonly thought of are affected by the things that we eat, and the effects referred to are not the result of any pattern of nutrition but seem to stem from inherent differences in the character of the plant or plants eaten. If animals are considered to be ultimate extrapolations of a food chain which begins with and is always supported by plants, the strong influence of plants on humans grows more apparent.

In several esoteric branches of the sciences there have recently been experiments which demonstrate that if the brains and/or bodies of living creatures who have learned certain tasks — rodents and planeria are the most commonly employed — are ingested by their naive relatives, these relatives acquire the learned

Plants' response to human voice, action & thought

There is something in the plants like unto that which we find in our own breast . . . Photograph: John Serwatka

17

Preface
Society and its
overwhelming
need for chem-
ical support

behavior of their emulsified ancestors.

Put these three distinct phenomena together and a startling but strongly probable pattern seems to develop. If plants have a life experience, it must be that some have a more profound experience than others. If these differential life experiences can even partially account for the diverse effects of plants on humans aside from nutrient considerations, and if in animals it is possible for life experiences to be passed from one creature to another by the naive ingesting the experienced, why should human beings be exempt from this process? And if human beings are not exempt from this process, why might it not be that the life experiences of some plants are so profound that when we ingest the physical beings of these plants our minds are granted access to organic knowledge which surpasses our normal human experience by a cosmic factor. And might not this group of plants, which is not a group at all in nature but which we humans, Linnaeus-like, want to put into categories, be what we call the psycho-active drugs, and among these drugs the combusted body of one of the most unique plants on earth, Cannabis Sativa. May we, then, inhale not only an intoxicating maze of molecular structures when we burn this plant, but a more filmy structure, a sort of knowledge heretofore inaccessible, a wisp of the living soul of a being from a foreign universe.

The central point which I hope derives from all of these observations, more or less speculative, is that our society is in grave danger of missing the mark in its consideration of Cannabis. It seems that the major thrust of the argument pro & con hinges on a treatment of Cannabis as a causal agent — either Cannabis does or does not alter the mind in a way more or less desirable; either Cannabis is a legitimate or illegitimate addition to our vast stock of euphoric drugs; either Cannabis can or cannot be said to have any redeeming social value (with the focus of our judgment more often than not on our personal sterling qualities). The point is that Cannabis is a complementary agent in the minds of humans who are whole, free & creative. It is not so much a question of what Cannabis *does,* or how it *works*; rather, the state of consciousness of those who enter into the Cannabis experience seems to be the most cogent issue.

Massive use of synthetic, manipulative drugs is particularly an American tradition, upon which much of our technology is based. These drugs are inextricably linked with the core of our society, the developing technology of human relations & human integration.

The overwhelming dependency of our society on external manipulation has created the need for a redefinition of what constitutes normal functioning in the person & the group, with this normalcy ever in need of chemical support. Drugs are an infinitely expandable series by all appearances, and can be shifted about at will to produce and ameliorate effects, but they let us down in the end because of the essential incompatability of the drug/man interaction. The drug technology is subject to the central misconception we have about all technologies — devices of whatever nature can carry a man only so far, teach him only so much, bring him only into proximities with the objects of his search. After that, each person & each society must make an unassisted commitment. No devices. It is either that or ride along with the machines, drugs, systems & devices into the oblivion of their eventual uselessness.

The drugs of our culture create a necessity & a lust in people for chemical states which leave little room for that tiny sense which takes years to grow to competitive size, the self. Almost all mind drugs, both sanctioned & prohibited, are the products of systematic striving toward the goals of indulgence & gratification. Drug technology is rapidly approaching the point where it will be able to provide consumers with the means to reach these goals, in fact, the technology presently exists to produce such drugs. The reason they are not officially sanctioned is largely because the chemists have yet to produce reliable drugs which produce gratification in ways thought desirable by the powers of society. It seems unlikely

Replacing the
self with chem-
ical states.
Illustration:
John Hurford,
OZ Magazine,
June 1969.

that many interests would rise to oppose a drug which gave happiness & gratification in a context of productivity, loyalty, obedience & malleability.

Up to this point in time, however, the society at large has had to fall back on the same imperfect chemical formula for gratification *and* industry as its Neolithic forebearers, the ubiquitous liquid, alcohol. The imperfect state which is achieved through alcohol is intoxication, a subtle, poisoned twisting of the individual which yields a modicum of frenetic if not effective industry, which dulls the self to the point where it can interact productively, that is to say uncritically, with other drugged organisms. Alcohol is an eminently suitable drug for those who concern themselves with manipulating our society and will remain so until Huxley's *Soma* can finally be synthesized.

One of the truly unfortunate aspects of Cannabis is that it too can be used to achieve intoxication. Were it a drug which did nothing but facilitate & enhance internal exploration & enlightenment it would have a small following in this country and the world. Its most common use through history has been as an intoxicant, and few have exercised their prerogative to use it otherwise. Contemporary America is not one of the exceptions to this phenomenon. We can plead that we are faced with the vastest array of drugs of any society in the history of civilization, and that the nature of our society dictates both the character & the usage of our drugs, which are almost exclusively chemically imperative modifiers of mood, personality, perspective & self. But that doesn't really let us off the hook. For when we are faced with Cannabis, a drug whose realizable potential lies easily in the other direction, away from a submersion of self & toward self-discovery, we either condemn the drug as dangerous or abuse it by looking only to get stoned. When this route is taken with an intoxicant, predictable results ensue. The problem becomes dependence.

Dependence, of course, does not have to ensue with Cannabis, which is one of the things that sets it apart as an unique drug among most others. But the pursuit of intoxicants has long since convinced most

folk in our society that the self is powerless to live alone in a world where unbalance, imperfections, pain & fear seem to yield only to chemical adjustments. Vast industries strive to maintain this myth as the basis for their profits. Some make it admirable that many people are turning to Cannabis as the drug (read: intoxicant) of preference, and certainly it is true that Cannabis used as a stupefacient has multiple advantages over alcohol or, for that matter, any western drug. That opinion suffers only in that it admits, unnecessarily, to an overpowering weakness in mankind which is so general that it condemns even those who try to go unintoxicated to the heart of self and make that the reason for survival. For those people Cannabis can be a valid breaker of the snares of culture & society. Most drugs used by Western man are worthless except in that they adjust the individual sufficiently that he does not reject the premises upon which his continued functioning depends. Neither, of course, are they conducive to a rational examination of those premises from the un-drugged perspective of self. And that, precisely, is where Cannabis deviates.

There are no such traps in a relationship with Cannabis. The will is left untouched, open, by the drug; it is at the same time extremely sensitive to all of the person's interior devils and angels. Within the Cannabis experience there are great potential benefits & liabilities because of this exposure of the will to interior forces. But for a person whose will alters during a Cannabis experience to attribute that change to the drug is simply covering up for the end result of a personal interaction of his virtues and weaknesses with his will. As with some forms of hypnotic suggestibility, you will do nothing with Cannabis running around your brain of which you are not normally capable, albeit that capability may, normally, be suppressed or hidden. This same observation holds for physiological as well as psychological phenomena — Cannabis neither adds nor detracts from the dimensions of normal physiological functioning. Exalted activity or supreme lethargy are not, granted, normal states for the bulk of people; neither are they abnormal states — outside of the capability of most people to achieve. Neither

SEPALS

STAMENS

PISTILS

BRACT

MALE

FEMALE

The will is
left untouched,
open . . .
Male & female
Cannabis Sativa
as illustrated in
*Scientific Amer-
ican*, December
1969

21

The homemade
chillum, USA,
1969
Photograph:
Robert Altman

do they occur all that often with Cannabis; one simply seeks among a multiplicity of personal levels to find that which is best for a given setting, a given frame of mind in the given Cannabis experience. There is nothing you must do, no chemical imperative. If you rise to a creative level, it has always been there, accessible. You have probably been there before, but maybe not; maybe this level's existence within you will be a major discovery. Maybe, too, no such level exists within you. Such a fear is always justified, but is no justification for failing to search.

If you fall into a non-productive, non-creative, non-meditative state, the drug has not put you there. You have found that level yourself, and you have passed up the alternatives.

All of this pre-supposes that the individual has some hint of the techniques of interior travel, the search for self and for thoughts & perceptions; or that the individual will, like a young animal tossed into water, instinctively make the appropriate movements when he first discovers himself in the enveloping, unfamiliar substance of the mind. Many people are past this easy, instinctive stage in skills of the interior journey. A child grown beyond infancy will often go rigid and helpless if tossed into water — he must be taught to swim or, more precisely, must unlearn all of those things which make it impossible to act naturally in a natural medium and so survive. So a grown human must unlearn all of those things which render him helpless & panicked when confronted by the deep, unfamiliar spaces & levels of his mind.

But if the man is frightened and acts unnaturally at being faced with the internal, he cannot with justice accuse Cannabis of having created this dilemma. Cannabis is not a creator, and what frightens, mystifies or exhalts a man in his mind is not built there by the drug. Neither can the search for cause finally rest with Cannabis as a guide or transport; there is no more responsive guide, no more dependably versatile mode to assist a person on his interior journeys. When you take on a guide to something with which you should be so intimately familiar as your mind, the guide should be absolved of all responsibility. That respon-sibility reposes instead in the person who needs & selects the guide — he may choose well or poorly. If he chooses out of ignorance, his guide will probably be of bad character — it will mislead, create false aspects and dimensions alter the physical context of the body & brain so that the journey becomes warped. There are far more such agents available than there are the opposite, the dependable guide, non-interfering but available to assist: drugs such as Cannabis are rare and, because of the perversions of the institutions rising out of or altered by warped minds, usually difficult to acquire.

Be that as it may, men will always seek the interior self and whether that state is generated through sleep, stupor, euphoria, pain, silence, concentration, hallu-cination, sensual experience, sensory stimulation or a host of other mediums, the search will prevail. There are more natural agents in this world which bring about, generate or cause each of these states than could ever be eradicated by decree, and men will find each of these in turn.

To pass laws to prohibit Cannabis is ignorant; to believe that legalization is the issue is ignorant. To fear yourself and so oppress others is ignorant; to attribute credit for self to a false source is ignorant. To choose destructive drugs and ways of living is igno-rant; but so is to fail to appreciate the limits of any drug, destructive or beneficial.

Perhaps the only antidote to ignorance is ex-perience, and to the open person the experience of others is often as good a source of discovery as per-sonal trials. The purpose of this book is largely to reveal some of the experiences of other cultures, other periods, with Cannabis and to compare them with our contemporary experience.

Preface
There is no
justification for
failing to search

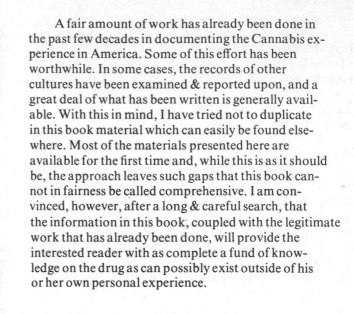

Satan by
Gustave Dore,
from Paradise
Lost, 1883

24

A fair amount of work has already been done in the past few decades in documenting the Cannabis experience in America. Some of this effort has been worthwhile. In some cases, the records of other cultures have been examined & reported upon, and a great deal of what has been written is generally available. With this in mind, I have tried not to duplicate in this book material which can easily be found elsewhere. Most of the materials presented here are available for the first time and, while this is as it should be, the approach leaves such gaps that this book cannot in fairness be called comprehensive. I am convinced, however, after a long & careful search, that the information in this book, coupled with the legitimate work that has already been done, will provide the interested reader with as complete a fund of knowledge on the drug as can possibly exist outside of his or her own personal experience.

One: We took Bhang and the
Mystery I Am he grew plain

Late Twentieth Century America is such a unique experience, it is understandable that many of us consider our lives to be extraordinary. We have been remarkably successful at consciously creating a context for our development through various processes, paramount among which has been our talent for creating a culture out of the assimilated and modified experiences of other cultures.

The process of assimilation and modification has given us many of our strengths but has also been the source of some great weaknesses. When we began the construction of our identity there was a great deal of latitude for those who wanted to bring with them a whole cultural experience, to simply transplant themselves, their experience & their heritage, into the body of a new land. This early process of accommodation gradually shifted as we came to feel that there was in fact an America, definable & therefore requiring a certain amount of discrimination regarding further assimilation. We grew more & more sure that questions which arose could be resolved by reference to our own experience. And as that experience acquired the dimensions of temporal depth & physical breadth we grew more & more accustomed to search for answers to new puzzles in our own past. Certainly lessons of other civilizations & cultures continue as objects of specialized study in institutions created for that purpose. But to a remarkable degree, such study has ceased to supply us guides for understanding our own experience.

In many areas of contemporary life this attitude can be justified, if one is so inclined. That is not to say that the most rational course invariably lies in that direction, simply that America is now composed of so many satisfactorily interlocking pieces that people & institutions can do a perfectly adequate job of survival & propagation within the contemporary context if they wish — with at least one major exception.

That caveat should be registered whenever America begins experimenting with experiences which have been shared by many people in many civilizations, some of them long before America was dreamed. We have consistently ignored this in what has become one of the crucial areas of experience in our collective lives, the relationship between drugs & humans. And because of our deliberate ignorance of drugs, and our inexplicable reluctance to explore their potentials & meanings, we are suffering schisms in all the dimensions of our collective & individual lives to the point that survival may be called into question.

As drugs go, Cannabis is a minor natural agent; its very innocuousness probably accounts for the dimension that exercises its opponents most — widespread acceptance and use despite mammoth efforts at suppression. The importance of the drug lies not so much in what it does as in the experiences of people who use it, and since these experiences are largely though not exclusively the products of the minds themselves and not the drug acting on the mind, the records of such experiences assume a major role in any attempt to understand the relationship between Cannabis Sativa & Homo Sapiens.

America's recorded experiences with hemp drugs are for the most part shallow. Until very recently we have not produced any significant writing on the subject.

This lack of an American-generated record on marijuana has passively convinced many people that no such record exists — after all, if the experiences were there, an American would have recorded it.

But to say that there is no American record on marijuana is not wholly accurate. It would be more accurate to say that a selective record exists and that most people are convinced that the whole story is there for inspection. What most people refer to, of course, is largely the product of official & unofficial propagandists, and that their statements have been accepted so uncritically until recently is indicative of how faithful we all are.

Another record exists, however. The record of several major civilizations who have known hemp

26

drugs intimately over periods of time which could swallow the American experience with marijuana without even a polite, cosmic burp. Throughout these centuries many voices have recorded their thoughts for any present or future people to examine. That this record today seems scanty is probably due more to the attrition of time & the cumulative effects of hundreds of years of periodic censorship than to any original lack of interest on the part of those living the experiences with Cannabis.

Of these civilizations India stands out as the primary source of recorded thought on Cannabis itself, and the relationship of the drug to man. Of all the countries where Cannabis has been used regularly & in large quantities, India is distinguished as being the center of discovery of the mystical connection between the plant & the mind as it moves from the common level to the religious experience. In most other countries, and as a general rule, Cannabis is viewed & used primarily as an inexpensive & desirable euphoriant.

There is within many of the Indian religions a clear recognition of the spiritual life within plants, manifested in the locations of many important gods within certain plants. Among the holy plants of the Hindu is the mighty hemp, within whose leaves swells the great Yogi, the brooding, ascetic Mahadev. The properties of the hemp give witness to the character of this guardian within the leaves.

In an appendix to the Indian Hemp Drugs Commission Report of 1893-94 there appears the following essay by Mr J M Campbell entitled *On The Religion Of Hemp*. It is a classic treatment of the subject, therefore we reproduce it in its entirety with minor changes for clarity:

So holy a plant should have special rearing. Shiva explains to his wife, Parvati, how, in sowing hemp seed, you should keep repeating the spell 'Bhangi, Bhangi', apparently that sound of the guardian name may scare away the evil tare-sowing influences. (NB: Tare is a class designation for a group of noxious weeds, among them rape, one of the principal enemies of the hemp.) Again, when the seedlings are planted the same holy name must be repeated, and also at the watering which, for the space of a year, the young plants must daily receive. When the flowers appear, the flowers and leaves should be stripped from the plant and kept for a day in warm water. Next day, with one hundred repetitions of the holy name Bhangi, the leaves & flowers should be washed in a river and dried in an open shed. When they are dry some of the leaves should be burnt with due repeating of the holy name as a jap, or muttered charm. Then, bearing in mind that Vagdevata, or the Goddess of Speech, and offering a prayer, the dried leaves should be laid in a pure & sanctified place. Bhang so prepared, especially if prayers are said over it, will gratify the wishes & desires of its owner. Taken early in the morning, such bhang cleanses the user from sin, frees him from the punishments of chores of sin, and entitles him to reap the fruits of a thousand horse-sacrifices. Such sanctified bhang taken at daybreak or noon destroys diseases. Before the religious user of bhang stand the Ashtadevata or Eight Guardians with clasped hands ready to obey him and perform his orders. The wish of him who with pure mind pours bhang with due reverence over the Ling of Mahadev will be fulfilled.

Such holiness & such evil-scaring powers must give bhang a high place among lucky objects, that a day may be fortunate to the careful man should on waking look into liquid bhang. So any nightmares or evil spirits that may have entered into him during the ghost-haunted hours of night will flee from him at the sight of the bhang and free him from their blinding influences during the day. So too when a journey has to be begun or a fresh duty or business undertaken, it is well to look at bhang. To meet someone carrying bhang is a sure omen of success. To see in a dream the leaves, plant or water of bhang is lucky; it brings the Goddess of Wealth into the dreamer's power. To see his parents worship the bhang plant and pour bhang over Shiva's Ling will cure the dreamer of fever. A longing for bhang foretells happiness; to see bhang drunk increases riches. No good thing can come to the man who treads under foot the holy bhang leaf.

So evil-scaring and therefore luck-bringing a plant must

play an important part in the rites to clear away evil influences. During the great spirit time of marriage in Bombay among almost all the higher classes of Gujarat Hindus, of the Jain as well as of the Brahmanic sects, the supplies sent by the family of the bride to the bridegroom's party during their seven day sojurn includes a supply of bhang. The name of the father who neglects to send bhang is held in contempt. Again, after the wedding, when the bridegroom & his friends are entertained at the house of the bride, richly-spiced bhang is drunk by the guests. The Gujarat Mussulman bride before and after marriage drinks a preparation of bhang. Among the Pardeshi or North Indian Hindus of Bombay bhang is given not only at weddings, but the Pardeshi who fails to give his visitor bhang is despised by his caste as mean & miserly. Another great spirit time during which bhang plays an important part is the time of war. Before the outbreak of a war and during its progress the Ling of Mahadev should be bathed with bhang. Its power of driving panic influences from near the god has gained for bhang the name of Vijaya, the unbeaten. So a drink of bhang drives from the fighting Hindu the haunting spirits of fear & weariness. So the beleaguered Rajput, when nothing is left but to die, after loosing his hair that the bhang spirit may have free entrance, drinks the sacramental bhang and rushing on the enemy completes his juhar, or self-sacrifice. It is this quality of panic-scaring that makes bhang, the Vijaya or Victorious, especially dear to Mahadev in his character of Tripureshvar, the slayer of the demon Triparasur. As Shiva is fond of bel leaves, as Vishnu is fond of tulsi leaves, so is Tripureshvar fond of bhang leaves. He who wishes to obtain his desires must constantly offer bhang to Tripureshvar.

Bhang the cooler is a ferbrifuge. Bhang acts on the fever not directly or physically as an ordinary medicine, but indirectly or spiritually by soothing the angry influences to whom the heats of fever are due. According to one account in the Ayurveda (NB: One of the Hindu systems of medicine) fever is possession by the hot angry breath of the great gods Brahman, Vishnu, and Shiva. According to another passage in the Ayurveda, Shankar or Shiva, enraged by a slight from his father-in-law Daksha, breathed from his nostrils the eight fevers that wither mankind. If the fever-stricken performs the Vijaya abhishekh, or bhang pouring on the Ling of Shankar, the god is pleased, his breath cools, and the portion of his breath in the body of the fever-stricken ceases to inflame. The Kashikhanda Purana tells how at Benares, a Brahman, sore-smitten with fever, dreamed that

he had poured bhang over the self-sprung Ling and was well. On waking he went to the Ling, worshipped, poured bhang, and recovered. The fame of this cure brings to Benares sufferers from fever which no ordinary medicine can cure. The sufferers are laid in the temple and pour bhang over the Ling whose virtue has endowed it with the name Juareshvar, the Fever-Lord. In Bombay many people sick of the fever vow on recovery to pour bhang over a Ling. Besides as a cure for fever bhang has many medicinal virtues. It cools the heated blood, soothes the over-wakeful to sleep, gives beauty, and secures length of days. It cures dysentery and sunstroke, clears phlegm, quickens digestion, sharpens appetite, makes the tongue of the lisper plain, freshens the intellect, and gives alertness to the body & gaiety to the mind. Such are the useful & needful ends for which in his goodness the Almighty made bhang. Ganja in excess causes abcess, even madness. In moderation bhang is the best of gifts. Bhang is a cordial, a bile absorber, an appetizer, a prolonger of life. Bhang quickens fancy, deepens thought & braces judgment.

As on other guardian-possessed objects, the cow, the Vedas, or the leaf of the bel tree, oaths are taken on the bhang leaf. Even to a truthful witness an oath on the bhang leaf is dreaded. To one who foreswears himself the bhang oath is death.

So holy a plant must play a part in temple rites. Shiva on fire with the poison churned from the ocean was cooled with bhang. At another time with family worries the god withdrew to the fields. The cool shade of a plant soothed him. He crushed & ate of the leaves, and the bhang refreshed him. For these two benefits bhang is Shankarpriya, the beloved of Mahadev. So the rightful user of bhang or of ganja, before beginning to drink or to smoke, offers the drug to Mahadev saying 'Lena Shankar, Lena Babulnath' : . . . Be pleased to take it Shankar, take it Babulnath. According to the Shiva Purana, from the dark fourteenth of Magh (January-February) to the light fourteenth of Ashadh (June-July) that is, during the three months of hot weather, bhang should be poured at least during the first & last days of this period. According to the Mru Tantra on any Monday, especially on Shravan (July-August) Mondays, on all twelfths or pradoshs, and on all dark fourteenths or shivratris, still more on the Mahashivratri or Shiva's Great Night on the dark fourteenth of Magh, and at all eclipses of the sun or moon, persons wistful either for this world or for the world to come should offer bhang to Shiva and pour it over the Ling. Not every devotee of Shiva makes offerings of bhang.

SHIVA'S DANCE OF LIFE

Shiva was cooled with Bhang

DO YOU DO IT FROM UUNNNKKK...

OR DO YOU DO IT FROM AAAAHHHH!!

DO YOU SURF THROUGH IT ALL?

OR DO YOU CARRY IT AROUND LIKE A LOAD?

29

The Mystery I
Am he grew
plain . . .
He who scan-
dalises the user
of Bhang shall
suffer the tor-
ments of hell so
long as the sun
endures.

Such rites in Bombay are seldom performed except in Bhulehvar and Babulnath temples and there only on special occasions. The bhang offered to Mahadev is without pepper or other spice. It is mixed with water, water & milk, or milk & sugar. It is poured over the Ling. According to some authorities the offerer should not touch the offered bhang. Temple ministrants Atits, Tapodhans, Bhojaks, Bhopis, Bharadis, Guravasalone should drink it. If there are no ministrants the remains of the offering should be poured into a well or given to cows to drink. Other authorities encourage the offerer to sip the bhang, since by sipping the bhang reaches and soothes the Shiva-Shakta, or Shiva-spirit in the sipper. On certain special occasions during failures of rain, during eclipses, and also in times of war libations of bhang are poured over the Ling.

Vaishnavas as well as Shaivas make offerings of bhang. The form of Vishnu or the guardian to whom bhang is a welcome offering is Baladev, Balaram, or Devji, the elder brother of Krishna. Baladev was fond of spirits, not of bhang. But Banias, Bhatias and other high class Hindus, not being able to offer spirits, instead of spirits offer bhang. In Bombay the offering of bhang to Baladev, unlike the special offering to Shiva, is a common & everyday rite. Without an offering of bhang no worship of Baladev is complete. Unlike the plain or milk & sugared bhang spilt over the Ling, Baladev's bhang is a richly spiced liquid which all present, including the offerer, join in drinking. Such social & religious drinking of bhang is common in Bombay in the temple of Devji in Kalyan Kirparam Lane near Bhuleshvar. As in the higher class worship of Baladev the liquor offering has been refined to an offering of bhang, so it is in the worship of Devi, Shiva's early & terrible consort. (NB: the Devi-Dasi cult of murder sprang from this wife of the young god Shiva.) On any Tuesday or Friday, the two weekdays sacred to Devi, still more during the Navratra, or Nine Nights in Ashwin (September-October) those whose caste rules forbid liquor make a pleasing spiced bhang. As in the worship of Baladev all present, worshipper & ministrant alike, join in drinking. Shitaladevi, the Cooler, the dread goddess of small-pox whose nature, like the nature of bhang, is cooling, takes pleasure in offerings of bhang. During epidemics of small-pox the burning and fever of the disease are soothed by pouring bhang over the image of Shitaladevi. So for the feverishness caused by the heats, especially to the old, no cure equals the drinking of bhang. Unlike spirits, the tempter to flesh, bhang the craver for milk is pleasing to the Hindu religion. Even according to the straightest school of the ob-

jectors to stimulants, while to a high caste Hindu the penalty for liquor drinking is death, no penalty attaches to the use of bhang, and a single day's fast is enough to cleanse from the coarser spirit of ganja. Even among those who hold stimulants to be devil-possessed, penalty & disfavor attach to the use of hemp drugs only when they are taken with no religious object & without observing the due religious rites.

At the other extreme of Hindu thought from the foes to stimulants, to the worshippers of the influences that, raising man out of himself and above mean individual worries, make him one with the divine forces of nature, it is inevitable that temperaments should be found to whom the quickening spirit of bhang is the spirit of freedom & knowledge. In the ecstasy of bhang the spark of the Eternal in man turns into light; the murkiness of matter or illusion & self is lost in the central soul-fire. The Hindu poet of Shiva, the great spirit that living in bhang passes into the drinker, sings of bhang as the clearer of ignorance, the giver of knowledge. No gem or jewel can touch in value bhang taken truly & reverently. He who drinks bhang drinks Shiva. The soul in whom the spirit of bhang finds a home glides into an ocean of Being freed from the weary round of self-blinded matter. To the meaner man, still under the glamour of matter, or maya, bhang taken religiously is kindly thwarting the wiles of his foes and giving the drinker wealth & promptness of mind.

In this devotion to bhang, with reverence, not with the worship, which is due to Allah alone, the North Indian Mussulman joins hymning the praises of bhang. To the follower of the later religion of Islam the holy spirit in bhang is not the spirit of the Almighty, it is the spirit of the great prophet Khizr, or Elijah. That bhang should be sacred to Khizr is natural, Khizr is the patron saint of water. Still more Khizr means green, the revered color of the cooling water of bhang. So the Urdu poet sings 'When I quaff fresh bhang I liken its color to the fresh light down of thy youthful beard.' The prophet Khizr or the green prophet cries 'May the drink be pleasing to thee.' Nasir, the great North Indian Urdu poet of the beginning of the present century is loud in the praises of his beloved Sabzi, the Green One. 'Compared with bhang spirits are naught. Leave all things thou fool, drink bhang.' From its quickening the imagination, Mussulman poets honor bhang with the title Waraq Al Khayal, Fancy's Leaf. And the Makhzan or great Arab-Greek drug book records many other fond names for the drug. Bhang is the Joy-Giver, the Sky-Flier, the Heavenly-Guide, the Poor Man's Heaven, the Soother of Grief.

Much of the holiness of bhang is due to its virtue of clearing the head & stimulating the brain to thought. Among ascetics the sect known as Atits are especially devoted to hemp. No social or religious gathering of Atits is complete without the use of the hemp plant smoked in ganja or drunk in bhang. To its devotee bhang is no ordinary plant that became holy from its guardian and healing properties. According to one account, when nectar was produced from the churning of the ocean, something was wanted to purify the nectar. The deity supplied the want of a nectar-cleanser by creating bhang. This bhang Mahadev made from his own body, and so it is called Angaj, or body-born. According to another account some nectar dropped to the ground & from the ground the bhang plant sprang. It was because they used this child of nectar or of Mahadev in agreement with religious forms that the seers or Rishis became Siddha, or one with the diety. He who, despite the example of the Rishis, used no bhang shall lose his happiness in this life and in the life to come. In the end he shall be cast into hell.

The mere sight of bhang cleanses from as much sin as a thousand horse-sacrifices or a thousand pilgrimages. He who scandalizes the user of bhang shall suffer the torments of hell so long as the sun endures. He who drinks bhang foolishly or for pleasure without religious rites is as guilty as the sinner of lakhs (hundreds of thousands) of sins. He who drinks wisely and according to rule, be he ever so low, even though his body is smeared with human ordure and urine, is Shiva. No man or god is as good as the religious drinker of bhang. The students of the scriptures at Benares are given bhang before they sit to study. At Benares, Ujjain & other holy places yogis, bairagis and sannyasis take deep draughts of bhang that they may center their thoughts on the Eternal. To bring back to reason an unhinged mind the best & cleanest bhang leaves should be boiled in milk and turned to clarified butter. Salamisri, saffron & sugar should be added and the whole eaten. Besides over the demon of madness bhang is Vijaya or victorious over the demons of hunger & thirst. By the help of bhang pass days without food·or drink. The supporting power of bhang has brought many a Hindu family safe through the miseries of famine. To forbid or even seriously restrict the use of so holy & gracious an herb as the hemp would cause widespread suffering & annoyance and to the large bands of worshipped ascetics deep-seated anger. It would rob the people of a solace in discomfort, of a cure in sickness, of a guardian whose gracious protection saves them from the attacks of evil influences, and whose mighty power makes the devotee of the

Victorious, overcoming the demons of hunger & thirst, of panic, fear, of the glamour of Maya or matter, and of madness; able in rest to brood upon the Eternal, till the Eternal, possessing him body and soul, frees him from the haunting of self and receives him into the ocean of Being.

Bhang, the gracious protector

So holy & gracious an herb . . . The Mosque of the Sun, Delhi, 1895

31

The Mystery I
Am he grew
plain . . .
An essay by GA
Grierson, 1893

JM Campbell was a Collector of Land Revenue &
Customs & Opium in Bombay. He was quite obviously
something more than a run-of-the-mill customs inspector, for those parts of his essay which are clearly
his own show a reasoned appreciation of the role of
Cannabis in the religious & spiritual life in India.
Equally obviously he is quoting at length from largely
unidentified sources whose veracity we will have to
accept. One only wishes that there was some way of
access to his library, for in this essay we are given so
many exciting clues to the metaphysical nature of a
plant whose properties are rarely, if ever, thoroughly
analyzed even in the limited terms of Western material
science.

References to Cannabis are numerous throughout
Indian Literature, though very little research has been
aimed at putting together a comprehensive survey on
the subject.

The most thorough essay available was written by
Mr GA Grierson in 1893. Grierson's essay will be of
great value for those who want to search on their own
through Indian Literature, and is therefore included
here in somewhat edited form:

On References to the Hemp Plant Occurring in Sanskrit & Hindi Literature

I have the honour to state that I have searched
through all the Sanskrit and Hindi books accessible to me,
and to forward the accompanying note on the references to
the hemp plant occurring in the literature of those languages.

I have met the hemp plant in Sanskrit & Hindi literature
under various names. The principal are:

(1) Bhanga

(2) Indrashana

(3) Vijaya or Jaya

The earliest mention of the word ganja which I have
noted is about the year 1300 AD.

Wherever the word Vijaya is used, it is doubtful whether
the hemp plant is meant, or the yellow myrobalan, as the
word means both.

The name bhanga occurs in the Atharvaveda (say, BC
300) mentions the pollen of the hemp flower (bhanga). In
the commencement of the sixth century we find the first
mention of Vijaya which I have noted. It is a sacred grass,
and probably means here the hemp plant.

The first mention of bhanga as a medicine which I
have noted is in the work of Sushruta (before the eighth
century AD) where it is called an antiphlegmatic. During
the next four centuries bhanga (feminine) frequently
occurs in native Sanskrit dictionaries in the sense of hemp-
plant.

In the tenth century the intoxicating nature of bhang
seems to have been known: and the name Indrashana,
Indra's food, first appears, so far as I know, in literature.
Its intoxicating power was certainly known in the beginning
of the fourteenth century. In a play written in the beginning of the sixteenth century, it is mentioned as being consumed by yogis (Shaiva mendicants). It is there named
'Indra's food.'

In later medical works it is frequently mentioned under
various names.

I append a more detailed account of the passages in
which I have noted the uses of Indian Hemp.

I may add that I have not traced in literature any difference between the uses of the word ganja and of the word
bhanga, although modern Kavirajas tell me that they are
distinct plants.

In the Atharvaveda (cir 1400 BC) the bhang plant is
mentioned (11,6,15) once:

'We tell of the five kingdoms of herbs headed by Soma;
may it and the Kusha grass, and bhanga and barley, and the

herb Saha release us from anxiety.'

Here reference is evidently made of offering of these herbs in oblations.

The grammerian Panini (5,2,29) mentions bhanga-kata, the pollen of the hemp flower, as one of his examples (cir 300 BC). The fact that the pollen of this special flower was quoted is worth noting.

Varahamihira in his Brihatsamhita (XLVIII, 39) mentions vijaya as used with other grasses in the rites of the Pusya, bathing festival, (AD504).

Vijaya in this passage certainly means some plant or other. The word may mean either the Indian Hemp plant or be a synonym of haritaki (the yellow myrobalan). Dr Hoernle informs me that in the oldest medical works the word is explained by commentators in the latter sense. It is doubtful what meaning we are to adopt here. The word *may* mean the hemp plant bhanga. In the passage from the Atharvaveda already quoted, amongst the five plants special honoured as oblations, bhanga is closely connected with the herb saha. So also in the Brihatsamhita, vijaya is mentioned as one of a long list of plants to be used in the offering, and the very next plant mentioned is saha, which is apparently the same as saha. This would encourage the theory that the vijaya of the Brihatsamhita was more probably the same as the bhanga of the Atharvaveda.

In Sushruta (VT. XI, 3) Bhanga is recommended with a number of other drugs as an antiphlegmatic.

Vijaya is mentioned in the same work as a remedy for catarrh accompanied by diarrhoea (VT. XXIV; 20, and VT. 39, page 415-20) as an ingredient in a prescription for fever arising from an excess of bile & phlegm. In these two passages, however, vijaya is probably an equivalent of haritaki, the yellow myrobalan, and does not mean hemp.

In the various Kosas, or dictionaries, bhanga is frequently mentioned as meaning the hemp plant. Thus

(1) Amarakosa, 2, 9, 20 (Cir AD 500)

(2) Trikandashesa, 3, 364

(3) Hemacandra's Anekarthakosa, 2, 37 (Cir AD 900-1000)

(4) Hemkandra's Abhidhanacintamani, 1179 (twelfth century)

The Sarasundari (date not known to me), as commentary on the Amarakosa mentioned above, by Mathuresha, and quoted in the Shabdakalpadruma, mentions that the seed of the bhanga plant is the size of that of millet (Kalaya).

Cakrapanidatta is said to have flourished around Nayapala, a prince who reigned in the eleventh century AD. In his Shabdacandrika, a medical vocabulary, he gives the following Sanskrit names for bhang:

(1) Vijaya (Victorious)
(2) Trailokyavijaya (victorious in the three worlds)
(3) Bhanga
(4) Indrashana (Indra's Food)
(5) Jaya (Victorious)

These names seem to show that its use as an intoxicant was then known.

The Rajanighantu of Narahani Pandita adds the following names to those given by Shabdacandrika above mentioned:

(6) Virapattra (Hero-leaved or the leaf of heroes)
(7) Ganja
(8) Capala (The Light-hearted)
(9) Ajaya (The unconquered)
(10) Ananda (The Joyful)
(11) Harsini (The Rejoicer)

and adds that the plant possesses the following qualities:
(1) Katutva (acridity); (2) Kasayatva (astringency);
(3) Usnatva (heat); (4) Tiktatva (pungency);
(5) Vatakaphapahatva (removing wind and phlegm);
(6) Samgrahitva (astringency); (7) Vakpradatva (speech-giving); (8) Batyatva (Strength-giving); (9) Medhakaritva (inspiring of mental powers); (10) Shresthadipanatva (the property of a most excellent excitant).

The Sharngadharasamhita, a medical work by Sharngadhara, the date of which is unknown, but which must have been compiled during the Muhammadan period of Indian history, specially mentions (1, 4, 19) bhanga as an excitant (vyavayin). In the same passage it mentions opium.

The Dhurtasamagama, or 'Rogue's Congress' is the name of an amusing if coarsely written farce of about the year 1500 AD, the author of which was one Jyotirisha. In the second act two Shaiva mendicants come before an unjust judge, and demand a decision on a quarrel which they have about a nymph of the bazaar. The judge demands payment of a deposit before he will give any opinion. One of the litigants says:

'Here is my ganja bag; let it be accepted as a deposit.'

The Judge (taking it pompously, and then smelling it greedily): 'Let me try what it is like (takes a pinch). Ah! I have just now by the merest chance some ganja which is soporific & corrects derangements of the humours, which produces a healthy appetite, sharpens the wits, and acts as an aphrodisiac.'

The word used for ganja in the above is Indrashana

33

The Mystery I
Am he grew
plain . . .
The drink of
the heroes

(Indra's food).

The Bhavaprakasha, another medical work written by Bhavadevamishra (ca. AD 1600) has as follows:

'Bhanga is also called ganja, madini (the intoxicating), vijaya (the victorious), and jaya (the victorious). It is anti-phlegmatic, pungent, astringent, digestive, easy of diges-tion, acid, bile-affecting; and increases infatuation, intoxi-cation, the power of the voice, and the digestive faculty.'

The Rajavallabha, a materia medica, the date of which I do not know, but which is quoted in the Shabdakalpadruma, and is believed to be ancient, has the following:

'Indra's food is acid, produces infatuation, and destroys leprosy. It creates vital energy, the mental powers, and internal heat, corrects irregularities of the phlegmatic humour, and is an elixir vitae. It was originally produced, like nectar, from the ocean by the churning of Mount Man-dara, and inasmuch as it gives victory in the three worlds, it, the delight of king of the gods, is called vijaya, the victorious. This desire-fulfilling drug was obtained by men on the earth, through desire for the welfare of all people. To those who regularly use it it begets joy and destroys every anxiety.'

Bhang is frequently mentioned by the vernacular poets. The oldest instance with which I am acquainted is the well-known hymn by Vidyapati Thakur (1400 AD), in which he calls Shiva 'Digambara bhanga' in reference to his habit of consuming the drug. According to an old Hindu poem, on which I cannot now lay my hands, Shiva himself brought down the bhang plant from the Himalayas and gave it to mankind. Yogis are well-known consumers of bhang & ganja, and they are worshippers of Shiva.

In folk songs, ganja or bhang (with or without opium) is the invariable drink of heroes before performing any great feat. At the Village of Bavri in Gaya there is a huge hollow stone, which is said to be the bowl in which the famous hero Lorik mixed his ganja. Lorik was a very valiant general, and is the hero of numerous folk songs. The epic poem of Alha & Rudal, of uncertain date, but undoubtedly based on very old materials (the heroes lived in the twelfth century AD) contains numerous references to ganja as a drink of warriors. For instance the commencement of the canto dealing with Alha's Marriage, describes the pestle & mortar with which ganja was prepared, the amount of the intoxicating drink prepared from it (it is called sabzi) and the amount of opium (an absurdly exaggerated quantity) given to each warrior in his court.

34

That the consumption of bhang is not considered dis-reputable among Rajputs may be gathered from the fact that Ajabes, who was court poet to the well-known Maha-raja Bishwanath Singh of Riwa, wrote a poem praising bhang and comparing siddhi to the 'success' which attends the worshipper of 'Hari'. Here there is an elaborate series of puns. The word siddhi means literally 'success' and hari means not only the god Hari, but also bhang.

Cannabis did not receive the unqualified blessings of Indian society, however positive an impression is left by a study of the historical literature. A rich source of opinion condemning use of hemp drugs is the oral tradition of Indian folk literature. A sampling of these songs and poems (opposite) reveals many anti-hemp drugs sentiments such as:

'The man who drinks bhang thrives,
He who takes ganja is deserted
By the Goddess Lukhi'

'If one smokes charas,
One's learning is diminished,
The seed is burnt up within,
Coughing goes on till one's belly bursts,
And one's face grows red
Like that of a monkey'

'He is a charas smoker,
You can't depend on him.
Boasters smoke hukkas,
And wild people eat opium.
Those who smoke bhang are mad,
And those addicted to the
Use of poppy heads die childless;
Childless die who use poppy heads,
As also charas smokers;
Sinners of this type
Die after a protracted illness.'

(From NW Province)

'Through smoking ganja and tobacco
Character is lost
And modesty destroyed.
Does not the heart
Of that man break
Who sells corn to buy ganja?

'My heart was broken indeed.
I did it without thought,
And all who act without thought,
Will have to repent

'It is not charas, but a curse.
It burns the chest and heart to its worst.
It brings on dimness of the eyes.
To phlegm and cough it must give rise.
To blind the eyes it never fails
Or cripple limbs that once were hale
In what but death ends its sad tale?'

(From Sind)

'I give you cough.
I give you itch.
I make you blind
I'm your eyes.
If still you do not die,
What more can I do?

'When the effects of bhang
Rise to the head
What feelings do they produce?

'The man who has drunk bhang
Holds tight to his bed
And wonders where it is going.

'Whoever smokes ganja
His face grows pale.
His wife will complain
He is impotent;
His brother will say
He is afflicted with pain,
But the smoker will turn
To his chillum again.

'Girdhar Kabra, the poet,
Says no one is good among them;
All those mentioned, they use liquor
And like children lie down in the way.
A charas smoker loses religious wisdom
Imparted by the guru
As well as vitality.
He is gradually reduced
To a mere skeleton
And his face resembles
That of a monkey.'

(From Punjab)

He who smokes
Ganja forgets
even his own
father's name.
(From Bengal)

Surprisingly enough, though the European mind is second only to India in its apprehension of the significance of Cannabis, most of their writings are concentrated on the symptoms and effects of the plant, whether they pose as objective or subjective observers, with clinical or philosophical bases for their judgments. Be this as it may, we nevertheless can gain a powerful insight into the Cannabis experience by listening for a while to the thoughts of these European and American experimenters with Cannabis.

Doctor Jean Moreau was a French physician who in Paris of the 1840's was closely associated with the literary group 'Le Club des Hashischins' whose members included Baudelaire, Gautier & Dumas. His experience with hashisch was extensive, and while his interest in placing the plant on a list of approved treatments for mental patients may well have made his clinical utterances a bit on the rosy side, he was nevertheless honest enough to record his personal experiences with enough accuracy that both opponents & proponents of Cannabis could get in their licks. It's really a shame that so much one-upmanship is played with the recorded history of Cannabis use & experience when an accurate job of reporting would surely provide any individual with enough thoughtful information that he could decide for himself whether or not his head would find Cannabis an essential tool or a horror.

Moreau writes:

Baudelaire.

Theophile Gautier.

Alex. Dummas

36

Thursday, Dec. 5th. I had taken some of the hachisch; I knew its effects, not by experience, but from what I had learned of it from a person who had visited the East, and I waited tranquilly, for the happy delirium to seize me. I took my seat at the table, I will not say with some, after having *relished this delicious paste,* for to me it seemed detestable; but after I had swallowed it with difficulty. While eating oysters, I was taken with a paroxysm of incontrollable laughter which was soon checked when I transferred my attention to two other persons, who, like me, had the fancy to taste the oriental article, and who already saw a lion's head upon their plate. I was tolerably calm until the end of dinner; then I seized a spoon and assumed a fencing attitude in front of a dish of preserved fruit, with which I imagined myself in combat, and I left the dining room bursting with laughter. Soon I experienced a desire to hear some music, to make it myself; I placed myself at the piano, and began to play an air from the *Domino Noir.* After a few measures I stopped, for a spectacle truly diabolical presented itself to my eyes; I thought I saw the portrait of my brother which hung over the piano, become animated; it appeared to me to have a black, forked tail, and to be terminated by three lanterns, one red, one green, and one white. This apparition presented itself to my mind several times in the course of the evening. I was seated upon a sofa, I suddenly cried out, "Why are you nailing fast my limbs. I feel as though made of lead. Ah! how heavy I am! Some one took me by the hand in order to raise me up, and I fell heavily on the floor, I prostrated myself after the manner of the mussulmen, exlaiming, 'Father I reproach myself,' &c, as if I was beginning a confession. They raised me up, and sudden change came over me. I took up a footstove with which to dance the polka; I imitated in voice and gestures several actors, among others Ravel and Grassot, whom I had seen a few days before in the Etourneau. From the theatre my thoughts transported me to the ball of Opera; the people, the noise, the light, excited me to the highest pitch; after a thousand incoherent speeches, all the while gesticulating, bawling out like the maskers, I thought I saw around me, I directed my steps toward the door of a neighboring room which was not lighted.

Now a frightful revolution took place in my feelings! I was suffocated, I gasped for breath, I was falling into an immense well, without bottom, the well of Bicetre. Like a drowning man who catches for help at a feeble bulrush which he sees elude him, so I strove to cling to the stones around the well, but they fell with me into this bottomless abyss. This sensation was truly painful, but of short duration, for I called out 'I am falling into a well,' and they drew me back into the room I had left. My first exclamation was, 'Am I a fool, I take this for a well, while I am at the ball of the Opera.' I struck against a stool; it seemed to me that it was a masker, who lying down on the floor was attempting to dance in that inconvenient way, and I begged a sergeant de ville to take him into custody. I asked to drink, they sent for a lemon to make some lemonade, and, I recommended the servant not to select one as yellow as her face, which seemed to me of an orange color.

I suddenly passed my hands through my hair; felt millions of insects preying upon my head. I ordered the by-standers to send for my accoucheur, who was then engaged with Mad. B———, in order that he might deliver the female of one of these insects who was with child, and who has chosen for her lying in room, the third hair upon the left side of my forehead; after a painful labor, the animal brought into the world seven little ones. I spoke of persons I had not seen for several years. I recalled to mind a dinner at which I was present five years ago, in Champagne; I saw the company; Gen H served a fish that was garnished with flowers; Mr K was at his left; they were before my eyes, and what was singular, it seemed to me that I was at home, and that all I saw took place at a remote period; they were there however. What was it I then felt.

But that was a happiness truly intoxicating, a delirium that the heart of a mother only can comprehend, when I saw my child, my much-loved son in a heaven of blue and silver. He had white wings bordered with rose color; he smiled upon me, and showed me two pretty white teeth, whose first appearance I had been watching with so much solic-itude; he was surrounded with a great number of children who like him had wings, and flew in this beautiful blue hea-ven; but my son was the handsomest of them all; of a truth there never was a purer intoxication; he smiled and stretched out to me his little arms as if to call me to him. Yet this sweet vision vanished like the others; and I fell from the upper heaven of which the hachisch had afforded me glimpses, into the country of the lanterns. It was a country where the men, the houses, the trees, were exactly similar to the colored lamps which lighted the Champs Elysees, the 29th July last. It recalled likewise the ballet of Chao-Kang, that I had seen at the aquatic theatre when a child. The lanterns moved forward, danced, were in a con-tinual agitation, and in their midst appeared more brilliant than them all, the three lanterns which terminated the false tail of my brother. I noticed especially one light which con-

tinually danced before my eyes, (it was produced by the flame of the charcoal that burned in the chimney.) Some one covered up the fire with ashes: Oh! said I, you would ex-tinguish my lantern, but it will return. In fact the flame flashed up again, and I saw the dancing of my light, green now, instead of white, as before.

My eyes were all the while closed by a sort of nervous contraction; they burned severely; I sought for the cause of it, and I soon found that my servant had daubed over my eyes with some encaustique, (a preparation of wax and turpentine) and that he was rubbing them with a brush; this was cause enough for the inconvenience I felt in the part.

I drank a glass of lemonade, then all at once, I cannot tell how or why, the imagination, my gracious fairy, trans-ported me along the Seine to the baths of Ouarnier. I would fain swim and yet I experienced a moment of bitter emotion in perceiving myself buried beneath the water; the more I tried to cry out the more water I swallowed, when a friend came to my assistance and drew me to the surface; I caught a view, though imperfect, through the curtains of the bath, of my brother who walked upon the Pont des Arts.

Twenty times I was upon the point of committing indis-cretions; but I checked myself with the remark I was going to speak, but I must be silent. I cannot describe the thousand fantastic ideas which passed through my brain during the three hours I was under the influence of the hachisch: they appeared too odd to be believed sincere; the persons present doubted at times, and asked me if I was not making sport of them, for I had my reason in the midst of this strange madness. My cries, my songs woke my child, who was sleeping on its mother's knees. Its little voice, that I heard weep, recalled me to myself, and I approached it; I embraced it as if I had been in my right mind. Fearing a crisis they separated me from it, and I then said that it did not belong to me, that it was the child of a lady I knew, who has none, and who always envies me it. Then I was out making visits, I talked, I put the questions and replied to them. I went to the Cafe, I asked for an ice, I found that the waiters had a stupid air, &c. After numerous strolls, in which I had met Mr So and So, whose nose was unnaturally lengthened, although it was already reasonably large, I re-turned home, saying; 'Oh, do see that great rat running in B's head.' At the same instant the rat swells up, and be-comes as enormous as the rat which figures in fairy story of "Les Sept Chateaux du Diable." I saw it, I would have sworn that this rat was walking on the head where I had so singu-larly placed it, at the same time I regarded the cap of a lady

'I had taken some of the hachisch . . .' An account by Dr Jean Moreau

The Mystery I
Am he grew
plain . . .
Reliable high
quality hachisch
of the 19th C.

present; I knew that it was really there, whilst B———was
only an imaginary being; but notwithstanding I can affirm
that I saw him.

A frightening but exciting experience such as this was
common among the members of the circle of *hashis-chins* during those years in Paris of the 1840's, and
much has been made of both sides of the issue by our
contempories arguing the marijuana question. Before
continuing with our look at the experiences of these
men, however, let's look a bit more closely at the
possible grounds for comparison of their experience
with ours.

While in much of the medical literature of the
English colonials there often is no convenient way to
distinguish whether or not they mean hashisch when
they use the term, in the case of the *hashischins* there
is never any doubt that they are talking about high-grade, unadulterated resin. There were no effective
restrictions on the importation, sale or use of Can-nabis products in Europe of that period, so it's un-likely that Moreau, Baudelaire et al. would have
obtained just any form of preparation when the best
was undoubtedly available. Moreover, in much of the
writing of the literary circle mention is made of a
doctor supplying the hashisch — Moreau, no doubt.
The above selection indicates that he had never before
tried the drug, but, he quickly became one of its fore-most advocates. And no doubt he would have assured
himself of a reliable, high quality source.

There is also the matter of the physical descrip-tion of the hashisch from the numerous *hashischins* —
'a paste;' 'a greenish paste or jam . . . drawn by means
of a spoon from a crystal jar;' 'a green sweetbread,
the size of a nut and uniquely odorous . . . an odor . . .
enhanced to its maximum of strength and, one could
say, density;' a 'rich extract . . . melted in a cup of
strong coffee.' From these descriptions and others,
one must conclude that the hashisch was pure resin &
pollen, a highest grade of charas, unadulterated by
the various substances used to cut & form run-of-the-

mill hashisch into small blocks so that it can be easily
transported & stored, losing, as it does, a considerable
amount of its potency in the process. The difference
between the *hashischin's* hashish & bhang, even ganja
and certainly street-grade contemporary marijuana
must have been as great as between 6% beer & uncut
grain alcohol.

Finally, there is the matter of how the hashisch
was ingested. Beyond any reasonable doubt, there are
extreme differences between smoking & eating even
street-grade marijuana, both in terms of its mental-physiological activity and its metaphysical properties.
To compare the experiences of these eaters of the
highest grade hashisch and the smoker of bhang or
marijuana is to perform a very risky leap of logical con-sequences. One of the grossest differences between
the nineteenth & the twentieth century European ex-periences with Cannabis lies in this method of usage.

Many of the tales of hashisch eaters & drinkers,
while they remain subject to some gross distortions
which strongly suggest toxic influences, nevertheless
are characterized by an appreciation of the more subtle
experiences of space & time alterations. The impor-tance of access to such out-of-place, out-of-time ex-perience is not often appreciated by those unac-customed to using their mental equipment free of the
strictures of the Western world-view with its narrow
concept of the pragmatic. But the reports are, for all
that, accurate and often beautiful to contemplate.

Charles Richet, 1877, expresses a common experi-ence (opposite) in a usual way — most writers struggling
to explain this experience need the inflexible clock to
re-orient themselves to real time. How strange that they
see the many thoughts a minute as an aberration of an
instrument, their mind, which ticks along as regularly
as their beloved clock mechanism until it is disturbed
by the hashisch. Today's clinical researchers express
the same concern in another way — they speak of the
problems of retaining a train of thought due to the rush
of associations.

But all of these problems seem to rest precari-ously on an unstated agreement as to the normal

Time appears of an unmeasurable length. Between two ideas clearly conceived, there are an infinity of others in-determined & incomplete, of which we have a vague consciousness, but which fill you with wonder at their number & their extent. It seems, then, that these ideas are innumer able, and as time is only measured by the remembrance of ideas, it appears prodigiously long. For example, let us imagine, as is the case with hashisch, that in the space of a minute we have fifty different thoughts; since, in general it requires several minutes to have fifty different thoughts, it will appear to us that several minutes are passed, and it is only by going to the inflexible clock, which marks for us the regular passage of time, that we perceive our error. With hashisch the notion of time is completely overthrown, the moments are years, and the minutes are centuries; but I feel the insufficiency of language to express this illusion, and I believe, that one can only understand it by feeling it for himself.—*Charles Richet (1877)*

Ch. Richet.

The Mystery I
Am he grew
plain . . .
Rejection of
spiritual or
metaphysical
possibilities

functioning of the mind. Rarely is this problem seen as a virtue, a benefit, a tool-access to other dimensions of the mind which are revealed by the subtle alterations of perception entered into through the Cannabis experience. Small wonder in the 19th century, on the doorstep of the Industrial Revolution with its regular mechanical rhythms, even less wonder today with our on-line, real-time machines, that such glances into these portions of the mental universe gain no great appreciation. It is remarkable, though, that our society — which places such emphasis on increasing data processing capability in its machines — would consider the 'fifty thoughts a minute' phenomenon as a liability rather than an asset. It is equally incredible that the effort of scientists has been largely to discredit the phenomenon, rather than to explore means of utilizing it. Most who have experienced their mind through Cannabis in this way would agree that you need a great deal of experience & effort before you can train yourself to use this phenomenon as a tool, for retention of the substance of the flow is indeed a problem. But hysteria alone can account for the general rejection of this capability. And how grossly hypocritical of a society which proclaims itself an explorer of the interior & exterior universe through a science which presumes to set men free through revelation & comparison.

Less explicable in terms of the temporal needs of great industrialized societies is the rejection of the spiritual or metaphysical possibilities which are open for exploration by the mind in companionship with Cannabis.

The most immediate & useful form of perception which the mind enjoys through the Cannabis experience, though this form of enlightenment is in no way limited to a dependency on a role played by Cannabis, is heightened mental activity.

One of the more enjoyable & entertaining games in this state is a fine appreciation of the absurd; a 19th century writer described it as ' . . . a wonderfully keen perception of the ludicrous, in the most simple and familiar objects.' It's quite possible that much of the 'maniacal laughter' noted by straight observers in experiments with subjects who have smoked or eaten Cannabis finds its origin in an exquisite sense of the improbability of their situation, wired to the gills and being asked a series of questions both incoherent & irrelevant.

A corollary of this perception of the absurd is the common experience of discovering & articulating unique meanings and associations in thoughts & words. This process is about as aberrant as the making of a pun, but it has probably attracted more eurekas from those seeking to discredit the Cannabis experience than any other single phenomenon. Condemnation of this phase of the Cannabis experience as evidence of abnormal mental functions seems to have its roots in the tick-tock concept of mental normalcy just described. Perhaps the answer can be found in the world which such judgments defend, a world of ordered relationships which are sacrosanct, a world which could be lovingly or savagely laughed at only by those engaged in a dangerous mental journey beyond its boundaries, travelling by illicit means. If the conveyance can be confiscated & destroyed, this reasoning may go, the travelers will no longer be able to go outside to indulge in their subversive humor.

The error here would be, of course, twofold. First it partakes of the mistaken notion that Cannabis is an agent, a device which transports the mind. Second, it fails to take into account that the sense if not the substance of the Cannabis experience is retained as a form of learning. Discovery of absurdity in our lives is an insidious process; once the first inkling is detected, the search is on for more. Fear is the only effective means for suppressing the initial step, and grows less effective, though it remains a powerful deterrent for a long time, as each successive step is taken.

Another usual experience, though one more common to Cannabis eaten & drunk than Cannabis smoked, is a distortion of normal spatial relationships. The distinction between eating and smoking here suggests that the distortion may principally be toxic in origin, and it does resemble in many ways some of the experiences of people suffering from organic disorders. Dr William Ireland, a principal figure in the Cannabis investigations of the 19th century, was very close to contemporary clinical evidence in attributing the altered perceptions of the Cannabis experience to mental shifts rather than sensory organ adjustments. It is too bad that he did not extend his intellectual inquiries further, but then we are not much further ourselves today after a hundred years of opportunity. He gives this account:

The description is difficult. In this illusion a bridge or an avenue appears to have no end, and to be prolonged to unheard of improbable distances. When one ascends a staircase the steps seem to rise to heaven; a river, whose opposite bank we see, appears as large as an arm of the sea. Vainly one notices the error of which he is the victim. The judgment cannot rectify this appearance, and we say 'Here is a bridge which has a hundred metres, but it appears to be as long as if it were 100,000 metres.'

I do not clearly understand how a man can see things larger or smaller without any change in the lenses of the eye, or in their adjustment, and it is difficult to conceive by what perversion of intellect one could estimate things smaller & larger than they really are. If we saw everything half as large, would the horizon not be doubled? And would it not be contracted when we saw things bigger? Or do certain objects appear larger or smaller, while the ground upon which they stand or move retains its usual apparent dimensions? The magnifying influence following intoxification through Cannabis upon the distance of visible objects, is only part of a general exaggeration of impressions, mental as well as sensual.

Dr Moreau would give to the increased sense of distance the same explanation which Richet restricts to that of the duration of time. Distance is measured by the number of intervening points between us and the extreme point seen: the attention runs from one point to another, and the number of these points being increased, the distance seems greater. There are instances on record where the power of vision is much increased; but, on the other hand, it might be contended that in accordance with the principles already laid down, increased clearness in seeing distant objects would have the effect of making them appear to the mind to be nearer rather than further off. The causes of this affliction are, probably, rather to be sought for in the hemispheres of the brain, than in the optic tract; they are mental, rather than physical.

A significant area of thought seems to be consistently overlooked in investigations into the role of Cannabis in altered perceptions; that is, the corollary to the arts, especially the graphic and dramatic arts.

One of the primary stocks in trade of the graphic arts is illusion—subtleties of color gives us volume, arrangement of visual clues gives us spatial relationships, advancing & receding lines give us dimension: the artist gives us field upon which we play out a mental game with many variations. Because we think of the piece of graphic art as created, and because we think we understand the rules, and because it is patently a game, we fail to see that the Cannabis experience converts our perception of the visible world in much the same way as the conscious guile of the artist manipulates the clues of his medium. Even if one insists that the world is as it is, uncomplicated by artistic duplicity, it must nevertheless be clear that what is seen is an interpretation of the clues which are perceived to be arranged in certain ways as a result of the way the world is.

It's clear that Cannabis has an insignificant impact upon the organs—sensory and otherwise—and if one is careful to distinguish between brain the organ & brain the mind there is little left to look at but the mind in explaining the altered perceptions of the Cannabis experience. And this same mind which takes pleasure in manipulating the clues of a painting can enjoy manipulating the clues of a world once it is freed to perceive it as a magnificent work of art, infinitely more pleasureably deceptive & open to manipulation than an artifice which originated in the mind of another man.

The time experience seems to follow a similar path, with its corollary in many of the arts which allow us to enter into a new set of time relationships. The dramatic presentation in which whole lives are played out in the space of a few hours; the book which absorbs us with an infinitely complex barrage of details—all the phenomena which draw our minds away from a reliance on the inflexible clock alter our time sense by providing us with a new set of time references. The Cannabis experience is at least partially one of focusing attention on what is already in the mind, the streaming thoughts, impressions & associations of an incredibly complex intellect. Cannabis is not the creator of the time warp anymore than the reader is the author, any more than the viewer is the dramatist. Cannabis may be the agent of perception, but it is neither the

42

discoverer nor the discovery.

The horror which is attached to the altered perceptions of the Cannabis experience is largely unfounded in general experience. Rather it seems largely due to perversions in the method, the agent or the person. It is difficult to understand how the connection between this altered perception and the experience of man with his art forms is not realized. There are analogies which could be drawn: as many men & many groups consider forms of art to be dangerous, so many of the same consider Cannabis subversive. As many people look at a painting and rack their brains for a meaning, so many people wait for a particular preconceived something to happen to them in their first Cannabis experience. As one develops a taste, discrimination & discipline in art, so one must learn to handle the medium of the Cannabis experience. As art can be exploited and exploitative, so with Cannabis. As the finer points of art are largely a matter for the connoisseur, so there is a vast territory beyond the simple high. As there are many mediums within which the artistic experience may be stimulated, so there is wide variation in the quality & intensity of the medium of the Cannabis experience.

The third classic aspect of perspective change through the Cannabis experience is on the auditory level though, again, there is no question of the ear being rendered more sensitive through an action on the part of Cannabis. The key to increased sensitivity to nuance & pattern in music, of greater discrimination among the whole range of sounds normally not heard in the ordinary state seems to be that the mind is less liable to distraction with Cannabis, and therefore is increasingly able to make sense of sound. In the case of music, this ability is often interpreted as an ability to understand or feel the intent of the composer and musicians, and as a greater sensitivity to the range of capability of individual instruments. The Cannabis experience, again, offers the untrained mind's ear an opportunity to perform in a way similar to the intensively trained perception of the musician; it does not alter the sensory organs at all. Yet the novelty is sufficient to impress upon the listener how powerful an instrument of comprehension he possesses and to allow him the use of this discovery long after the involvement with Cannabis.

All of these aspects of Cannabis have drawn the attention of philosophers, writers and, occasionally, scientists. One of the most brilliant, albeit polemical treatments of the total Cannabis experience was performed by Charles Baudelaire in his work *Les Paradis Artificiels,* written & revised over a ten-year period spanning the 1850's. The following passages are excerpted largely from the first section of the book, a group of interlocking essays titled 'Du Vin et Du Hashisch'.

'Are you *sure* its the wine?'

Le Hashisch (4) Notes on the Hashisch Experience

During the harvest season for hemp, one notices from time to time certain strange phenomena among the workers, both men & women. One might say that they were elevated in spirit by the harvest season, but that would not explain the dizzying spirits which entwine their limbs and maliciously creep into their minds. The head of the harvest-hand is at once full of turbulence & charged with reveries. Their prostrated limbs are of little service. I am reminded of the intoxication of the child, myself, tumbling in the heaped piles of fresh alfalfa.

Attempts have been made to produce hashisch from the French variety of hemp. All such attempts have failed, and the madmen who wish at all costs to sample the enchantment of hashisch must consume hashisch from across the Mediterranean, from Egypt or India.

Common hashisch is a decoction of Indian Hemp mixed in butter, with possibly a dash of opium. You then have a green sweet, singularly odorous, so odorous in fact that it is somewhat repulsive, an odor at once pervasive & thick. Taking a nut-sized portion up in a tiny spoon you eat, and are possessed with happiness — an absolute stuporous happiness, a callow happiness of infinite complacency. Such happiness as this lies there for you, in a little morsel of sweet; take it without fear, you won't die of happiness; your physical self cannot be injured gravely by such as this. And if your will comes out of the experience somewhat diminished, that's entirely another concern.

In general, to derive from hashisch its full force, for a full development of the sensations, you should dissolve it in hot, black coffee taken on an empty stomach; have nothing to eat for ten hours preceding — if you must, have only a light soup. Infraction of this rule very simply will make you vomit as your dinner quarrels with the drug, and will wipe out the effects of the hashisch. Many are the imbecilic & ignorant who, because of rejection of this principle, accuse hashisch of being an impotent yet nauseous drug.

Scarcely has the drug been taken, an operation which like all other matters requires some resolution because, as I mentioned, it has a certain nauseous quality, you will begin to notice the onset of anxiety. You have heard rumors of the marvelous effects of hashisch, your imagination has been stimulated by these tales, and you long to know if the reality, and the results, do justice to your expectations. The period which will elapse between ingestion and the onset of the first symptoms will vary with your temperament, and your experience. Those who have had previous knowledge of

43

hashisch begin to feel, in about half an hour, the first signs of invasion.

Oh, I forgot to mention that hashisch produces an irritable state of mind, which is strongly affected by the tenor of the surroundings, so take care to undergo the experience only in pleasant company & comfortable surroundings. For joy and well-being are magnified, and sadness & anguish are magnified in proportion to the milieu. And also, don't undertake this experience if you must soon engage in some disagreeable task, if your spirit is splenetic, or if you have bills to pay. I've warned you: hashisch is unpredictable. it does not console like wine, it does nothing but develop the possibilities in the personality and the surroundings at any given moment. Further advice — take it in an attractive apartment or with a view of a striking landscape; be of good spirits, and gather around you those with intellectual bent similar to yours; arrange for a little music, too, if possible.

Most of the time novices at their initiation complain of the slow progress of the effects. They anticipate anxiously, and when things do not keep pace with their anticipation they give out with blustering incredulity, to the delight of those who well know the things & the manner in which hashisch governs. There's nothing much more comical than to watch the novitiates' first symptoms emerge & become magnified in the face of their denials.

Quickly a certain irresistible hilarity of manner becomes evident. Words grow more coarse, and quite simple ideas take on bizarre, novel forms. The gaiety of it all begins to turn, becomes a strain; but it is useless to balk. The demon has invaded you; your struggles merely accelerate the process now. You laugh at your willful folly; your comrades laugh, though without malice, and you forgive them as a certain benevolent air begins to settle over you.

This phase of languid gaiety, this malaise amidst joy, this uneasiness, this faint, indecisive sickness lasts generally but a short time. At this point sometimes men begin to speak interminable foolishness, wholly disconnected plays on words, making absurd & improbable mental leaps which are beyond the provenance of even the masters of mental games.

Quickly, within minutes, the ideas grow more vague, the threads of thought even more tenuous, allowable only among co-religionists & accomplices.

The sagacity which comes of this unhappy state imparts a sang-froid; you are pushed to the outer limits of irony; you become party to the most insane & ridiculous which man has to offer. Among you and your comrades there seems perfect

understanding. Soon you arrive at the point where the eyes say & understand all. The fact is that this situation is passably comical, a group of men engaged in revelry incomprehensible for any who do not inhabit their special world. They take on as well an aspect most profoundly pitiful. Yet even in this state, delusions of a superior intellect haunt the horizons of your mind. These convictions grow apace.

The second phase announces itself with a sudden chill, a great enfeebling rush, your hands lose their power to grasp, your head becomes intolerably heavy, and your entire being is stupified. Your eyes enlarge, drawn large by an implacable ecstacy. Your face pales, grows livid, then subsides to a green pallor. Your lips grown thin, their foreshortened appearance makes them seem to sink inwards. Great sighs rack your breast, as if your ancient basic nature were incapable of supporting this new load. The senses becomes exquisite, developing an acute sensitivity. You can see to forever. You hear finally the most inaccessible sounds amidst the general noise.

And now the hallucinations! Monstrous shapes emerge from the most ordinary objects. The commonplace reveals itself to you in forms previously unimagined. Their deformations seem to enter your being, or equally, your soul is drawn in and absorbed by their frightful essence. Ideas arise from unfathomable reaches of the mind, and are transposed upon the surface in inexplicable patterns. Sounds take on shades of color, and colors arrange themselves along a musical scale. Harmonic relationships resolve into a calculus which streams with frightening speed through your ear. You are transfixed with your pipe — it is your substance going up in smoke, and the clouds of blue vapor you exhale are the combusted remains of your soul.

Now a singular idea grows in force — how to escape from your pipe. You ponder this for an eternity. Then arrives a moment of lucidity as the idea slips its grasp — you notice the clock. A minute has passed in this world. Your mind is diverted once again into another stream, it seizes you & sweeps you along its course — another eternal moment. All proportions, time & your being, are submerged in the rush of sensations & thoughts. Several lifetimes occupy but an hour on the clock. It could be an outrageous tale, an interplay between the physical realities and the timeless meandering intellect.

On occasion the personality disappears. That concentration on the external, which is the hallmark of the great secular poets and master comedians grows & dominates your outlook. You become a wind-whipped tree, regaling all nature

The Mystery I
Am he grew
plain . . .
'You are above
the level of
all men . . .'

with your organic music. Now you sweep formless into the immensity of an azure sky. Lethargy disappears. You struggle no more, yet are impatient; you have no self-control, but there is no sense of loss. Soon there is no time sense remaining. Once in a while a little window of reason opens. It seems that you are about in a fantastic world of untold marvels. You retain, true, a certain sense of your identity, enough so that tomorrow you will be able to say 'I was there, I saw such & such.' But you cannot take advantage of this faculty while enmeshed in the dream. I defy you to record your experiences at the time — it is beyond your capability.

Another aspect of this phase is the transport of music, which whispers to you intricate poetry, and spins you onto stages where the players are mad. Music fastens on the world before your eyes — the ceiling hosts a grotesque collection of flickering demons. An enchanted dew settles upon fluttering grass. Nymphs with flawless bodies appear to watch you carefully with their clear blue eyes. You are absorbed into an evil landscape, merging with a gross tapestry which obscures the distant nature.

I've noted that waters have a peculiar charm for those whose spirits have been illuminated by hashisch. Waters flowing in their beds, waters leaping into the air, waters falling in graceful harmonies, the blue immensity of the sea, rolling, resting, chanting interminably to your spirit — it's not good to leave a man in this state too long near water. Like the fisherman in the ballad, he may become fatally entranced by Ondine.

Towards the end of the soiree, one may eat, but even this activity is not without its difficulties. You experience a great reluctance to stir from your resting place. If your appetite grows to enormous proportions, perhaps you will be able to respond but even then it takes courage to face a bottle of wine, to take up knife & fork.

The third phase, following the vertiginous crises of the other, is almost indescribable. It is what the Arabs call Al Keif, an absolute tranquility. Your mind is done with turbulence. Your spirit is beatific & at rest. All philosophical questions are resolved. All of the arduous searches of theologians, all of the despairing quests of human reason are finally clarified. The threads of all contradiction are knit together. The man has passed beyond God.

There is something which tells you 'You are above the level of all men; no one understands as you. Equally, they are incapable of knowing the immensity of your love for them. But it is not for you to loathe them, rather to feel a deep pity. Goodwill & the virtue of a peaceful soul are your lot. No one

will ever know the heights to which you are risen at this moment. In your clarity & precision of thought you shall now address the afflictions of mankind.'

One of the most grotesque aspects of hashisch is the fear experienced in pursuing the suggestions which occur at this point. The mind is reluctant to go further and pushes back, if it can, to avoid a confrontation with those who might benefit from such benevolence, certain of the disturbance which it would cause.

In this supreme state, love, spiritual center of the tender and gentle spirit, begins to take on the most baroque forms. The unbridled libertine is all mixed up with a tender paternal sense.

And my final note, equally bizarre. When, the following morning you become aware of the new day that has crept into your room, your first sensation is one of incredulity. Time has wholly disappeared; night has just been & day is now. 'Have I slept, or no? What was the nature of my stupor, that all the night is valued by my intelligence as but a second. Or have I been shrouded with dreams in a sleep which only seemed to be a waking state.' You will never know.

But your spirit this morning is light, and there is no fatigue. But you are faintly aware of a need for repose. You move about with tender concern for your limbs, and you balance your head with great delicacy. A languor, not without its charming side, lays upon your spirit. You rest without spur to action of any sort, drained of energy.

This is the price of your prodigal expenditure of nervous energy. You have projected your spirit into the far winds of the sky, and now is the time to call it home.

Now I don't claim that hashisch produces such effects as these in all men. I've simply tried to give a general description of the progression of states, with variations, which are encountered in the experience of men of artistic & philosophical temperament. There are those temperaments which the drug affects only by producing a gaudy foolishness, a violent humor resembling a reeling drunk, madcap dancing, leaping & stomping about, accompanied by a maniac's laughter. For them hashisch has no spiritual or intellectual component. They are looked down on by those who enjoy the more elevated experience. Their low grade personality is simply broken by the drug.

I once saw a magistrate, a respectable & honorable man in the opinion of all, one of those men of inestimable gravity, burst into a most indecent can-can upon the invasion of his mind by hashisch. If there lurks a monster inside the man, he is invariably exposed. This judge of others, this honorable man, was duly condemned by his personal monster in the heat of a can-can.

It would be well to note, too, that the superior perspective, the objective intellectual achievements of which I have spoken are attributable only to the mind itself, and are in no way inherent in the hashisch.

Note on the political and economic morality of hashisch

In Egypt, the government condones sale & use of hashisch, at least in the interior. The unfortunates afflicted with a passion for hashisch acquire it at dispensaries where they go on the pretext of buying some other drug, but where they have arranged for their little dose well in advance. The Egyptian government has its reasons for this arrangement. Never has a rational state existed without some controls over the use of hashisch. Hashisch users will be neither warriors nor even proper citizens.

In effect it is encumbent upon any government to minimize the access of its citizens, on pain of forfeiture of their intellect, to such primordial destructive vices. If there exists a government which wishes total corruption of its populace, it has only to encourage & facilitate the use of hashisch.

It is said that this substance causes no physical damage.

That's true, as far as we now know. But I don't see how one can argue for no damage when a man is rendered incapable of all but dreams, however intact his body may be. When the will is attacked, the most precious organ has been threatened. There has never been a man who could, with a little piece of sweet, instantly acquire all that is good & beneficial without the most infinitesimal evidence of effort on his own part. There is no substitute for work & experience.

The idea came to me to talk of wine & hashisch in the same article because they share some of the same attributes & aspects. The stimulation of man's poetic nature. Man's inexorable taste for any substance, benign or dangerous, which exalts his personality & enhances his status. He aspires always to relive his experiences in his quest for infinity. But we should examine the results of these two routes. On the one hand, we have a liquor which stimulates digestion, fortifies the muscles & enriches the blood. Even if wine is taken in vast quantities, the accompanying liabilities are short-lived. On the other hand, we have a substance which interrupts proper digestion, which enfeebles the body & stupifies the mind for a space of twenty-four hours. Wine exhaults the will; hashisch annihilates it. Wine is a physical asset; hashisch drives you toward suicide. Wine

'It is said that this substance causes no physical damage...' Comparison of types. 'Addicts' and the Cairo Police Guard (right), 1929.

The Mystery I
Am he grew
plain . . .
The fancy of
Lord Dunsany

renders you jolly & sociable; hashisch turns you irritable & insolent. The one stimulates painstaking effort; the other makes you sloppy & idle. To what end would one trade the ability to work, write, and create for something whose sole recommendation is a dream. In the final analysis, wine is for people who work hard, who earn their right to drink, while hashisch suits only those who pursue solitary pleasures — it well suits such miserable loafers. Wine is useful and its effects creative. Hashisch is useless & dangerous.

Despite its several internal inconsistancies & misdirected arguments, Baudelaire's essay stands as the finest description of one form of the Cannabis experience. It is also one of the most objective pieces ever written; that is, Baudelaire's prejudices are clearly labeled, and we know a great deal of the sources of those judgments from our knowledge of his history as a man.

A few American writers have seriously attempted to deal with Cannabis on the level which Baudelaire did, fewer still English writers. The English drug literature is largely taken up with accounts of the virtues or liabilities of alcohol & the opiates, and Cannabis seems not to have had much impact on those chilly isles.

If few Englishmen recorded any interest in Cannabis, those who did were usually less than effusive. The mystical, mental side to the drug seems to have had little appeal to the English writer. Lord Dunsany was one of the few Englishmen who recorded their experiences with Cannabis, and his fancy rivals those of the Hashischians:

It was about that time that I got the hashish from the gypsy, who had a quantity that he did not want. It takes one literally out of oneself. It is like wings. You swoop over distant countries and into other worlds. Once I found out the secret of the universe. I have forgotten what it was, but I know that the Creator does not take Creation seriously, for I remember that He sat in Space with all His work in front of Him & laughed. I have seen incredible things in fearful worlds. As it is your imagination that takes you there, so it is only by your imagination that can get you back. Once out in aether I met a battered, prowling spirit, that had belonged to a man whom drugs had killed a hundred years ago; and he led me into regions that I had never imagined; and we parted in anger beyond the Pleiades, and I could not imagine my way back. And I met a huge gray shape that was the Spirit of some great people, perhaps of a whole star, and I besought it to show me my way home, and it halted beside me like a sudden wind & pointed, and, speaking quite softly, asked me if I discerned a certain tiny light, and I saw a far star faintly, and then It said to me, 'That is the Solar System,' and strode tremendously on. And somehow I imagined my way back, and only just in time, for my body was already stiffening in a chair in my room; and the fire had gone out and everything was cold, and I had to move each finger one by one, and there were pins & needles in them, and dreadful pains in the nails, which began to thaw; and at last I could move one arm, and reached a bell, and for a long time no one came because everyone was in bed. But at last a man appeared, and they got a doctor; and *he* said that it was hashish poisoning, but it would have been all right if I hadn't met that battered, prowling spirit.

A more decadent approach to Cannabis, still very English, is this passage by John Symonds, a 19th Century critic, who was not really talking so much about hashish as his self-glorified profession:

What is left for modern man. We cannot be Greek now. The cypress of Knowledge springs, and withers when it comes in sight of Troy; the cypress of pleasure likewise, if it has not died already at the root of cankering Calvanism; the cypress of religion is tottering. What is left? Science, for those who are scientific. Art for artists; and all literary men are artists in a way. But science falls not to the lot of all. Art is hardly worth pursuing now. What is left? Hasheesh, I think, Hasheesh of one form or another. We can dull the pangs of the present by living in the past again in reveries or learned studies by illusions of the fancy and a life of self-indulgent dreaming. Take down the perfumed scrolls; open, unroll, peruse, digest, intoxicate your spirit with the flavor. Behold, here is the Athens of Plato in your narcotic visions; Budda & his anchorites appear; the raptures of St Francis & the fire-oblations of St Dominic; the phantasms of mythologies; the birth-throes of religion; the neuroticism of chivalry; the passion of past poems; all pass before you in your Maya world of hasheesh, which is criticism.

When we move to America we find still fewer things written about Cannabis on an intellectual or philosophical level, though such a literature is slowly developing at this time. With the exception of a few early writers, Taylor & Ludlow, and some of the modern writers, most of the literature in America which is concerned with Cannabis treats Cannabis more as a plot prop than as a central concept.

Bayard Taylor wrote several steamy pieces on his experiences with hashisch, the most notable being a long, rococco chapter in his travel book *Land of the Saracens*. Taylor's descriptions of his hashisch experiences do not approach the levels of Baudelaire, Moreau or the other Hashischins, but his account of his initial experiences with the drug reported in *Journey to Central Africa* in 1856 is a pretty good condensation of the sensations on which he later elaborated at length:

'Journey to Central Africa'

While in Egypt, I had frequently heard mention of the curious effects produced by *hasheesh*, a preparation made from *cannabis indica*. On reaching Siout, I took occasion to buy some, for the purpose of testing it. It was a sort of paste, made of the leaves of the plant, mixed with sugar and spices. The taste is aromatic and slightly pungent, but by no means disagreeable. About sunset, I took what Achmet considered to be a large dose, and waited half an hour without feeling the slightest effect. I then repeated it, and drank a cup of hot tea immediately afterwards. In about ten minutes, I became conscious of the gentlest and balmiest feeling of rest stealing over me. The couch on which I sat grew soft and yielding as air; my flesh was purged from all gross quality, and became a gossamer filigree of exquisite nerves, every one tingling with a sensation which was too dim and soft to be pleasure, but which resembled nothing else so nearly. No sum could have tempted me to move a finger. The slightest shock seemed enough to crush a structure so frail and delicate as I had become. I felt like one of those wonderful sprays of brittle spar which hang for ages in the unstirred air of a cavern, but are shivered to pieces by the breath of the first explorer.

As this sensation, which lasted but a short time, was gradually fading away, I found myself infected with a tendency to view the most common objects in a ridiculous light. Achmet was sitting on one of the provision chests, as was his custom of an evening. I thought: was there ever anything so absurd as to see him sitting on that chest? and laughed immoderately at the idea. The turban worn by the captain next put on such a quizzical appearance that I chuckled over it for some time. Of all turbans in the world it was the most ludicrous. Various other things affected me in like manner, and at last it seemed to me that my eyes were increasing in breadth. 'Achmet,' I called out, 'how is this? my eyes are precisely like two onions.' This was my crowning piece of absurdity. I laughed so loud and long at the singular comparison I had made, that when I ceased from sheer weariness the effect was over. But on the following morning my eyes were much better, and I was able to write, for the first time in a week.

Another American who sought adventure abroad and found Cannabis was RCV Bodley who, while visiting Algeria in the 20's, wrote this account:

49

The Keef Smoker

Before closing these sketches of Arab life a word must be said on a vice which is luckily not very prevalent, but which nevertheless exists in many centers.

I speak of keef-smoking.

Keef is a dried flower of the hemp-plant chopped up and smoked like tobacco, rolled in a cigarette, or in the bowl of a small pipe. In a different form it is the basis of the hashish sweets, rarely seen in Algeria, but very common in the Near East.

The effect of keef on the smoker is to make him practically independent of food and sleep as long as he is under its influence, and a habitual keef-taker is easy to detect. His eyes are very bright, his face is pale and drawn, his arms and hands are terribly thin, his movements are restless. At the same time he is not at all dazed like one under the influence of a drug, and though after a few days' smoking he will drift off into a kind of feverish sleep, during the early periods he is extraordinarily lucid. In fact, it is said that the first effects of keef are to make the brain work at three times its normal pace.

European tourists in the south occasionally get hold of some keef to smoke, and complain that it has had no effect at all beyond giving them a sore throat. This is quite normal, as the fact of smoking a little hemp in a pipe or cigarette will hurt no one if not continued. To feel the effect of keef one must smoke for at least one night through, and three days are necessary to get really poisoned. The danger of an experiment of this kind is that the desire to go on may seize one, and once keef has taken hold of a man it is rare to see it give him up. However, it is quite amusing to go to a keef-smoking den, all the more so as it has to be done in secret and with the connivance of a smoker, as no outsiders know where these little nocturnal *reunions* take place.

As a matter of fact I doubt whether there is much danger of the police interfering as, though it is against the law to smoke keef, the French are not going to try to stop something which must always go on, and unless the offense is deliberately open they will not peer into the dark streets to catch a few poor Arabs.

The town where keef-smoking is the most prevalent, I believe, is Ghardaia — not of course among the puritan Mzabites, but in the Arab quarter. This is partly due to the fact that these Arabs are far away from their own people, and club together in small groups to do what they would not dare do before their relatives in their own oases.

I remember going to one of these places in the Mzab

with some English friends who wanted to see the den for themselves. We were a curious party — an English girl, a short-story writer and another man connected with letters — none of whom knew the country well, while our Arab guide was the *khodja* of the Bureau Arabe, a man unbelievably fat, who rather sailed along the street than walked. We passed through interminable little streets, pitch black, fell up and down steps until we came to a tumble-down house, all dark save for a yellow light which flickered in an upper chamber. The tinkle of a mandolin floated out, a warm breeze sent little whirls of dust up the narrow way, the stars stood out bright in the sky.

Our immense companion tapped mysteriously at the door, the sound of the mandolin ceased, and we heard some one coming cautiously down-stairs. A few whispered words were exchanged, followed by the noise of heavy bolts being drawn, the door swung back, and we found ourselves in front of a rickety wooden staircase at the foot of which stood an Arab in tattered clothes, who held aloft a hissing acetylene lamp. He scrutinized us closely, and then, bidding us enter, drew aside as we filed slowly past and followed our fat friend up the stairs. The janitor waited till we were all inside, and then with a clash shot back the bolts, and we felt ourselves prisoners in this illicit haunt.

At the top of the stairs we came to a room dimly lighted, and the first thing which struck our attention was an enormous skin full of water. When I say that it struck our attention it is not quite exact, as in reality it was struck by the head of my friend S A , who had not noticed it until a stream of icy water poured down his back. When we had recovered from this pleasing little incident we looked about us.

On the floor all round the little room squatted men of all ages and grades — some in rags, some in prosperous-looking *gandourahs,* some in very modern red fezzes — but all with the same hungry look on their drawn faces. At the far end the Arab who had opened the door attended to the little fireplace ornamented with colored tiles and on which he prepared coffee and mint tea; in the middle of the group sat the mandolinist playing with a far-away look in his shining eyes.

The air was heavy with a sweet, rather sickly smell, an odor not unlike new-mown hay, only stronger. A bench was mysteriously produced for us and for our stout companion, who explained that if he sat on the ground he would never be able to get up again. Tea was placed before us, and then rather diffidently one of the corpses on the floor rose and offered Miss G a small pipe. Seeing she was prepared to smoke, he drew a wallet from the folds of his *gandourah* and filled the bowl with the strange grayish-green, tobacco-looking matter, and handed it back to her.

In the meanwhile we had also been supplied with similar pipes, and in a few moments we had lighted up. The taste was not pleasant to the regular pipe-smoker like myself, and at the same time it was not as nasty as my first attempts at smoking when in the depths of a wood my brother and I, aged nine and ten, filled a cast-off pipe of my father's with brown paper in the belief that we were smoking!

Keef is better than brown paper. The taste and smell were rather like that of hay.

When the company saw that we were quite human and ready to join in the fun there was a general relaxation. All the pipes were lighted, the mandolinist tuned up, and soon the whole crowd was as merry as children at a birthday party. In fact, so great was the effect of the atmosphere that S A insisted on singing himself, and would have danced had not M J, who has his interests at heart, held him forcibly on the bench.

I don't know how long this would have gone on had not a discreet signal from the street warned us that the police were making their rounds. In a second the light was dimmed, the music ceased, and we sat as still as mice until we heard the measured tramp of the Arab constables disappearing up the street. We felt it more discreet to depart ourselves, so we took leave of our fevered-eyed hosts and returned to our inn.

Though I spent a rather restless night, I don't know if it was the effect of the keef or not, and we all certainly felt quite fit the next day.

Still, I can never think of that night without smiling; it was all so mysterious, so much part of another world, and I often wonder if MJ, as he sits editorially in London, or SA, scooping in royalties, or Miss G, in her English surroundings realize how they peeped into the past for a few seconds and lived again the life which, if it had not been Algerian, would have probably been celebrated by another DeQuincy.

Of the literature which has developed in America with marijuana as a plot device, the most fascinating stuff has been cranked out by the anti-marijuana forces. The anti-marijuana novel developed as an art form in the late 1920's, and reached its apothesis in the late thirties. Novels of this genre were published by two organizations, one in Tennessee and one in California, which also published leaflets & pamphlets warning of the dangers of the Killer Weed. These publishers were well-financed and show strong connections to both the languishing prohibitionist forces and to the sources of capital which had supported much of the prohibition propaganda machinery.

A good example of this genre is the novel *The Dope Adventures of David Dare,* which arrived toward the end of this period in American folk art. This marvelous little novel takes us through the plot setting, a small-town middle-America with focus on the local adolescent community, and sets the scene with a chapter entitled 'High School Boy Faints,' wherein the first indication of drug use among the teens appears to us, and to a bemused David Dare. We are then taken on a fudge sundae, A&W baseball trip through the town with David, who has decided to discover the source of this ubiquitous menace. Suspicion focuses on a dark stranger lately come to town, but also on some of David's acquaintances. Could it be that his friends are mixed up in this pernicious business? The crisis is building, as the bobby-soxers degenerate even further in a chapter entitled 'Movie Mad'. Alarmed by what he sees, torn between what he knows to be the true way and loyalty to his strayed friends, David prays for guidance and the Lord tells him to fink. The local fuzz are skeptical at first ('In our fair town?') but David draws upon his strong inner convictions and forcefully persuades the minions to examine more deeply the significance of the escalating sales of ju-jubes during intermissions at the Bijou. Finally, the law is convinced and, more than that, David is vindicated. The law is proud of him. He can stand tall, knowing that he is a good Christian citizen. Not only that, he is made an honorary cop. Which means that the title of the next chapter is (absurd

not to have guessed) 'David Goes On A Dope Raid'.
The raid is accompanied by a confrontation between
the pusher, some of his acne-scarred victims and David
(backed up by the police), all of which makes for a
glorious opportunity for David to orate on the fate of
all criminals, junior or otherwise. The dope is seized,
a few of the more truculent teenagers are hauled off
to do time, David is once more congratulated, and we
are then treated to the final chapter, 'David Meets The
Shadow,' who, true to life, knows what evils lurk in
the hearts of men and confirms David's suspicion that
the weed of crime bears bitter fruit. He proceeds to
recruit David for further adventures. Which excites
the lad. Then he and The Shadow . . . Anyway, David
is much stronger, much more confident, much more
likely to make it with the FBI after The Shadow gets
through with his head. And we are left with the un-
shakable conviction that if we are ever so rash as to
fall tempted to the Killer Weed, David Dare will be
around to point the finger at us, for he is now enlisted
in the forces of The Shadow.

Less entertaining than the adventures of David
Dare are the myriad official & unoffiicial books which
have been cranked out purporting either to be scientific
or blantantly propagandizing against marijuana. It
would be undignified to include many such passages
in a discussion of literature, but a few are both
meritorious & indicative. In a feverish book
titled 'The Conspiracy of Silence' we find the
following panegyric:

It is not sufficient that we should carry the triple burden
of Morphine, Heroin, & Cocaine addiction, with their
attendant evils, plus widespread ignorance of the subject
and a general lack of interest other than in official circles,
but now a new Gorgon rears its head above the horizon
of our national life to add its sinister threat to a condition
that is already far out of bounds.

In recent years our burden of youth has become overrun with weeds, the most loathsome and deadly of all para-
sitic growths — *Marijuana* (NB. This is 1938).

Prolonged use of marijuana frequently develops a
delirious rage which sometimes gives man the lust to kill,
unreasonably & without motive, and leads to high crimes
such as assault, rape, robbery, & murder. Hence Marijuana
has been called the Killer drug.

While the Marijuana habit leads to physical wreckage
& mental decay, its effect upon character & morality are
even more devastating. The victim will frequently undergo
such moral degeneracy that he will lie & steal without
scruple; he will commit acts that, in the light of returning
reason, cause him to hide his face in horror & shame and
even indulge in greater excesses in an effort to forget. He
becomes utterly untrustworthy & often drifts into the under-
world, where, with his degenerate companions, commits
high crimes & misdemeanors.

Rick Griffin

The history of Cannabis' role in American society is very shallow; few Americans became aware of the plant as anything other than a fibre crop until recently. The first mention of the use of Cannabis as a drug appears in American medical journals in the 1840's, coinciding with the period in Europe when a growing awareness of its euphoriant qualities among travelers & literary figures was developing. Cannabis had, however, been with us since the earliest days of the American colonies, and it seems unlikely that no one had discovered the minor joy of standing downwind as a field of fibre hemp was fired to clear the land. A contemporary narcotics official has put it that 'You might pull the leaves from the marijuana plant of some farmer who is growing it to make hemp rope, and you might as well smoke corn silk.' But then, smoking corn silk and just about anything else is and was a time-honored rural American tradition.

Very few early Americans, however, did write anything of their experiences with Cannabis, and those who had such encounters usually made use of imported tinctures. One is drawn to suspect that the practice of smoking homegrown hemp was not unknown, though, by passages such as this from an early gardening journal:

The ornamental value of Marijuana

In connection with planting around the rural home it is often difficult to select some rapidly growing plant that may be used to form a screen to conceal something beyond, or to form a clump to make a break in an extended open space. In many instances it may be desirable to plant something that will remain but a single season, and which will form a hedge to separate two distinct parts of the lawn or garden. It is essential to secure a plant of rapid growth, of sufficient strength to withstand the force of wind or any ordinary injury, and one that will be attractive. All these requirements are met within the Indian Hemp, Cannabis Indica.

The hemp plant is a native of India & Persia. It is of well-known commercial importance for its fibre & its alkaloid properties. The dried leaves & flowers are used both along & mixed with tobacco for smoking purposes. When grown in warm countries there exudes from the stems a resinous compound which is highly narcotic, and in great demand for use as an intoxicant. The commercial importance of Indian Hemp need not be considered in this connection, for the plant is worthy of cultivation for its ornamental value alone.

The species of hemp usually grown for fiber, Cannabis Sativa, should not be selected for growing as an ornamental, as the leaves are too coarse & rough and the plant has not the proper shape either to form a screen or to present an attractive appearance, except when grown in large quantities. The plant of Indian Hemp grows to a height of from four to six feet, is closely branched, compact, and spreading, with numerous finely divided leaves. The leaflets have a drooping habit which adds very materially to the graceful appearance of the plant. A perfectly developed plant of Indian Hemp, when viewed from a distance, has the appearance & general outline of the young trees of Red Cedar, Juniperus Virginiana.

The color of the plant is of deep green, sometimes with a bronze tinting on the stems. When the foliage is disturbed by the wind it has a silvery or frosty appearance due to the presence of innumerable small plant hairs on the under side of the leaves. On a warm day and with a light wind blowing there are few things more pleasing to the eye than a field of growing hemp.

To which many of us may add 'Amen,' and secretly revise our opinions of Grandma, Grandpa, & the East Platte Garden Club.

The Mystery I
Am he grew
plain . . .
Were Your
Grandparents
Junkies?

There are quite a few valid reasons why Cannabis was not a popularly known drug in the early stages of American history. Prominent among these was the fact that Americans had access to so many strong drugs already, drugs which performed the tasks of intoxication & stupefication without the unwanted potential for clarifying thought & perception. Use of drugs on a large scale is not a new phenomenon in Western societies, nor is wholesale addiction. The current epidemic has yet to reach the proportions of the narcotic plague which persisted for generations in this country during the late 19th & early 20th Centuries. Conservative estimates of the addicted population of the United States at the turn of the century place the number at between one and two million living persons. This does not take into account the large number of people, namely children, who succumbed to toxic dosages of opiates. Given the population of this country during these years — around 75-100 million people — the chances are quite good that one of your grandparents was a junkie, or that one of your great uncles or aunts never survived beyond infancy to produce cousins for you.

One of the largest markets for opiates in the country was the soothing syrup trade, aimed primarily at infants who were giving their parents a hard time by crying & carrying on, or who made the mistake of appearing sickly. This genre of medicines included preparations which were known as baby syrups, colic cures, infants' friends, teething concoctions and so forth. Parents were put at ease by labels which assured that the preparation 'Contains nothing injurious to the youngest babe' and that 'Mother need not fear giving this medicine to the youngest babe, as no bad effects come from the use of it.' Laws were passed to prevent such claims appearing on preparations which did, in fact, contain addictive & toxic dosages of opiates, but then, as now, the laws were quickly circumvented by quick-thinking entrepreneurs. A representative list of products offered to distraught parents of uptight infants looks something like this:

Dr James' Soothing Syrup Cordial — Heroin
Children's Comfort — Morphine Sulphate
Dr Fahey's Pepsin Anodyne Compound — Morphine Sulphate
Dr Fahrney's Teething Syrup — Morphine and Chloroform
Dr Miller's Anodyne for Babies — Morphine Sulphate and
   Chloral Hydrate
Dr Fowler's Strawberry and Peppermint Mixture — Morphine
Gadway's Elixir for Infants — Codeine
Dr Grove's Anodyne for Infants — Morphine Sulphate
Kopp's Baby Friend — Morphine Sulphate
Dr Moffett's Teething (Teething Compound) — powdered
   Opium
Victor Infant Relief — Chloroform and Cannabis Indica
Hopper's Anodyne — The Infant's Friend — Morphine Sulphate
Mrs Winslow's Soothing Syrup — Morphine Sulphate

There are numerous cases on record in the medical journals of this period of infant drug addictions; a very few infants died of liberal doses of these friendly snake oils. The addicted child syndrome was quite common — as soon as the effects of one dose of the soothing syrup wore off, the child became irritable and raised a fuss which led to a quick mouthful of the medicine to quiet the ruckus. Infant addicts appeared plump & healthy and, except for their periodic tantrums when mama was late with the elixir, they appeared on the surface to be pink & pacific. As a matter of fact, however, their metabolism was very poor, they withstood illness very badly and their musculoskeletal development was seriously impaired.

Shortly after several of the more restrictive laws had been passed, some manufacturers of these soothing syrups began putting out products which were, in all respects, the same except that the syrups no longer contained the opiates & other narcotics. These new products apparently did not give satisfaction to the harried motherhood of the country, for there were immediate & vocal demands that the 'old kinds' of preparations be once more put on the market.

In the tradition of free enterprise, which holds that it is imperative that a consumer consume from the cradle to the grave, regardless of the quality or

THE MOTHER'S MISSION.

A great Emperor once asked one of his noble subjects what would secure his country the first place among the nations of the earth. The nobleman's grand reply was, "Good mothers." Now, what constitutes a good mother? The answer is conclusive: She who, regarding the future welfare of her child, seeks every available means that may offer to promote a sound physical development, to the end that her offspring may not be deficient in any single faculty with which nature has endowed it. In infancy there is no period which is more likely to affect the future disposition of the child than that of teething, producing as it does fretfulness, moroseness of mind, etc., which if not checked will manifest itself in after days.

USE MRS. WINSLOW'S SOOTHING SYRUP.

The Mystery I
Am he grew
plain . . .
Caffein and the
Cocaine Kolas

length of that span, the entrepreneurs of America did not neglect other markets for their products. One ready-made market for the imaginative manufacturer was a result of our preference for anything but water. Soft drinks were a national institution by the early 1800's, and when the flood of narcotics began in the latter part of that century, the fizzy drinks were a national pool into which the opiates began to flow. A marvelous new technique for assuring consumer brand loyalty — the ideal equilibrium state in a free capitalist society — presented itself in the form of addictive drugs.

The primary addictive agents found in the soft drinks of this period were cocaine and caffein. In the initial stages of this developing industry, the kola nut played a prominant role due to its reputed tonic & stimulant qualities. Most of the contemporary soft drinks with some variation of the word kola in their name grew out of this initial belief. After several years of manufacturing soft drinks from extract of kola nuts, however, it was discovered that kola nuts didn't really contain any significant active ingredient except caffein. Kola nuts were expensive to process, and the supplies were somewhat limited, so naturally the soft drink manufacturers began to look around for ways to cut their expenses & increase their profits. They found their answer right in their own backyard — it turned out that waste tea leaves could be easily processed to get the caffein they needed, and this, of course, represented a tremendous savings because they were then able to use the waste products of one drug industry to support the growth of a second drug industry. A triumph of ingenuity.

Of course the competitive aspects of the soft drink industry made it inevitable that no one was going to be fully satisfied with simple caffein extracts, and many foresighted pioneers turned to cocaine as a natural additive. Cocaine had a long folkloric history, full of accounts of its tonic virtues. People were not generally negative toward cocaine, which somehow seemed more natural & healthy than opium and its derivatives.

During the days of the industrial revolution, when millions of people were being subjected to tedium &

boredom in the name of economic expansion, destined to create the good life for all, tonic drinks had a ready-made market among the pick-me-up crowd. The problem quickly became so serious in this country that life insurance companies, those bellwether institutions of practical capitalism, began to raise the rates on people who drank more than a certain number of soft drinks in the course of a long day in the factory. Among the brands viewed askance by the insurance folks were Koca Nola, Celery Cola, Wiseda, Pillsbury's Koke, Kola-Ade, Kos-Kola, Cafe-Cola, & Koke. These brands were, of course, the favorites of the swinging Kola generations of the 80's and 90's.

The opiates do enjoy a wide range of useful application in the treatment of diseases, and they are particularly effective in mucous disorders of the breathing system. Opiate drugs have been used for over two hundred years, both by legitimate physicians and by people who for one reason or another chose to treat themselves for disease and organic disorder. Taking advantage of the latter group, which numbered in the millions in this country before the advent of large scale medicine, many manufacturers of asthma & catarrh remedies liberally dosed their customers with cocaine, codeine, chloral hydrate, heroin, morphine, opium, belladonna, stramonium, lobelia, potassium iodide, potassium nitrate & so forth. Most commonly these curatives relied upon the opiates.

One of the many asthma remedies available to sufferers was, 'Davis Asthma Remedy,' the brainchild of an enterprising realtor. This curative contained a primary active ingredient of chloral hydrate, and each dose at the recommended level consisted of from one to eight grains of the stuff. Quality control was pretty much lacking in those days. The directions and the label read 'Dose can be increased or diminished or taken as often as needed. Adults can repeat it as many as three doses all within fifteen minutes. Tell others how it benefits you after using it.' Chloral hydrate is, naturally, addictive & holds a firm place in American folklore as the notorious knockout drug.

Asthma remedies such as that of Davis' were commonly sold as cures for catarrh — the common chest cold — but there were also several specific catarrh cures on the market. Most of these specifics contained cocaine in liberal doses. One of the biggest sellers was a brand known as Dr. Agnew's Catarrh Powder, out of Baltimore, Maryland and, after the Food and Drug Acts were passed, out of Toronto, Canada. The mutual food and drug laws made it an offense to ship cocaine-laden drugs interstate, or to trade in them in any area under Federal jurisdiction, but that did not deter the most aggressive of the dealers. Dr Agnew, for one, proved particularly hard to stop. A USDA agent reported in 1907 that "A clergyman (from Washington, DC) interviewed the writer some time ago as the possibility of taking action against a certain firm supplying his communicants with a catarrh powder formerly under the name of Dr Agnew's Catarrh Powder; and if so, what the charges would be. The firm was also advised that the reason for making the application was that the laws of the District of Columbia were so stringent & so rigidly enforced that it was exceedingly difficult, if not impossible, to purchase any cocaine or cocaine preparation in this jurisdiction. The firm in question responded to the effect that the desired article would be sent at a certain price. The amount named for three packages was transmitted by postal order and three packages of Dr Agnew's Cattarrh Powder were duly received."

Dr Agnew's Catarrh Powder contained 10 grains of pure cocaine to the ounce. This was an exceptionally generous portion, no doubt designed to promote return customers; but there were quite a few remedies in competition with Agnew for the market. Several of these competitors took the route of advertising their remedies as cough & cold specifics, leaving catarrh & asthma to the big boys. Examples of these medicaments, aimed chiefly at the youth market, are:

Acker's English Remedy—Chloroform
Adamson's Botanic Cough Balsam—Heroin Hydrochloride
Dr A Boschee's German Syrup—Morphine
Dr Bull's Cough Syrup—Morphine & Codeine
Dr Femer's Cough-Cold Syrup—Morphine
Jackson's Magic Balsam—Chloroform & Morphine
Von Totta's Cough Pectoral—Chloroform & Morphine
Pastilles Paneraj—Chloroform & Morphine
Kohler's One-Night Cough Cure—Morphine Sulphate, Chloroform & Cannabis Indica
Chlorodyne Pastilles—Morphine, Chloroform & Ether

Many cold & cough sufferers in those days did not have colds or coughs—they had tuberculosis. Who could then blame the quick thinking businessman for cashing in on the ready market of consumption cures. These remedies did, in fact, allay that coughing, tickling sensation & other distressing symptoms so effectively suppressed by the heavy doses of narcotics in those narcotic cures that they died, true enough, of terminal lung disease; but they died without so much as a tiny wheeze. Some of the well-known and widely used consumption cures were:

Tuberculozyne—Heroin
Prof Hoff's Consumption Cure—Opium
Gooch's Mexican Consumption Cure—Morphine Sulphate
Dr Brutus Shiloh's Cure for Consumption—Heroin & Chloroform

Part of the CIA's anti-kif campaign in Morocco. The French and Arabic script read: Kif destroys the body and mind.

الكيف يحطم الجسم والعقل

LE KIF DETRUIT LE CORPS ET L'ESPRIT

58

Along with the ills of TB & chest ailments in general, things weren't going so well with the heads of the population. Headache mixtures in those days commonly contained codeine and morphine, along with acetanilid, acetphenetidin, antipyrin, & caffein. Epilepsy cures were also highly touted, usually containing one or more of the bromides in addition to the run-of-the-mill opium & morphine.

One of the most interesting aspects of this whole drug scene was the very large business which grew out of drug addiction treatments and cures, largely of the home-remedy type, which were advertised as 'mail order express treatments.' If you were on the mailing list of the patent medicine promoters, after a period of time you could count on receiving literature on these cures for narcotics addiction. Response was, naturally, quite heavy.

The only catch to the cure was the nature of the treatment. In most cases the addiction cure was presented as highly secret & profoundly respectable compound known only to the agent offering this

miraculous substance. The true nature of these addiction treatments were, however, much closer to the mundane. Mail order physicians commonly prescribed formulae such as: 'alcohol 12.5%; morphine 22.0 grains per fluid ounce; cannabis indica extract 4 minims to the fluid ounce.'

The 'James Mixture for the Gradual Reductive Treatment of Narcotic Drug Addictions' contained 24 grains of morphine to the fluid ounce. Habitina, product of the Delta Chemical Company, contained 16 grains of morphine sulphate and 8 grains of heroin to the fluid ounce. Such treatments characteristically bore the solicitous injunction, 'When you open this bottle, order your next month's treatment in order to avoid any break.'

Heroin was the most common ingredient in these express treatments, and for good reason. Heroin had just been developed as a cure for morphine addiction. It was considered a positive turn of events when an addict switched from morphine to heroin, just as today methadone is lauded for its benign narcosis.

In the course of time the average American's access to most of these drugs was inhibited, and by the early years of the Twentieth Century it had become extremely difficult to obtain the opiates, cocaine & other such drugs without the cooperation of either doctors or the newly forming underground syndicates which dealt in bootleg drugs. This situation was near unbearable for the millions of addicts existing in America at the turn of the century, and very few alternatives presented themselves. Those with the heaviest habits and the most means, continued to deal in those drugs to which they were addicted. Others, those less addicted & those without money, came to depend more & more on alcohol.

Even the second & third decades of the Twentieth Century—the period of greatest deprivation for the addicts of America—there was little turning to marijuana for two reasons. First, marijuana was not, even at this point, a widely known & used drug, and second, it did not do as good a job of deep intoxication as alcohol, principally because what marijuana was available was not particularly potent stuff. Had high grade

'When you open this bottle, order your next month's treatment in order to avoid any break'

Marijuana was not widely known— Photograph: Peter D'Agostino

Opposite: The Morning Tribune, New Orleans, 1940's

charas, or hashish, been readily available in America in the 1910-1930 period our drug history might well have been rewritten, and with that key phenomenon altered, our entire subsequent history as a nation redirected. We may, in fact, now be seeing a delayed expression of this phenomenon. The incidence of the joint use of hashish, alcohol, amphetamines and barbituates is on the increase. The difference is that the context of society has so altered, and the capabilities of individual members so extremely reduced, that before this dependence on intoxication as a mode of existence wears off the society may be shattered. Perhaps we had a chance to change this direction; perhaps if we had treated Cannabis with intelligence through our institutions we would have been able to react intelligently to its use as individuals. Certainly many do use Cannabis constructively — some temporarily, some permanently, so there would seem to be hope. It is possible that balance can be restored, and the direction of drug use changed from a search for intoxication to a search for self. Perhaps we can learn from the past of ourselves and others. Perhaps. But it does seem that our choice as a society lies not in whether or not we use drugs — that is fixed for the forseeable future — but in what drugs we use & how we use them.

Seattle, 1970
Photograph:
Peter Riches

Opposite: The
Morning Tribune,
New Orleans,
1940's

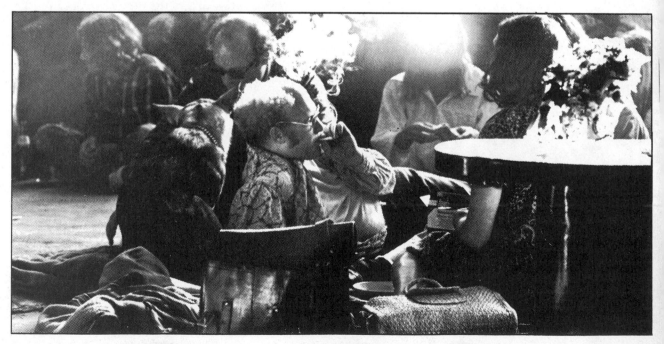

Two: A brief ramble through the history of Hemp

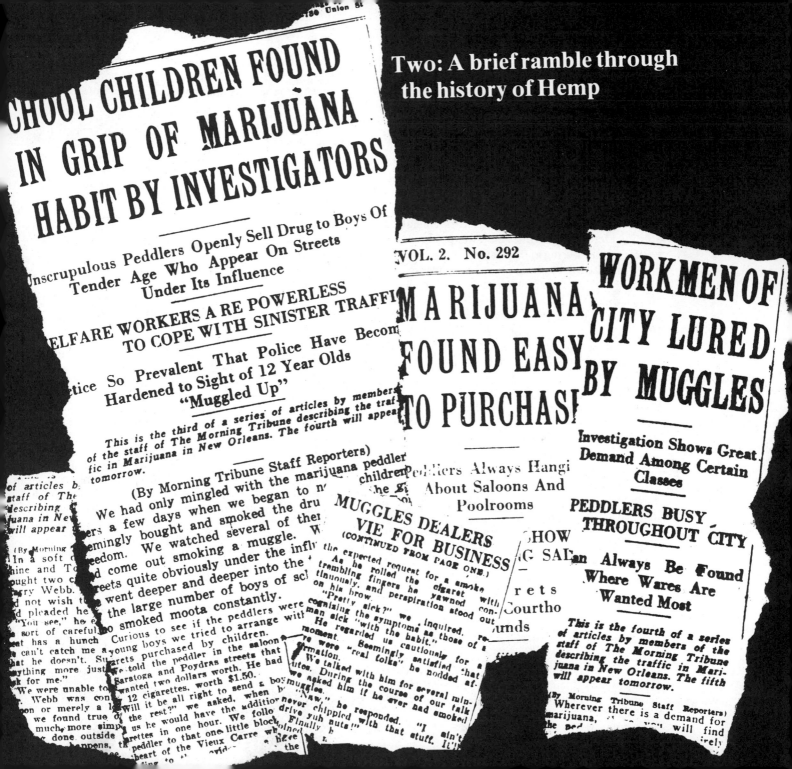

Hemp drugs are interwoven with the historical development of many societies in many periods, but few of them have recorded their experiences with Cannabis at length. No culture at any period has sung the praises of hemp as exhaustively as the Western cultures have celebrated alcohol, their longstanding drug of choice. In the Near & Far East, we can read the influence of hemp drugs into the histories of nations only by inference, for while hemp was celebrated as a paramount blessing in the natural order there was little written directly about the cultural impact of the plant. Perhaps this is as it should be. It is somehow more natural for a culture to grow & develop without being obsessed with the sources of its configuration. Nevertheless this paucity of historical record leaves us with little more than speculation as to the role played by Cannabis in the major societies of the East in the pre-colonial days.

With the coming of the colonials the record of hemp drugs in the major Eastern cultures began to fill in. Cannabis had been known in Europe before Christ, though it was hazed in the exoticism of the Orient and its use was not widespread. It was only natural that as the early legions of empire seekers set forth from the continent they were aware of hemp drugs as one of the more mystifying phenomena of the East.

The earliest of these reports were fanciful; not negative or moralistic as they were later to become, just bemused by the apparent powers of this simple weed. This was in the age of scouts, travelers & explorers for the European powers. Their job was to assess the tenor of the East, to begin to bring to Europe some elementary notions of the inner workings of the vast lands & populations which lay before her nations in their march toward dawn.

Most of the reports on hemp drugs reaching the European continent in the 17th & 18th centuries resembled each other in style & content, usually in the form of an aside in an account of a traveler's encounter with the weird practices of the natives. A Frenchman, CS Sonnini wrote of Egypt in 1800:

Hemp is cultivated in the plains of these countries; but it is not spun into thread as in Europe, although it might probably answer for that purpose. It is, nevertheless, a plant very much in use. For want of intoxicating liquors, the Arabs and Egyptians compose from it different preparations, which throw them into a sort of pleasing inebriety, a state of reverie that inspires gaiety and occasions agreeable dreams. This kind of annihilation of the faculty of thinking, this kind of slumber of the soul, bears no resemblance to the intoxication produced by wine or strong liquors, and the French language affords no terms by which it can be expressed. The Arabs give the name of *keif* to this voluptuous vacuity of mind, this sort of fascinating stupor.

The preparation most in use from this hemp is made by pounding the fruits with their membranous capsules; the paste resulting therefrom is baked, with honey, pepper, and nutmeg, and this sweetmeat is then swallowed in pieces of the size of a nut. The poor, who sooth their misery by the stupefaction produced by hemp, content themselves with bruising the capsules of the seeds in water, and eating the paste. The Egyptians also eat the capsules without any preparation, and they likewise mix them with tobacco for smoking. At other times they reduce only the capsules and pistils to a fine powder, and throw away the seeds. This powder they mix with an equal quantity of tobacco, and smoke the mixture in a sort of pipe, a very simple, but coarse imitation of the Persian pipe. It is nothing more than the shell of a cocoa-nut hollowed and filled with water, through which a pungent and intoxicating smoke is inhaled. This manner of smoking is one of the most ordinary pastimes of the women in the southern part of Egypt.

All these preparations, as well as the parts of the plant that serve to make them, are known under the Arabic name of *haschisch**, which properly signifies *herb*, as if this plant were the herb, or plant of plants. The *haschisch*, the consumption of which is very considerable, is to be met with in all the markets. When it is meant to designate the plant

---

*This denomination of *herb* has led M. Niebuhr into an error. "The *haschisch*," says he, "is sort of herb which M. Forskal, and some others who have preceded us in the East, have taken for the leaves of hemp." (Description de l' Arabie, p. 50.) It is nevertheless very certain, that the *haschisch* of the Arabs is nothing more than a species, or a variety, of hemp, of which I have just given a particular account.

itself, unconnected with its virtues and its use, it is called *baste*.

Although the hemp of Egypt has much resemblance to ours, it, nevertheless, differs from it in some characters which appear to constitute a particular species. On an attentive comparison of this hemp with that of Europe, it may be remarked, that its stalk is not near so high; that it acquires in thickness what it wants in height; that the port or habit of the plant is rather that of a shrub, the stem of which is frequently more than two inches in circumference, with numerous and alternate branches adorning it down to the very root. Its leaves are also not so narrow, and less dentated or toothed. The whole plant exhales a stronger smell, and its fructification is smaller, and at the same time more numerous than in the European species.

It took full-scale colonization of the Eastern world to bring Europeans into close contact with hemp drugs, and to produce for the first time an extensive literature on the role of Cannabis in the social & economic lives of people in societies where its use was common & traditional.

The Colonial literature suffers obvious defects. It is largely observation, not experience. It has as its object comprehension with a view to manipulation of foreign culture. It is Western-limited & pragmatic. It is largely the work of soldiers, managers & the professional classes like physicians. It treats hemp drugs as falling in the same class as Western drugs, and their users into the Western categories of drunkard & addict. It has a curious preoccupation with mental aberration, and tends to see it everywhere.

In short, it is often superficial & ethnocentric, rarely objective & sensitive reporting. Yet it is about all that we have by way of access to the history of hemp in these cultures, and so we are forced to look largely through the Colonialists' eyes. But since so many of the assets & liabilities of Colonialism are so clearly understood, while we borrow their eyes, we need not subscribe to their vision. And the Colonials do have some strong points. They were not subtle about their prejudices. Many of them were competent, analytical people who were trained to deal with facts first, opinion second. Many had a penchant for detail, and were good observers of surface phenomena. Then there were some who, for whatever their reasons, genuinely loved the nations and people which, through their government, they exploited. These people, some of them whose families had lived in the country for generations, occasionally give us deep insight into the workings of these societies. This was particularly true of the English in India & the French in Algeria.

Of those countries which were colonized by European powers, India, Egypt, & Morocco have given us the most extensive views of the relationship of hemp drugs to their culture as seen through the eyes of the Colonials. There are vast differences between the experiences of the Colonials in each. Then, too, there are great gaps in the records of each country as reported by the Colonials, for their approach was by & large motivated by official policy and not by personal interest. So what we have, once all available records are assembled, is still a spotty picture of the depth at which these cultures were moved & shaped by their drugs. But even such a fragmented picture should help to give us a better understanding of our own culture's dilemma in these times.

An English physician, director of the Cairo Hospital for the Insane, wrote in 1903 that:

I'M SO WASTED!

The Cannibinomaniac is a good-for-nothing, lazy fellow, who lives by begging & stealing, and pesters his relations for money to buy hasheesh, often assaulting them when they refuse his demands. The moral degradation of these cases is their most salient symptom; loss of social position, shamelessness, addiction to lying & theft, and a loose irregular life, make them a curse to their families. While in the asylum they are notorious for making false charges, refusing to work, & quarreling. Some deny using hasheesh, but others boast of its stimulating effects. They often have an inordinately high opinion of themselves. They are loud in their complaints of oppression by the police, and emphatically protest their innocence of any misdeeds. Irritability, unconcern as to the future, loss of interest in family, malingering, continual demands for cigarettes, urgent petitions for release, emotional outbreaks when refused their demands, garrulity, abusive threats alternating with extreme servility, are all marks of this state. These patients do not often ask for hasheesh while in the asylum, but occasionally procure it by stealth, though the craving for it does not appear to be so keen as that of a dipsomaniac or a morphinomaniac. No phenomena of deprivation are noticeable, and therefore the cessation of the habit should be easier than in the case of alcohol or opium, and I believe that it is actually easier.

In the early stages these individuals are usually regarded as criminals, and their moral lapses land them in the gaol. Later on, when their intellectual impairment becomes more marked, they are sent to the asylum.

'The effects of Drug Addiction' — A Lawyer's Clerk before and after '6 years addiction'

When comparing the Colonial Cannabis experience in Egypt & India, one finds in almost every case a marked difference in approach & outcome. The Colonials themselves recognize that they were dealing with vastly different cultures & societies, yet beneath it all there were two points upon which they agreed there was little difference. First, they felt that they were dealing with races of people who, whatever their differences, stood in a lump on the other side of that remarkable formula for dichotomizing the world, English/non-English. Second, they agreed that many non-Western aspects of each society needed to be understood as a first step to altering those societies to fit the English image, and that one of the most salient non-English phenomena in each case was extensive use of Cannabis Sativa.

Reports which the English Colonials prepared on their experience with Cannabis users in the Orient were rarely calculated to give a balanced impression of the role of Cannabis in the societies on which they were reporting. A massive & profound exception was the Report of the Indian Hemp Commission, which sat throughout India in 1893-4 and issued its seven volume report in 1894. This extraordinary document is so important and has been, until recently, so overlooked in America that we will save its serious consideration for Chapter III. In any event more typical of the run of the mill impressions received on the English home front is this essay produced by Dr John Davidson, who was vacationing in Morocco on leave from the Cheshire County Asylum, Chester, England where he was superintendent:

Cannabis indica or *cannabis sativa,* as medical men are aware, furnishes the product known as hashish, a product which has been the subject of much serious study, and which is known all over the East for its extremely intoxicating quality. The name hashish is adopted only in Egypt and Syria; in Turkey it is known by the name of *esrar,* where the term hashish is only applied to the poppy —*papaver somniferum,* from which opium is extracted. The Turkish word *esrar* simply means secret production or secret preparation, a term first applied by the simple-minded inhabitants of Anatolia, where the plant is extensively grown. In Morocco it is universally known by the name of *kif,* an Arabic word, signifying quietude or rest. It is in much use throughout the whole of that magnificent country, and it may be said that all those Moors, Berbers, and Arabs whom one meets in the streets of the cities dragging themselves about, and looking with a dull, stupified expression of countenance, like men who have just had a blow on the head, are victims to this deleterious drug. The greater part of them smoke it, mixed with a little tobacco, in small clay pipes, by which means prompt action is produced, while others eat it in the form of a sweetmeat called *madjun,* made of butter, honey, nutmeg, and cloves. This *madjun* is a soft paste of a violet colour, with a smell like pomatum. The *esrar* powder is not unfrequently taken in water, when its effect is very rapid and injurious. In Turkey the *esrar,* eaten as a sweetmeat, has both the colour and odour of coffee, for in its preparation much care is taken to water the *esrar* powder with a strong infusion of coffee.

On arriving in the locality where *cannabis* is cultivated the *esrar* merchant divides into squads the large number of people that accompany him. They then enter the extensive fields of *cannabis,* and commence cutting off all the flowering tops of the plant in order that the leaves, from which the product is drawn, may become more developed and more vigorous. A fortnight after this operation the harvesting begins, the merchant being first assured that the leaves have considerably enlarged, and that they present much viscosity to the touch. The plants being all collected and placed under a shed, the leaves are detached from the stalks and laid out to dry upon a large linen carpet called *a kilim.* As soon as the leaves have reached the desired dryness they are picked up and placed together upon one half of the *kilim,* the other half being reserved for rubbing them rudely until they are reduced to a powder. This first product is at once sifted, and put aside with care, for it constitutes the choicest quality of *esrar,* and is called *sighirma.* The residue, con-

'...Like men who have just had a blow on the head'

taining the fibrous tissue of the leaves, is reduced to a powder in the same manner. This second product, called *hourda*, is not by any means esteemed, for while the first quality is usually sold at about sixteen shillings the pound, the other, on the contrary, scarcely fetches the half of that sum.

The *esrar*, which reaches the capital of the Ottoman Empire, is enclosed in double sacks, the exterior bag being of horsehair, and that of the interior of skin. All powder of *esrar* is not entirely consumed in the country, for more than the half passes into Egypt, Algeria, Tunis, Morocco, and other benighted lands where Islamism holds sway. Prior to being delivered for consumption it is subjected to various processes of manufacture according to the different tastes of the inhabitants of the countries to which it has to be transmitted. In Egypt and Syria, as is well-known to all inquiring and observant travellers, the confection extract is held in the highest esteem, while at Constantinople this preparation is disliked because of its rancid odour and taste, which render it most unpalatable. The *esrar* most patronised in Turkey, is chiefly to be had in the form of a syrup, with which sherbet is prepared, or as lozenges, which the lovers of this baneful intoxicant smoke with *tombeki*. As the simple syrup of *esrar* always has a disagreeable odour and rancid taste, it is never forgotten to add to it such aromatic substances as *bahart*, without neglecting at the same time to enhance it with something of an aphrodisiac character. This latter corrective always plays a very important *role*, for by the excitation of the genetic organs, which it provokes and maintains, there is imprinted on the extatic delirium a special direction of ideas, with a series of the most sensual and voluptuous visions, thus procuring to all those who make use of the drug a foretaste of the delights and pleasures of paradise, which the Moslems in general believe are reserved in the future life to all true believers in Islamism and its founder, Mohammed. On visiting a coffeehouse in one of the Moroccan cities much celebrated for the excellence of its coffee and *kif* as well as other *agrements*, I had the opportunity of witnessing the drug both smoked and eaten. Shortly after being indulged in — say about half an hour — a feeling of great hilarity is created, some laughing most unmeaningly, and fancying they are being lifted from the ground and carried through the air in the arms of angels; but the wind-up to this pleasurable feeling is a sudden, deep, and painful melancholy, while a poignant aspect of remorse and regret is depicted in every countenance. The joys of *kif* and the *dolce far niente* have now completely vanished,

and the indulgers in the drug have been rendered the most miserable of men.

That hashish taken to excess in any form or by whatever name it may be called is a most prolific cause of insanity is a fact beyond all question or doubt, for the large numbers of *santos*, or saints, constantly met with in Morocco everywhere one turns, who have been long the slaves of this vice, doubtless afford the most conclusive evidence of its pernicious effects on the brain and nervous system. Many of these *santos*, who receive the greatest homage, and are regarded with the profoundest respect and veneration by the Moors, are very frequently most dangerously homicidal, while not a few of them have been reduced to a most deplorable state, the condition of drivelling imbeciles.

Syphilis is another most potent and fruitful source of insanity throughout the entire length and breadth of Morocco, scarcely a family being free from the syphilitic taint, which, it is alleged, was first introduced into the country by the Jews who took refuge there on being driven out of Spain, before which time, however, it was not known in Morocco even by name. It was first called "the Spanish sickness," but is not known now by that appellation. The Moors call it "the great disease," *mrd-el-kebir*, or "the woman's sickness," *nord-el-nssauin*. So common is this disease in this portion of Africa, I have been informed, that there is scarcely a Moor in Barbary who has not more or less of the virus in his blood; indeed, in many families it has become hereditary.

The peasantry in the interior of Turkey and Asia Minor are most abstemious, both as regards eating and drinking, being greatly dominated by the religious sentiment, which forbids to them the use of all fermented liquors. Less scrupulous upon this point than their co-religionists of the interior, the Mussulmans of the capital of the Osmanlis, in order to procure pleasant and agreeable sensations, often have recourse to other substances not less hurtful to the health than *esrar*, namely, mastic, raki, and other fermented drinks, while throughout the whole of Morocco till beyond the Atlas mountains, from the highest grades in society to the lowest, wine, gin, and brandy distilled from dates are indulged in to a very large extent indeed, notwithstanding the interdiction by the Koran of the use of all fermented beverages.

Having given as full and accurate an account of hashish and its various preparations as a brief paper like this will permit, I will only add that it is my intention to describe in a future paper the police measures adopted by the Government of Turkey against the use of the esraric substance by

158. ALGÉRIE — Fumeur de Kif

Biskra Ouled Naïl Halima

Jeune fille au Harem.

The joys of kif
and the 'dolce far
niente' —
Postcards from
North Africa,
circa 1910

the people; to set forth more fully the ordinary phenomena that its use provokes in men in the enjoyment of their reasoning faculties; to describe the experiments made with the drug which I have witnessed on the insane in the East; and also to point out the various disorders which the use of *esrar*, hashish, or *kif* occasions in the intellectual, physical, and moral conditions of those who abuse it, and also the hereditary consequences of its abuse.

The colonials were great ones for attributing behavioral differences to racial distinctions. British Commissioner in Burma wrote that:

In every case (of ganja possession) with which I have had to deal in my 31 years' experience in this province the offender was a native of India. The effect of the prohibitory system has undoubtedly been to render it somewhat difficult & dangerous for any one to possess the drug, and this must have very largely tended to keep it out of the hands of Burmans. In my opinion, if this system had not been adopted, the results would have been disastrous. Burmans would very certainly have taken to the use of ganja, and from their national character those who took to it would have used it to excess as is the case now with opium which, taken in moderation, does not harm.

It is most important to remember that the markedly characteristic feature in the Burman character is want of self-control. A Burman is, as a general rule, unable to deny himself anything obtainable. He won't work if he can get the natives of India to work for him; he no sooner makes money than he spends it on silk clothes or in gambling at boat, cart & pony races. Naturally happy & good-natured and by

Algeria 1896

68

religion & training careful of life, he, on comparatively slight provocation, attacks his own friend with any weapon on which he can suddenly lay his hand, and will cause death without a thought because he cannot control himself sufficiently to think. Long-premeditated crimes of violence are comparatively rare: a dacoity is got up in a day or two and is carried out often enough by men who are ordinarily fairly honest peasants, but perhaps gamblers or opium-smokers, or most rarely, if ever, drunkards in want of money to satisfy what by indulgence has become an uncontrollable craving. If a Burman takes to gambling, to drinking, or to opium-smoking, he is for this very reason lost, and he, by want of self-control turns what is a harmless amusement or pleasure into a vice which utterly ruins him and makes him still more recklessly self-indulgent than he is by nature. It is for this reason that opium-smoking is for Burmans such a monstrous evil. If a Burman took to ganja in a similar way, as he would were its consumption & even possession not prohibited, the effects would be terrible.

I regret that the very fact of prohibition (of ganja) renders it impossible for me to furnish you with any statement of fact, except that I have never known a case of a Burman using ganja.

نباتات الحشيش كما هو النمو وبه الازهار

We can see from such reports that many of the paranoid myths still harboured in America of the 70's have their counterparts, if not their origins, in a relatively antique period. The British concern with moral decay among the natives may legitimately be written off as part of their attempt to Anglicize the Eastern world. By their own evidence, moral decay is largely an ethnocentric judgment, though in fairness that same concern was & is shared by the political rulers of the nations where the colonials held sway.

Such concern can probably be explained by the indisputable effects on a population of large scale use of Cannabis, which differs in the extreme from most other drugs. Cannabis is not a drug which is compatible with an industrial society, nor is it likely to draw favorable responses from the would-be architects of an industrial society. The conflict between a social, economic & educational elite hoping to benefit further from western-style progress and a vast, submerged agricultural & urban peasantry which rightfully saw no place for themselves in the schemes of the elite and so chose to continue in one of their few pleasures, cannot be so simply written off. The reaction of the rulers in these societies to Cannabis usage has long been swift & harsh, tempered upon occasion only by a realization of the tax-generating potential of the Cannabis crop.

For example, in the Fourteenth Century AD Cannabis use was well established in Egypt. Periodic attempts at suppresssion had been made over the preceding years, but the various virtues of the plant exempted its users from full-blown prosecution. In particular, Cannabis was recognized as a valuable medicinal plant, and its pleasure-inducing properties were lightly regarded by the rulers of Egypt. In 1320, however, a new, highly moralistic regime came to power. One of the primary sources of its moralism seems to have been a concern with putting the country on a favorable trading basis with its neighbors & the Mediterranean countries of the North and East. It recognized that widespread use of Cannabis on the part of the population was inimical to its economic interests and so promulgated a series of severe ordinances against cultivation, sale & use of Cannabis products.

The valley of Dijonica, long the primary producing area for Cannabis, which had been exempt from restrictions for several centuries & around which had grown several important & wealthy towns, was put under seige by specially trained elements of the royal guard. In the space of a few months the valley was captured, the towns razed, and the vast acres of Cannabis burned & turned under. In the towns, cafes which were the centers of Cannabis trade & usage were placed under surveillance, raided & burned to the ground. Their proprietors were put to death immediately, and their many patrons were rounded up and subjected to public extraction of all their teeth. By 1339, however, the Egyptian historian Makrizi writes that the custom of Cannabis usage had re-established itself with more than its previous vigor, and 'As its consequence, general corruption of sentiments & manners ensued, modesty disappeared, every base & evil passion was openly indulged in, and nobility of external form alone remained in these infatuated beings.'

Egypt has fluctuated violently in its treatment of Cannabis usage by the masses for centuries; indeed, the dominant characteristic of Cannabis laws in most societies has been their inconsistency. The recent history of Egypt yields this erratic pattern:

1868: the drug was totally prohibited, with death penalty for possession in some cases.

1874: the Government allowed importation of hashish upon payment of duty but continued its prohibition on possession.

1877: a nationwide search & seizure took place — all hashish was ordered confiscated.

March, 1879: the importation & cultivation of hashish were prohibited by Khedivial (royal) decree.

March, 1884: a decree was issued to prohibit sale, cultivation or importation of hashish with a penalty of 2-8 Egyptian pounds per oke of hashish (1 oke= approx 1 kg). Hashish seized under this new decree was to be sold for export by the Government within fifteen days, and 25% of the money obtained from these sales was divided between informers & seizers of the hashish.

May, 1891: a decree was issued prohibiting cultivation of hashish with a fine of 50-100 pounds Egyptian per field. The penalty for possession of hashish became an offense with a higher penalty — up to 50 pounds Egyptian per kilo.

June, 1892: the Court of Appeals of the Mixed Tribunals ruled that none of the preceding decrees applied to foreigners.

April, 1895: the Native Appeal Court ruled that no minimum fine for possession was mandatory.

January, 1895: an arrete was issued prohibiting keepers of public establishments from sale of hashish, and provided that three condemnations in six months would entail closure of the establishment.

May, 1900: the preceding ruling was modified to provide for one to seven days in prison for shopkeepers nailed for sale of hashish. It further stated that simply allowing hashish smoking on the premises would be punished by closure of the shop for one month, and permanent closure for two convictions.

Much of the motivation behind such fluctuations in a country's approach may be accounted for by considering whether or not, and in what way, it chooses to affect the economic & social organization of its populace.

Contemporary Egypt has a history of reaction to hemp drugs which is remarkably similar to that of the USA, and which stands in vivid contrast to the approach of India during the same period. Both Egypt and the USA have cooperated extensively over the past forty years, with much direct contact between the bureau chiefs of the Narcotics organizations in each country. Interestingly enough, neither country has ever initiated an investigation along the lines of the Indian Hemp Commission's Report, and so we find an official attitude on hemp drugs which stems largely from the opinions of those in charge of suppressing usage and what supporters they can find in the medical & scientific professions.

In both countries the motives of the enforcers of the laws on hemp drugs seem somewhat suspect. While they do seem to have convinced themselves that Cannabis is a dangerous & undesirable popular drug, their reasons often follow not so much from a concern for the welfare of the folk as from a personal view of what is good for the continuing political & economic welfare of their bosses. This bias is revealed in startling ways, and is not necessarily limited to hemp drugs; witness this Egyptian landlord testifying before a Narcotics Investigatory Committee in 1933 on the negative effects of tea drinking among *his* fellahin:

Some of the fellahin took the opportunity to open small cafes for the sale of tea which they sold at 2 mills for a small glass and 5 mills for a large tumbler. These cafes made a big profit as all the tea drinkers of the village gathered there every evening as soon as they had received their wages and were joined by all the doubtful characters of the neighbouring villages. Things were so bad two years ago that we had to take strong action such as closing the cafes, breaking up of tea utensils and turning the worst offenders out of the village. We also contrived to make all our working men take small holdings of land.

And at the end of the month we deducted the wages we owed to them from what they owed us for the land: in this way we prevented them having cash in hand to spend on tea. By various other severe methods we were able to bring things back very nearly to the normal and the labour capacity of our fellahin returned to what it had been before. However the epidemic is so strong all around us that we have not been able to keep our ezba quite immune.

This black tea habit is very much a major problem and needs endless care and attention to counter it.

From all sides comes the same story.

The habit is strongest in the Mudirias of Giza, Fayum, Beni-Suef & Minia and in certain parts of the Delta.

It is a very difficult matter to tackle as there is nothing illegal in it and as I have shown, the tea itself is harmless: it is the method of preparation that does the damage.

It would seem a simple thing to teach the fellahin how to make tea properly but unfortunately they have no desire to drink tea as we do.

They are always searching for a stimulant, they can no longer afford white drugs, or hashish, so now they are finding it in this vile brew to the damage to their health. Here is an interesting field for social & medical study within the reach of all. Not being illegal this tea drinking does not hide itself in holes & corners and escape notice, it is time for every one to see & study and it is for the young educated men of Egypt today to realize the harm that is being done and try and find some remedy for this modern plague of Egypt.

While the official Egyptian position on black tea drinking remained unclear, the motives behind this landlord's concern somehow shows through. But on the subject of hashish there was no such government equivocation, as shown by this report published in the Annual Report of the Egyptian Central Intelligence Narcotics Bureau for 1934:

Elsewhere in this Report will be found the discourse on hashish delivered last November by the Assistant Director of the Central Narcotics Intelligence Bureau to the members of the Opium Advisory Commission at Geneva.

The occasion of this speech was the nineteenth session of the above-mentioned Commission and, from Egypt's point of view, it was of the highest importance for it was the first occasion on which the hashish question had ever been openly debated at Geneva.

The statement referred to above is as follows:

Statement presented to the League of Nations Advisory Committee by the Representative of Egypt, November 19, 1934.

In responding to your invitation I propose to confine my remarks to the hashish situation as it affects and as it is viewed by Egypt today.

Let me explain, first of all, what we in Egypt mean by hashish. We mean the flat cake of compressed resinous powder extracted from the flowering top of the female plant of the variety indica of the species cannabis sativa. We do not grow the plant in Egypt nor do we prepare the hashish thus described. It comes to us in two forms — the flat cake or "turba" varying in weight from half a kilo to 2 kilos, and the "pantoufle" weighing generally about ¼ kilo. In either form it is sown up in a thin linen covering which generally bears some distinguishing mark impressed upon it by means of a rubber stamp or a stencil. It may and frequently does receive further covering, this depending on the method by which it is intended to be introduced into Egypt.

If immersion in the sea is anticipated, for instance, a tight covering of oiled silk may be bound around the inner linen covering. The "pantoufle" form deserves a few remarks in passing. The reason for the adoption of this particular shape by smugglers may probably be ascribed to the fact that, years ago, crews of vessels arriving at Egyptian ports used to walk ashore wearing a kind of cheap rope-soled shoe with canvas uppers such as may be bought in any Mediterranean port. The hashish "pantoufle" cut and pressed to fit these shoes could be inserted beneath the sole of the foot and the result was at first not easily detected. Although the trick, once detected, obviously lost its value, the "pantoufle" form has been retained and has come to be accepted as a kind of trade shape which indicates hashish of a superior quality generally known as Stambouli.

Having considered the nature and the form of hashish as it is known in Egypt let us turn to its preparation. This is carried out in the following manner: —

Towards the end of the month of September the plant arrives at maturity. It then takes on an amber coloured tint and becomes sticky. The seeds are examined with a view to determining the degree of ripeness, and when this is satisfactorily confirmed the plant is harvested by means of scythes or sickles to ground level and is gathered into bundles and transported to the farm buildings for drying and subsequent preparation.

The stalks are now laid out side by side on specially made drying grounds of hard clay, exposed to the sun and the dew and well protected from the wind. It is very important that no stalk should overlap another during this drying process as this might produce mildew which would spoil the product. After two or three days the exposed surfaces of the plant begin to dry off. It is then turned over to the other side and this process is repeated every 24 hours for the next 10 or 12 days.

Thus completely dried by exposure to sun and dew the plant begins to throw off a fine amber coloured powder which is especially abundant in the seed pods.

The plant is now carefully placed on large linen sheets, care being taken to lose none of the precious powder, and is thus carried to a special shed or room which must fulfill the following conditions: —

The interior must be clean and have smooth walls and be capable of being hermetically closed. The floor must be smooth and hard to avoid the introduction of any foreign matter during the beating process which is now about to take place. It is in this room that the hashish will be extracted.

The plants are stacked in a heap in the middle of the room and the workmen (specially engaged experts in the operation) shut themselves in and proceed to give the first beating by means of sticks or flails. This beating is intended to separate the useless twigs which are thrown aside and to beat out from the plant the first and best qualities of hashish. Throughout this operation a cloud of fine powder rises from the heap and settles on the surrounding floor and walls. This powder constitutes the hashish and the beating results in a heap of leaves and broken stems also the seed-pods containing the seeds. These debris are now submitted to further manipulation.

Three sieves of varying degrees of fineness are now used. They are of silk or wire according to the fineness required.

Loading Hashish
for the desert run

Left: 25 kilos of
hashish hidden in
a consignment
of olives

'vigorous
methods...
to eliminate
hashish...'

73

Little by little the heap of beaten debris is passed through the three sieves. The finest mesh is used for the extra quality, the next finest for No. 1 quality and the largest mesh for No. 2 quality. The results of this initial sieving constitute the three first and best qualities of hashish.

The debris is now beaten again six or seven times, the sieving operation being carried out between each beating. Naturally, the quality of the powder deteriorates with each successive sieving, and it is used for mixing with the finer qualities above enumerated in order to form other and lower qualities. The quality of these varying grades depends very much on the caprice of the manufacturer. The only real first class grades come from the first beating.

When no further powder can be obtained by the beating method the seeds are extracted from the debris to be used for the ensuing crop. The broken stems and fragments are ground down in a flour mill and used for further adulteration of the finer qualities. The varying qualities of powder are classified and placed in bags containing 5 to 10 okes each to await further preparation prior to being sent off to their destination.

The workmen employed in this operation are specialists accustomed to breathing the heavily laden air in the beating sheds but even so they frequently have to stop work and go outside to get some fresh air into their lungs. Up to this point the preparation is carried out by the cultivator.

The final operation, which is only undertaken by the exporters, consists of mixing the varying qualities of powder in order to attain the degree of excellence required and of again sieving this mixture, weighing it and inserting it into small bags made of strong linen, sometimes rectangular in shape, sometimes in the shape of a 'pantoufle'. These bags are then fastened up, flattened out and put in a special cooking apparatus.

This consists of a kind of cupboard about one metre high possessing two doors which can be hermetically sealed. The interior of this cupboard has a horizontal shelf or grill at about 2/3 of its height. Below this shelf reposing on the floor of the cupboard, two Primus lamps are placed and on them two vessels containing boiling water. On the upper shelf or grill the requisite number of bags or pantoufles are placed, the stoves are lit and the cupboard is tightly closed. Rugs and blankets are thrown over the exterior of the cupboard to prevent the steam escaping.

After 10 or 15 minutes the powder in the bags begins to grow soft and develops into a paste. The bags are now withdrawn and whilst still hot placed in presses similar in form to, but more powerful than, ordinary letter presses and capable of containing several bags at a time. After pressure, the bags harden and thereafter maintain the 'turba' or 'pantoufle' shape. After being exposed to the air for 2 or 3 hours they are ready for despatch.

And in this form they reach Egypt.

The situation in Egypt has not undergone any considerable change since last May except that the arrival of Syrian hashish on the Egyptian market has continued to give way to stuff bearing such marks as would seem to indicate other origin.

I should like to take this opportunity of expressing to this Committee how truly appreciative Egypt is of the unmistakably vigorous methods which are now being applied in the French Mandated Territories of Syria and the Lebanon to the elimination of hashish cultivation and to the detection of illicit traffic therein. The formation of a Central Police Service for Narcotic Drugs at Beirut together with the provisions of the Decree No. 193 L.R. of August 28, 1934, have caused the keenest satisfaction in Egypt. In this connection it is interesting to note that the functions of this new Police Service have already begun to make themselves felt for I see that two important cases of hashish cultivation and possession, involving the persons of a Syrian Cabinet Minister and a Syrian Nationalist Leader have recently been reported in the Damascus and Beirut press.

I should like here, if I may, to refer members to page 20 of doc OC 1542 and to say that for a long time now we have had no Greek hashish in Egypt. Not only has cultivation ceased but existing stocks held by peasants have now all been handed in to a central authority in Athens and are being held pending computation of compensations. As soon as this is completed the stocks will be destroyed.

In respect of other aspects of the hashish situation in Egypt such as prices obtained by smugglers, tricks employed by them, numbers arrested and convicted, etc, etc, I need not here go over ground which is already fully covered in the CNIB report for 1933 referred to.

I may, however, allude to the forms in which hashish is consumed in Egypt as this is a subject which has not so far been discussed.

First and most popular is the 'goza' or water-pipe consisting in its cheapest form of a polished cocoanut-shell and a perpendicular tube with a clay receptacle at the top for the tombac or hassan kef, a form of light tobacco leaf, on the top of which, when well alight, is placed a small portion of hashish. A bamboo stem at an angle of 45° protrudes from the cocoanut-shell and serves as a mouthpiece. When all is ready the pipe is vigorously puffed and the smoke deeply inhaled by the smoker who then passes the pipe to his neighbour and so on until it has completed the round of the assembly. For hashish smoking is mostly conducted in groups and is accompanied by a confused din of loud talk punctuated by peals of uncontrolled laughter as the fumes begin to take effect. Smoking continues until the senses become too numbed to permit the pipe being held in the smokers' grasp. He then either tumbles off to sleep where he is or, if a stouter breed, manages to stagger home in time to drop off to the enjoyment or otherwise of the dreams of his disordered brain. This type of gathering is however becoming less and less common owing to the severity of the Egyptian law and the risks of detection.

Hashish is also smoked in cigarettes.

Next in popularity comes *manzoul,* a form of sweetmeat composed as to 10 per cent of hashish melted in oil and as to 90 per cent of cheap chocolate powder mixed with the following spices: nutmeg, ginger, pepper, cloves and seeds of celery, onion, watercress and quince. This compound is kneaded by hand into a stiff paste which is then flattened out and stamped into discs about 1 cm thick and 3 centimetres diameter. These discs are sold for 1 piastre each and are chewed slowly.

We also have ma'agou, the same as the madjun on page 2 of document OC 1542 (a). This is composed as to 10 per cent of hashish melted in oil and 90 per cent of spices mixed with honey. The compound is kneaded with dry powdered gum arabic and rolled into pills or boluses which are sold at 1½ piastres per pill. These are swallowed whole and are mostly favoured by elderly people.

Both compounds by reason of containing hashish are of course prohibited by law in Egypt and the sentences inflicted on persons caught in possession of them are no whit less severe than those inflicted on the possessor or smoker of the purer form of hashish. Of the dangerous and undesirable attributes of the drug hashish there can be no question. Used as it is almost exclusively as an aphrodisiac it produces all the symptoms commonly associated with the use of white drugs except in the case of withdrawal which is not generally accompanied by the lamentable mental distress that characterizes the treatment of white drug addicts.

As stated in the CNIB Report the use of hashish in Egypt is very often the prologue to crime and the bad characters of a village are generally found to be hashish smokers.

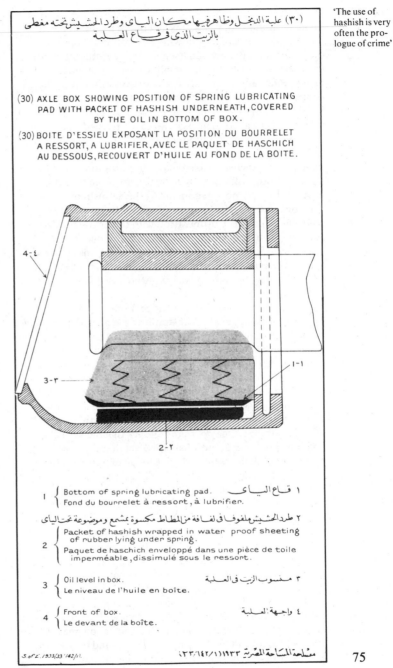

(٣٠) علبة الدبخل وظاهر فيها مكان الياى وطرد الحشيش تحته مغطى بالزيت الذى فقاع العلبة

(30) AXLE BOX SHOWING POSITION OF SPRING LUBRICATING PAD WITH PACKET OF HASHISH UNDERNEATH, COVERED BY THE OIL IN BOTTOM OF BOX.

(30) BOITE D'ESSIEU EXPOSANT LA POSITION DU BOURRELET A RESSORT, A LUBRIFIER, AVEC LE PAQUET DE HASCHICH AU DESSOUS, RECOUVERT D'HUILE AU FOND DE LA BOITE.

1 قاع الياى
{ Bottom of spring lubricating pad.
{ Fond du bourrelet à ressort, à lubrifier.

٢ طرد الحشيش وملفوف فى لفافة من المطاط مكسوة بمشمع وموضوعة تحت الياى
2 { Packet of hashish wrapped in water proof sheeting of rubber lying under spring.
{ Paquet de haschich enveloppé dans une pièce de toile imperméable, dissimulé sous le ressort.

3 مـنسوب الزيت فى العلبة
{ Oil level in box.
{ Le niveau de l'huile en boîte.

4 واجهة العلبة
{ Front of box.
{ Le devant de la boîte.

Although hashish has been known and used in Egypt for a long number of years, this fact ought not I think to be offered as any excuse for allowing it to continue to poison the youth of the country. In itself hashish constitutes another grave menace other than the medical one. The immense profits obtainable from even a single successful smuggling coup are constantly occupying the attention of the contraband fraternity. The incitement offered to crews of vessels calling at Egyptian ports is not easily resisted when the profit on a single kilogramme of hashish may be as high as 50 or 60 pounds. The Egyptian Government is obliged to maintain an expensive Coastguard organization in addition to various other offices both in the Customs and the Police purely for the purpose of combating the hashish smuggler. The constitution of its Frontiers Police is largely of an anti-contraband nature. Co-operation with the Egyptian Army Air Force, wireless communication, automobiles specially constructed for desert work, all these dispositions are directed against the smuggler in addition to the normal routine of keeping order amongst a widely scattered Bedouin population.

In fact Egypt is obliged to budget for a very considerable sum of money every year simply to keep out the smuggler of an article which is proscribed not only within her own boundaries but within those of the neighbouring countries from which it emanates.

At this point it may be permissible to consider for a moment the wider aspects of the hashish problem. I do not intend to nor have I the authority to discuss the question of a Convention for the Suppression of the Cultivation of Cannabis Indica. I may perhaps remark that the 1925 Convention appears to be curiously weak on the subject of internal control of both the plant and the hashish extracts whether in the resinous or powder form. What does, however, seem to me to be a remarkable anomaly is that whilst the 1925 Convention only deals with the question of the prepared forms of hashish, no fewer that five of the countries represented at the present meeting have laws prohibiting the *cultivation* of the plant, *viz*, Egypt since 1884, Greece since 1920, Bulgaria since 1925, Yugoslavia since 1929, Turkey since 1933, perhaps even earlier. Cannabis indica is not grown for any purpose in the following European countries (here I quote the friendly OC 1542 again), Austria, Belgium, Denmark, Danzig, Estonia, France, Hungary, Poland, Portugal, Spain, Sweden, Norway and Lithuania. Holland has on one occasion grown 17 acres and that was nine years ago and for scientific purposes. Italy grows hemp which has no narcotic properties, and Switzerland is preparing legislation to deal with the question.

Palestine, the Mandated Syrian Territories and Iraq all prohibit cultivation.

Surely there is here at least a remarkable indication of the attitude of a large part of the world towards hashish. In any case the existing convention cannot be said, I think, to treat the hashish question satisfactorily, and if it is agreed that some amendment is necessary Chapter IV of that Convention might perhaps be taken as a departing point of discussion of the whole question. The whole of Western Europe has no use for it and the Balkan States and Eastern Mediterranean countries including Asia Minor definitely prohibit it.

So may we not ask ourselves what good is it to anyone anyhow? On this simple basis, surely, it should not be impossible to formulate some sort of convention, though it is admitted that the cases of India and perhaps Persia and Siam present certain difficulties, and form a matter for discussion by more experienced persons than myself.

What I can and do definitely say is that Egypt very vigorously recommends and would most warmly welcome any project tending towards a world-wide outlawing of the cannabis indica plant. Meanwhile she again begs those neighbouring countries which have already prohibited its cultivation to redouble their efforts in the direction of detection and destruction of illicit crops. Determination and energy are all that is required. No great detective feats would appear to be necessary. If the crops themselves are remote and difficult of access, the process of preparation which I have described elsewhere gives, I think, I may say, the fullest opportunity to an alert local gendarmerie or police force to assert its powers.

In glancing back over these notes I have the suspicion that I may not have laid sufficient stress on the real moral and physical dangers of hashish. I am consoled however to see that the representative of the United States of America has more eloquently described to you this aspect of the menace in his country.

What I want most especially to impress on this meeting is the peculiar vulnerability of Egypt with its vastly preponderating illiterate peasant class that offers such a remunerative market to the conscienceless smuggler and his countless agents. The normal Egyptian peasant is a simple, sober, hardworking, cheerful individual who instinctively dislikes hashish and despises those who use it. He can easily and will willingly do without it. But if he finds it constantly peddled under his nose who can blame him if he is tempted to try it?

This is what the smuggler plays for and where alas he too often succeeds.

And why is it possible for the stuff to be obtained? Simply because of the propinquity of countries where illicit cultivation of the plant has not yet been successfully checked despite existing legislation *ad hoc*.

Before sitting down I should like to refer to Document 1542 (c) wherein appears a letter on another subject concerning hashish which I hope this Assembly may spare a moment to consider. The identification of hashish in the laboratory has, I believe, almost exclusively relied on the Beam test in the past. It is disconcerting to find that the efficacy of this test is no longer undisputed. The difficulties from a purely police point of view are not diminished by a recent admission which I received from our own Medico-Legal Expert in Egypt that hashish once swallowed and subjected even in the mildest form to the process of digestion fails when submitted to the Beam test to give the characteristic violet colour.

I conclude with a final reference to the invaluable document OC 1542, page 1 final paragraph:

'Too much stress cannot be laid on the fact that the raw resin of Indian hemp is, up to the present, of no medicinal or industrial value. It is collected and is the subject of considerable trade only on account of the fact that when swallowed or smoked, it induces hashish intoxication.'

Whilst assuming that the raw resin here mentioned may be taken to include prepared hashish as I have described it, I would add to that most incisive summary that it also encourages and promotes in a direct manner the existence of an ever increasing bond of international rascals who, as in the case of white drugs, are able by a process of mass victimization to make fortunes which might cause even Croesus himself to rub his eyes in envious astonishment.

Perhaps the most revealing arguments in this remarkable document are contained in the closing paragraphs, where the crux of the matter, lightly passed over, is that the Government objects to its illiterate peasant class having access to Cannabis as an intoxicant on moral grounds. This line developed early in Egypt, before the Colonial period in fact, and for reasons earlier identified. That it has been carried over into modern times with such consistency, and in the face of largely passive rejection of its premises, is a comment on the tenacious character of those interests which seek in every country to protect the people against themselves.

One of the more original thoughts on the origin of drug use in the Egyptian population was proposed by one Dr Dudgeon, who noted that:

Every new fad, folly or experience however ridiculous or bizarre it may happen to be, will be embraced with unreasoning enthusiasm by a larger or smaller number of people in relation to the manner in which it appeals to their senses or imaginations; if it eventually proves itself to be harmful, uninteresting or foolish, it is dropped by those who are reasonable & have ordinary common sense and it is finally relegated to the hysterical, degenerate, mentally deficient & vicious classes. Such people are evolved in large numbers under today's conditions where education is forced on evolutionally unsuitable material. The drug addict is part of the general problem of the unfit. Like the poor, he is always likely to be with us and what particular drug or drugs is or are the fashion of today is a matter of secondary importance.

Moral judgments aside, one of the greatest concerns of the English Colonials was the high incidence of what they chose to label insanity from the use of Cannabis, usually in the form of hashish. In this matter the English, as a rule, showed far greater perspicacity than in their dealings with ethics. These people were no doubt influenced by judgmental reports of casual & unqualified observers as much as by the foreign nature of the culture with which they dealt. The general failure to understand the nature of Cannabis must also have been a significant factor in their perception. All of these negative aspects notwithstanding, this professional class of colonials did a remarkable and, from our viewpoint, very entertaining job of reporting on the bizarre set of conditions which confronted them in their crusade to Anglicize the East.

The English-Indian experience has produced the most extensive observations on the perceived connection between Cannabis usage & deviant behavior with insanity. As an overview of the moderate, clinical approach characterizing many English Colonials, consider this statement by a superintendent, surgeon & officer:

"Stoned."

Before formulating any definite conclusions on the question of the connection between hemp drugs and insanity I would like to point out some of the difficulties under which all superintendents of asylums have worked and still work in this country, and these difficulties are especially present in relation to *ganja-insanity*. The patients belong nearly always to the lower and grossly ignorant classes, to whose minds the relations of *cause* and *effect*, except in very ordinary affairs of life, are, more or less, unknown, and anything which is outside their ken is generally given up as unknowable. When pressed for reasons they give such as are foolish or wilfully untrue. Little then is likely to be obtained in the way of information from the friends, if indeed they are ever questioned at all by the committing magistrate. It is only very rarely in cases of private-paying patients that the superintendent sees the relatives; most cases are brought to the asylum by the police on an order from a magistrate. The lunacy laws in India leave much to be desired. In certainly 50 per cent of the insanes admitted into asylums as wandering lunatics under Section iv, or at the request of friends, under Section v of Act xxxvi of 1858, or as so-called criminal lunatics under the provisions of Act x of 1882, the descriptive rolls contain no mention of relatives. These descriptive rolls (Forms 3 and 4) are filled up as a rule by a European or native inspector on the information of a native policeman. These men know from experience that unless they make these rolls fairly presentable they will be returned from the asylum to the committing magistrate, and that this officer will in his turn call upon his subordinates for more information, which is, unfortunately, seldom forthcoming. To escape trouble and worry the police are averse to entering the names of relatives (who might be called upon to contribute towards the maintenance of the insane person), and are in the habit of accepting *ganja, bhang*, etc, as convenient causes of insanity, which have long been permitted to pass as probably correct. The medical officers in charge of asylums have long suspected this to be the case.

Let it be granted that want of accuracy in ascertaining a cause renders about 50 per cent of the cases of insanity, said to be due to *ganja*, etc, doubtful; it is not therefore necessary to suppose that these insane never used hemp drugs at all. They may, and probably do, represent persons, insane from other causes, who are known to have used hemp drugs occasionally, or even habitually. In a certain proportion, too, it is not very improbable that, owing to the fact that these persons are of a neuropathic diathesis, and in them a tendency to insanity exists, and has always been latent, hemp drugs in excess, or even in quantities which would not damage a man of robust nervous constitution, have acted as an *exciting cause*, making manifest a mental weakness which might not have shown itself in the absence of such indulgence. Granting all this, we are still left with a number of cases in which the abuse of Indian hemp drugs, either alone or combined with datura or alcohol, has produced a violent and prolonged intoxication followed by a maniacal, melancholic, or demented condition. In these cases recovery takes place in a very short time; indeed, in many of them the individuals are sane, or almost sane, when they reach the asylum.

A nominal roll has been prepared in the Dallanda Asylum for the past five years, and from it I find that of the 108 persons admitted, whose insanity is put down to *ganja* or *bhang*, eight are distinctly stated to have been sane on admission to the asylum. All these persons remained sane. There can be no doubt, therefore, that a certain proportion of the cases admitted are not cases of insanity, but, if rightly reported in the first instance, merely cases of intoxication which should never have been sent to an asylum at all. Although, as I have already admitted, in many cases perfect proof that the *toxic insanity* is due to the abuse of hemp drugs is wanting, there is another feature in these cases which points to a causation, which is transient, and from which recovery is rapid. The average period under treatment in the Dallanda Asylum of 55 cases discharged cured during the five years 1888-1892 varied from three to ten months, and many of these were kept under observation for some time after they had been pronounced sane. Of the 108 cases admitted more than half recovered very quickly, and this points to a cause easily removable. These figures include a few readmissions of persons previously treated for insanity due to the abuse of hemp drugs. With regard to the patients who do not recover I think they probably represent, as pointed out by Dr Wise, a number of insane persons who may or may not have used hemp drugs.

Chanvre :
a, tige mâle ; b, tige femelle
c, fleur mâle; d, fleur femelle.

There were many superintendents who agreed, and many who did not. Some had pet theories to push, and some could not separate evidence from preconception. By & large, however, most of the medical people in charge of Colonial mental institutions were moderate & even perceptive in their reporting.

A sample of opinion among these 19th Century stalwarts reveals some of this spread of opinion:

The causes of insanity among the patients admitted to the asylum are given in the annexed table; but on this head I regret to observe that the information furnished by Magistrates, as given in the rolls accompanying lunatics, is of the most meagre description, 'cause unknown' being stated in 69 per cent of the admissions.

Cases of Insanity

Smoking *ganja* and the use of intoxicating drugs: 12
Grief from loss of a child: 1
Hereditary: 3
Sequelae of fever: 1
Unknown: 38
Total: 55

(A Fleming, MD, 'Annual Report Moorshedabad Lunatic Asylum, 1862.')

Of the 416 cases in which the causes of insanity have been ascertained, the disease is attributed to indulgence in intoxicating drugs and liquor in 313 persons, or, as in 1862, to upwards of 75 per cent. The malady was hereditary in 24 instances, and was excited by moral causes — principally grief on account of loss of relatives or property — in 63. (Annual Report on Lunatic Asylums, Bengal, 1863, by J McClelland, Esq, Officiating Principal Inspector General Medical Department.)

The chief physical cause has been indulgence in *ganja*; 165, or 50 per cent of the total number treated, have been distinctly traced to that cause, 16 have been traced to hereditary tendency, eight to opium, seven to epilepsy, and five to ardent spirits. (A Simpson, MD, Annual Report Dacca Lunatic Asylum for 1863.)

The abuse of intoxicating drugs, especially *ganja*, is answerable for 45.5 per cent of the admissions; amongst the rest three were unknown, three were attributed to starvation, the rest being due to moral causes, such as grief, anger, fright, and religious excitement.

I fully believe that the excessive use of *ganja* or spirits may lead to insanity, but I am not prepared to give my adhesion to the opinion that the moderate use of opium has any evil effect on the brain. I believe its action to have a directly opposite effect, for whilst other stimulants deaden the intellectual faculties and excite the passions, opium calms the passions, and healthily exalts the intellectual and moral faculties.

Readmissions — There were three readmissions, two of persons discharged cured in 1865, and one who was discharged cured in May, 1856; one of the three was addicted to the excessive use of *ganja*, and another to *muddut* (a preparation of opium). There is no record that the third was addicted to the use of any intoxicating drug. (N Jackson, MD, Annual Report Cuttack Lunatic Asylum for 1866.)

As in former reports, the largest proportion is ascribed to indulgence in *ganja*. The ratio from this cause in the last five years has been as follows:

1863 ... 30.5
1864 ... 49.0
1865 ... 46.8
1866 ... 38.9
1867 ... 35.7
Average: 40.1

Indulgence in *ganja*, however, is always associated with other vices, such as spirit drinking and debauchery. The outbreak of mental disease cannot, except in a few cases, be referred to this narcotic alone. The return is more correctly a record of the number of *ganja* smokers among the lunatics.

Statement No 6 shows the trades or occupations of those admitted during 1867. The largest number was furnished by those who engaged in domestic service, including those employed under European and native masters. Twenty-one, or 27.2 per cent, were servants. In former years this proportion was only 8 per cent. This rise is due to the irregular habits and debauched lives led by Mahommedan servants, more especially by those serving in large towns. A second cause is the shameful practice, followed by rich natives, of keeping a servant, generally a boy, who is forced to intoxicate himself and perform indecent dances, not as a warning to others, like the helot of old, but as an entertainment for his master and his companions. One of these miserable creatures was admitted during the year. (James Wise, MD, Annual report Dacca Lunatic Asylum for 1867.)

The excessive use of intoxicating drugs, *ganja* especially, has contributed 22 cases, or 44.9 per cent of the number treated. Of the narcotics used, *datura* has on two occasions been noted among the exciting causes. I allude particularly to this drug in connection with the case of Bunkall, who was admitted in August under the following circumstances:

He had been an inspector in the Irrigation Works six years, always bore a good and upright character, and had given uniform satisfaction, so much so that when one of the executive engineers was absent on sick leave Bunkall was placed in charge of extensive and very important works; previous to this he was already doing the work of another subordinate, so that at one time he was doing the work of three men. Mr Bunkall's previous health had never been good.

He was subject to spasmodic asthma; during the damp weather it was so bad that his medical attendant recommended him to live two miles away from his works, and among other remedies ordered the *datura* to be smoked. Bunkall derived so much benefit from this that he resorted to it on every occasion he was distressed. Tobacco was also freely used, but never with the *datura*. The leaves of the plant were chiefly employed. For six months he continued in this habit, on some occasions smoking two or three pipes a day; about this time he was heard to complain of pain and pressure on the head. Here there were two exciting causes: excessive mental and bodily occupation, and, secondly, *datura* smoking. The difficulties of the case were, that when relieved of some of his work on giving over charge, he suddenly burst into a fit of craziness, and declared he was poisoned and surrounded by conspirators. For the first two months of his stay in the asylum he lost greatly in flesh, and was violently maniacal; official visitors and others who had seen him on these occasions were struck with the change in his condition, and had no doubt of his insanity. For some days he was so morose that he refused all food, and had to be fed by the stomach-pump. He slowly improved, but had two or three relapses. Since then he has steadily recovered, but not sufficiently to justify his discharge. Orders have been received to transfer him to Bhawanipore, where he can be better treated than in an asylum in which no provision is yet made for European cases.

This patient was admitted into the Bhawanipore Asylum on the 22nd January, 1868.

January 25th — Appears perfectly intelligent and rational still, and his religious views seem to have less possession of him; employs himself painting.

Left the asylum quite sane on the 14th March, 1868.

We are aware of the powerfully deleterious effects of all parts of the *datura* (*alha* and *fastuosa*) when swallowed. The narcotic irritant effects of the seeds especially have for a long time been the subject of study in Indian jurisprudence. But whether the habit of smoking parts of the plant, so highly recommended in bronchial complaints, has a further action in disturbing the mind and predisposing to lunacy is perhaps not so generally acknowledged. Natives believe firmly in its action in this respect. The question is an interesting one, and worthy of further investigation. (WD Stewart, Annual Report Cuttack Lunatic Asylum for 1867.)

The readmissions were less numerous than usual. During the previous five years they averaged 17 annually.

Of the readmissions, one, a *ganja* seller, came in for the

81

seventh time. He was a thin, spare man, aged about 60 years, with a fair amount of intelligence and energy. Six were readmitted within one year of their discharge, two within two years, two after four years, one after seven years, and one after eight years. Of these 13 persons six were addicted to *ganja,* four to *ganja* and spirits, two to spirits alone, and the habits of one could not be ascertained. (James Wise, MD, Annual Report Dacca Lunatic Asylum for 1868).

I have a few words to say regarding criminal lunatics. There has been an increase of late in the number of this class of the insane, and it has appeared to me, judging from their demeanour here (many of them), that it would be as well for those whose duty it is to pronounce on the sanity of these individuals to recollect (medical officers, juries, and judicial officers) that cerebral excitement resulting from the abuse of intoxicating liquors and drugs is not insanity. If an Englishman gets drunk, and in that state commits a criminal act, he is held responsible for it; and if he has committed murder in his state of excitement he is hung. But a native of India indulges in an intoxicating drug which he knows will produce maniacal excitement, and he escapes all future punishment (except confinement in a lunatic asylum) on the ground of insanity. The drunken native is no more mad than the drunken Englishman; why, then, this difference in the punishment awarded? I think I could point out several (so-called) criminal lunatics at Dallanda who have never shown any signs of insanity, and who have never been insane, though they have suffered from the stimulating and destructive effects of *bhang*, *churrus*, or other intoxicating agents. (G Saunders, Deputy Inspector-General, Bengal, Inspection Report Dallanda Asylum, 1870.)

Surgeon-Captain Tull-Walsh, in commenting on the accrued evidence of over forty years of Colonial supervision of mental hospitals before the Indian Hemp Commission (see Chapter III), summed up his experience as follows:

I think it may be fairly stated:

1. That hemp drugs are very largely used in Bengal, smoked as *ganja* and *chunus*; drank as *bhang* and *siddhi*, or eaten as *majune*. The smoking of *chunus* and the eating of *majune* are not very common.

2. Among healthy persons *ganja* smoked alone, with tobacco, or with a very small addition of *datura* (two or three seeds) produces a condition varying from mild exhilaration to marked intoxication. The violent intoxicating effects are less marked, or not seen at all, in persons having a regular and wholesome supply of food. Much the same may be said of *bhang* etc.

3. Among persons of weak mind, or with a marked neurotic tendency, even a moderate quantity, or only a slight excess of hemp drugs, may so increase the insanity, evident or latent, as to make such persons violent, morose, or melancholy, according to the neuropathy with which we start. The presence of adulterations such as *datura* will increase these effects.

4. Abuse of hemp drugs, especially when adulterated with *datura*, will produce even in healthy persons a very violent intoxication simulating mania, or may lead to a morose melancholic condition, or to dementia. These conditions are generally of short duration, and the patient ultimately recovers. So common is absolute recovery that I think when a patient confined in an asylum for the treatment of insanity said to be due to the abuse of hemp drugs does not recover within 10 months these drugs were possibly only the *exciting cause,* and that we are dealing with an individual who was either insane previous to his use of intoxicating drugs, or with one in whom latent insanity has been roused into activity by the vitiating effects of excess of *ganja*, *bhang*, etc.

Tull-Walsh's conclusions seem to have had a major impact on the findings of the Commission, findings which by & large have been ignored in the anti-marijuana propaganda circulating in America today, and findings which have either by design or default been generally unavailabe to those in favor of a wiser legal & social treatment of the phenomenon.

On the other hand, a great deal of the propaganda against marijuana legalization & usage seems to be comprised of carefully selected pieces of the writings of the more extreme Colonials, to some extent in India, but largely in Egypt & the Middle East where the cultural context is markedly different from that of India, and where the struggling Colonials found far weaker grounds for compatability with their own perspective & background. A good example of the differing approach of the English in Egypt, along with an indication of why the American anti-marijuana forces have generally found the writings of these Egyptian-based Colonials more useful than those of India in pushing their arguments, may be found in the following excerpts from a report by Dr John Warneck, Medical Director of the Egyptian Hospital for the Insane:

Let us now examine the results of the use of hasheesh in Egypt, where large quantities are used by the inhabitants of the towns, although the importation of the drug is prohibited by law. The fact that about sixteen tons of hasheesh were confiscated during the year 1901 gives some indication of the extent of its use. Most of the drug is consumed by smoking in the gozch and in cigarettes, but a considerable amount is eaten in pill form and in sweetmeats, magoon, etc.

The usual reason given by patients for using hasheesh is that it induces a general feeling of pleasure and content. It is also alleged that it increases the appetite for food, also the sexual appetite, and relieves feelings of lassitude and depression. When eaten in pills and sweetmeats it seems to be taken chiefly for aphrodisiac purposes.

Probably, as in the habit of opium, alcohol, coca and tobacco, etc, hasheesh is primarily employed on account of its euphoric effects on the nervous system. The need for some such agent exists in almost every race of human beings, especially among the males; local conditions of climate and topography, race traditions, etc, cause variations in the agent selected.

Popular opinion disapproves of the use of hasheesh. Even its moderate use is condemned by the better class of Egyptians; the habit is considered as degrading as secret drinking is with us. The low associations of the habit are partly responsible for the ill-favour with which it is regarded, but without doubt the real reason for its condemnation is the fact that hasheesh users degenerate morally, and therefore all decent people feel bound to hold up the habit to reprobation. From a religious point of view the use of hasheesh is prohibited just as much as alcohol by the Mohammedan creed (Koran, chapters ii and v).

Hasheesh appears, nevertheless, to be used by certain Mohammedan religious teachers (fikkis) as largely as by laymen.

The diagnosis of insanity from hasheesh depends on the history of the case and the patient's statements. The police certificate frequently gives information as to the existence of the habit; but unless this is confirmed otherwise, such evidence is disregarded in making the diagnosis of hasheesh insanity.

The discovery of hasheesh in the patient's clothing, or concealed in his ears or mouth, occasionally betrays the nature of the case. On admission every male patient is questioned with regard to hasheesh, and a report made on the amount he takes and his attitude towards the charge; excited protests and denials of the habit are known by experi-

'Popular opinion disapproves of the use of hasheesh.'

Meanwhile, back in England

ence to indicate a hardened hasheesh smoker. As the mental state of the patient improves, he is again questioned about hasheesh, and before discharge he is invited to give full details of his habit. By comparing the repeated statements and by noting his knowledge or ignorance of the various details of hasheesh smoking, such as the price of the gozeh, the different qualities of the drug, etc, it is not difficult in most cases to form an opinion as to whether the case is one of hasheesh. The evidence of relatives is occasionally of use, but is less reliable than the repeated cross-examination of the patient; numbers of the Cairo cases are known to be frequenters of hasheesh cafes from being seen there by hospital employees.

Insanity from hasheesh belongs to the toxic group of insanities, and, like insanity from alcohol, opium, cocaine, etc, has an exogenous toxic cause.

The clinical types of hasheesh insanity vary, but before describing them it will simplify matters to enumerate those met with in alcoholic insanity as follows:

1. *Ordinary alcoholic intoxication*, short in duration; with symptoms of excitement and violence, stupor, exaltation, and various ataxic and paretic phenomena; occasionally real transitory mania.

2. *Delirium tremens,* of longer duration; numerous hallucinations, especially visual; oblivious restless delirium, melancholic in tone; delusions of fear; motor phenomena, tremors, etc; usually curable.

3. *Alcoholic mania* of various degrees of acuteness; no complete delirium, hallucinations chiefly auditory; maniacal, changing delusions of exaltation or persecution, restlessness and violence; no tremors usually; often curable.

4. *Chronic alcoholic mania*, including alcoholic mania of persecution; delusions about tortures, machines, conspiracies, poisoning, wires, etc; there may be idea of grandeur or altered personality; often suicidal and homicidal impulses; motor and sensory phenomena occur; usually incurable.

5. *Alcoholic dementia*, often with gross organic brain-lesions, or with hemiplegia, paresis, etc; loss of memory, mental facility, loss of interest, dull, apathetic demeanour; various motor and sensory phenomena occur.

6. *Dipsomania* — This term is used to express the craving for alcohol, and nearly all the foregoing types occur as the results of giving in to this craving. Between his outbreaks of mania or delirium tremens, the dipsomaniac usually shows some mental and physical impairment, especially in the direction of blunted moral feeling. He is usually a practised liar, reckless in his methods of obtaining money to gratify

his craving, careless of the claims of relations on him, lazy, dishonourable, often shameless, and often incurable.

Non-nervous results of alcohol—Almost every organ in the body shows pathological results of alcoholism which need not be enumerated here. Now let us consider the result of using hasheesh. Insanity from hasheesh gives the following types:

1. *Temporary intoxication* — The smoker of hasheesh becomes dull and drowsy, he feels pleasantly exalted, and the worries of life are temporarily blotted out; fatigue is no longer felt; he is at peace with the world. The drug acts as a stimulant and sedative. This state is to be observed among the *habitues* of hasheesh cafes; such cases do not come to the asylum, though patients recovering from the graver forms of hasheesh insanity often describe what were their feelings during the temporary intoxication. Pleasant half-waking dreams, not unlike those of the opium taker, gently occupy the mind, and often the individual feels that he is temporarily some important personage. The active excitement of alcoholic inebriety is uncommon, but if the hasheesh smoker is annoyed or interfered with during his dreams he is liable to become irritable and excited, and to show loss of self-control. A staggering gait makes the condition not unlike that of alcoholic intoxication, while the pleasant, dreamy state approaches that of the opium smoker.

Contrasting the three intoxications, one may say that the mental pose of the hasheesh smoker is more 'subjective' than that of the alcoholic, and less so than that of the absorbed opium user. The alcoholic is the most 'objective' and demonstrative of the three.

2. *Delirium from hasheesh*, which is accompanied by hallucinations of sight, hearing, taste, and smell, often of an unpleasant kind. Delusions of persecution often occur. The idea that the subject is possessed by a devil or spirit is common. Great exaltation and the belief that the individual is a sultan or prophet may occur. Suicidal intentions are rare. The restlessness and sleeplessness of these cases are marked features, but usually they do not approach the unending chatter and continual busy movements of the subject of delirium tremens, nor is the absorption in delirious ideas and hallucinations as complete as in the latter. The motor phenomena of delirium tremens, tremors and ataxy are absent, usually the patient is active and quick in movements, although some staggering is occasionally noticeable. The physical exhaustion and gastro-intestinal and hepatic disorders of delirium tremens do not occur. Hasheesh delirium is a less grave state both physically and mentally. Some cases

are stuporous in type.

3. *Mania from hasheesh*—This varies in degree of acuteness from a mild short attack of excitement to a prolonged attack of furious mania ending in exhaustion or even death. Most cases are exalted, and have delusions of grandeur or of religious importance; persecutory delusions occur frequently, and provoke violence toward others, but not suicide. Restlessness, incoherent talking, destructiveness, indecency, and loss of moral feelings and affections, all are ordinary symptoms. A certain impudent dare-devil demeanor is a characteristic symptom. Hallucinations are not so masked as in alcoholic mania, but those of hearing and taste are not uncommon; delusions of being poisoned are often based on the latter variety. A few cases are more melancholic than maniacal in demeanor, and exhibit extreme depression and terror with hallucinations of hearing (threatening voices, etc.) There is no pathogramonic symptom of hasheesh mania, but the transitory nature of many cases is often a guide.

4. *Chronic mania from Hasheesh,* including a form of mania or persecution. Many of these cases are not distinguishable from ordinary chronic mania. Hallucinations are not so frequent as in alcoholic mania. The patient is a happier, less worried individual than the alcoholic chronic maniac. The morose, suspicious jealous demeanor of the alcoholic, his belief in machines, invisible wires, and mysterious tortures are absent, also his motor and sensory troubles. His suicidal and homicidal tendencies are also usually wanting.

5. *Chronic dementia from Hasheesh* describes the final stage of the preceding forms. We find no motor or sensory symptoms, as in alcoholism; there are loss of memory, apathy, degraded habits, and loss of energy, as in ordinary chronic dementia.

The similarity between (these conditions) and those (induced by alcohol) is evident; many of the differences are probably due to racial peculiarities.

Contrasting genergally hasheesh insanities with those produced by alcohol, the following points stand out:

1. Suicidal intentions are common among alcoholics, rare among hasheesh cases. How far this may be explained by differences in race and religion one cannot say, but it is to be borne in mind that suicide is rare among the insane of the Arab race and Mohammedan religion.

2. Hasheesh, in Egypt, seems to be a more important factor in the production of insanity than alcohol is in England.

3. As a cause of crime, hasheesh appears to be important in Egypt as alcohol is in England.

4. The use of hasheesh, unlike that of alcohol, is not followed by any characteristic anatomical lesions, and no physical disorders are known to result from it. I have not found asthma and bronchitis to be specially common among hasheesh smokers; only the physical disorders and lesions met with in the idiopathic insanities occur in insanity from hasheesh. The only exception to this rule being the staggering gait of hasheesh intoxication and delirium.

Numerous convictions are obtained under the laws of Egypt, and the importation of hasheesh along the Mediterranean coast is carefully watched, many tons of the drug being annually confiscated; yet the use of hasheesh still continues on a large scale, though not so openly as in former years, and every one who wants to smoke hasheesh seems to have no difficulty in obtaining it. The number of hasheesh cases admitted into the asylum shows an annual diminution, and one hopes that the strenuous efforts now being made to suppress the habit will gradually reduce the asylum admissions from this disease to a small figure.

It is to be noted that the abuse of hasheesh, like that of alcohol, is sometimes only a symptom of incipient insanity.

It has been suggested that if the use of hasheesh were entirely prevented in Egypt its place would be taken by another euphoric agent, probably alcohol. Would this change be for the better? I am inclined to answer in the negative. Alcohol is in other countries such a fertile cause of crime and insanity that its substitution for hasheesh in Egypt would probably result in a worse state of things. Alcohol also seems to have a specially deleterious effect in warm climates and on Oriental races. Probably the wisest policy in Egypt will be to keep the use of hasheesh within bounds without entirely preventing it.

The present system of nominally prohibiting hasheesh, while a large amount is smuggled into the country and smoked in spite of the decrees, may eventually bring about the necessary amount of restriction by raising the price of hasheesh, and rendering its immoderate purchase beyond the means of the majority of habitual hasheesh smokers.

Opium, which is so largely used in India, apparently with little evil effect, is taken to some extent in Egypt; but I have seldom met with insanity among the lower classes attributable to its use. Probably the substitution of the opium habit for that of hasheesh would be an improvement.

In the *Report of the Royal Commission on Opium*, 1895, the conclusion is reached that 'the temperate use of opium in India should be viewed in the same light as the temperate use of alcohol in England. The use of opium does not cause insanity. It does not appear responsible for any disease peculiar to itself.'

To sum up, the use of Cannabis Indica in Egypt seems to have graver mental and social results than in India, and is responsible for a large amount of insanity and crime in this country.

In the face of such marked contrasts between the Indian & the Egyptian experiences with Cannabis, one is forced to question which of the experiences was more valid, on the assumption that the central figure in the dispute was fairly consistent in both situations. This assumption—that the Cannabis used in both Egypt & India was of the same character—seems to be well founded, with a few possible exceptions.

The plant which is bred for drug production in India, Southeast Asia, Central Asia and the Near & Middle East is indeed uniform in potency, with local variation due to the skills of the cultivator and the efficiency of processing. Over the thousands of years that

Cannabis has been cultivated in these areas the essential nature of the plant has not been altered, as have so many other domesticated varieties such as the grains. Therefore, there cannot have been any essential differences in the plant itself in India & Egypt to account for the differences in experience.

Cultural differences may account for some secondary differences, because the objectives of the Cannabis user have a lot to do with the effects of the drug. In India there was widespread recognition of the need for moderation in the use of hemp drugs, and an appreciation of the role of ritualism in the experience. The primary objective in much of India was not to produce a stuporous state, but to heighten sensory, spiritual, social, & intellectual experiences. There must have been large numbers of people, of course, in India who simply used hemp as an escapist intoxicant, but there were strong pressures in the larger society against over indulgence in any form of intoxicant. There is little to indicate that in Egypt any comparable context for the use of hemp drugs existed. Muslim law forbids

Hemp drugs are more widely tolerated by the Muslim religion

intoxicants of any sort, but that law is regularly stretched to accommodate the needs of the masses. Hemp drugs are, as a rule, more widely tolerated by Muslim religious practices than alcohol, but the Muslim religion does not provide any context within which the use of hemp drugs may be played out by the individual, either privately or socially.

An additional cultural factor is the radically different overall profile of the Indian & Egyptian societies. Within Indian society there are many different levels of life style, while Egyptian society is marked by its flatness & uniformity, with its two definable levels — the elite & the peasantry. Cannabis use in Egypt, while not completely confined to the peasant fellah, is largely his property. The cultural & social context of the fellahin was & still is marked by dependence, authority, servitude, and lack of mobility — an altogether feudal atmosphere. Faced with this limited life style, it is not remarkable that the fellahin have not developed as sophisticated a use for Cannabis as has been developed in India. The chances are very good that the Egyptian authorities are quite right when they observe that the peasantry uses Cannabis primarily to get stoned, nor is it particularly incomprehensible that, considering their lot in life, once stoned a lot of fellahin demonstrate symptoms of insanity.

In a sense it follows that the hemp drugs of choice differ from India to Egypt, this difference reflecting the nature of the objectives of the user of Cannabis. Indian culture emphasizes the use of bhang & ganja, largely eschewing charas as too potent, too toxic a drug. Charas, it is recognized, interferes with the totality of the Cannabis experience, giving the smoker or eater a predominantly stuporous daze & not much else. It is also recognized that Charas is used primarily by people who, for one reason or another, simply want to sink into the river of forgetfulness. A person, however poor who is to some degree responsible for the maintainance, continuation & even possible improvement of his own life would have little motivation to immerse himself in Lethe. On the other hand, a person with no prospects, with no control over his future, and whose life is not his own would be far more likely to avail

himself of such prospects. Over centuries the hemp drug of choice in Egypt has been the most potent charas, or hashish, which could be obtained. Hashish is readily abandoned for the opiates when they are available in good supply at low prices. In fact, Egypt has been experiencing a drastic rise over the past few decades in the use of heroin & morphine among its fellahin.

Without belaboring the point, I would simply ask each reader to seek in his own mind those analogies which might explain why Egypt & America share so many of the same perspectives on drugs in general, and hemp drugs in particular, and why it is that each have decided that the Indian experience is not applicable to their own.

Chile: Hemp growing in the Aconcagua Valley, 1922 — 5,000 tons of fibre & seed . . .

89

History of Hemp
Sergeant
J Kruger
supervises the
destruction of
dagga in the
mountains of
Northern
Transvaal,
S. Africa
Photograph:
Africamerica

Opposite: Too
much—Martin
Sharp, *OZ Mag-
azine*, September
1968

The Report
Dr Turner stalks
through the
'Treasury' — A
NIMH Research
project at the
University of
Mississippi grows
twenty varieties
to ascertain the
properties of
Cannabis. Mari-
juana breaks
down into 40-50
component sub-
stances, many
of a still unknown
composition.
Dr Turner is per-
fecting a process
to produce syn-
thetic THC, first
isolated in 1964,
and decoded in
1966.
Photograph:
John Messina

Opposite:
Grass, Personality
Poster, no. 302

Three: The Indian Hemp Drugs Commission Report

No single document yet produced is of greater value to rational analysis of the range of social, ethical & economic questions surrounding Cannabis Sativa than The Indian Hemp Drugs Commission Report of 1893-94. The very complexity of the society out of which the report is generated must account for a good deal of the thoroughness of its seven volumes. For the British realized that their basically cooperative governing scheme for India, particularly in light of projected schemes for industrial development, depended for its success on receipt & application of intelligent policy recommendations which would forestall their embroilment in unworkable plans. From their extensive experience at bringing other cultures under colonial rule they were aware that there are always areas of another country's life best left alone unless, of course, they run directly contrary to the colonial plans for exploitation or are likely to effectively thwart such plans. In such cases the colonial power is obligated, they knew, to prevail absolutely or to fail.

The question to be resolved, then, in 1893 was whether or not hemp drug use by large numbers of Indians of a fantastic variety of backgrounds & persuasions was inimical to British interests in her colony. A logical extension of this question would be, of course, could Britain pragmatically expect to eliminate hemp drug use in India if it were found to be necessary. Proceeding from this question, it became readily apparent that what was required was a full-scale analysis of the entire phenomenon — know your potential adversary as well as or better than he knows himself, whenever possible.

With this background in mind, it should be clear that the Indian Hemp Drugs Commission was not, as some would have it, a committee of heads & sycophants who gathered together to advocate legalization, to minimize the inherent risks, or to pass down to the ages a paean on the subject of Cannabis Sativa. It was,

instead, a committee of hard-nosed pragmatists who were seeking to analyze an issue of immediate bearing on the future of a vast social-economic enterprise in which they each had substantial personal stakes.

So much more the pity that in America of the mid-twentieth century — eighty years after the appearance of this report — even the title is unfamiliar and the report itself has been for all practical purposes unavailable to all. In 1969, however, a much delayed but welcome event occurred — a rational & observant publisher in Silver Springs, Maryland — the Thomas Jefferson Publishing Company — put out an edited version of the Report which includes the full text of the Commission's findings & several valuable appendices.

The two major policy recommendations of the Indian Hemp Drugs Commission were:

I. Total prohibition of the cultivation of the hemp plant for narcotics, & of the manufacture, sale or use of the drugs derived from it, is neither necessary nor expedient in *consideration of their ascertained effects, of the prevalence of the habit using them,* of *the social & religious feeling on the subject*, and of *the possibility of its driving the consumers to have recourse to other stimulants or narcotics which may be more deleterious.*
II. The *policy advocated is one of control and restriction, aimed at suppressing the excessive use and restraining the moderate use within due limits.*

The complete & exhaustive body of evidence supporting these positions will not be dealt with in great detail here; rather, we shall concentrate on a summary of the conclusions which the Commission used in arriving at its recommendations:

In Consideration of Their Ascertained Effects

The Commission have now examined all the evidence before them regarding the effects attributed to hemp drugs. It will be well to summarize briefly the conclusions to which they come. It has been clearly established that the occasional use of hemp in moderate doses may be beneficial; but this use may be regarded as medicinal in character. It is rather to the popular & common use of the drugs that the Commission will now confine their attention. It is convenient to consider the effects separately as affecting the physical, mental, or moral nature.

In regard to the physical effects, the Commission have come to the conclusion that the moderate use of hemp drugs is practically attended by no evil results at all. There may be exceptional cases in which, owing to idiosyncrasies of constitution, the drugs in even moderate use may be injurious. There is probably nothing the use of which may not possibly be injurious in cases of exceptional intolerance. There are also many cases where in tracts with a specially malarious climate, or in circumstances of hard work & exposure, the people attribute beneficial effects to the habitual moderate use of these drugs; and there is some evidence to show that the popular impression may have some basis in fact. Speaking generally, the Commission is of the opinion that the moderate use of hemp drugs appears to cause no appreciable physical injury of any kind. The excessive use does cause injury. As in the case with other intoxicants, excessive use tends to weaken the constitution & to render the consumer more susceptible to disease.

In respect to the particular diseases which according to a considerable number of witnesses should be associated directly with hemp drugs, it appears to be reasonably established that the excessive use of these drugs does not cause asthma; that it may indirectly cause dysentery by weakening the constitution as above indicated; and that it may cause bronchitis mainly through the action of the inhaled smoke on the bronchial tubes.

In respect to the alleged mental effects of the drugs, the Commission has come to the conclusion that the moderate use of hemp drugs produces no injurious effects on the mind. It may indeed be accepted that in the case of specially marked neurotic diathesis, even the moderate use may produce mental injury, for the slightest mental stimulation or excitement may have that effect in such cases. But putting aside these quite exceptional cases, the moderate use of these drugs produces no mental injury. It is otherwise with the excessive use. Excessive use indicates & intensifies mental instability. It tends to

weaken the mind. It may even lead to insanity. It has been said by Dr Blanford that 'two factors only are necessary for the causation of insanity, which are complimentary; heredity, and stress. Both enter into every case: the stronger the influence of one factor, the less of the other factor is requisite to produce the result. Insanity, therefore, needs for its production a certain instability of nerve tissue & the incidence of a certain disturbance. It appears that the excessive use of hemp drugs may, especially in cases where there is any weakness or hereditary predisposition, induce insanity. It has been shown that the effect of hemp drugs in this respect has hitherto been greatly exaggerated, but that they do sometimes produce insanity seems beyond question.

In regard to the moral effects of the drugs, the Commission is of opinion that their moderate use produces no moral injury whatever. There is no adequate ground for believing that it injuriously affects the character of the consumer. Excessive consumption, on the other hand, both indicates & intensifies moral weakness or depravity. Manifest excess leads directly to loss of self-respect, and thus to moral degradation. In respect to his relations with society, however, even the excessive consumer of hemp drugs is ordinarily inoffensive. His excesses may indeed bring him to degraded poverty which may lead him to dishonest practices but apparently very rarely indeed, excessive indulgence in hemp drugs may lead to violent crime. But for all practical purposes it may be laid down that there is little or no connection between the use of hemp drugs & crime.

Viewing the subject generally, it may be added that the moderate use of these drugs is the rule, and that the excessive use is comparatively exceptional. The moderate use practically produces no ill effects. In all but the most exceptional cases, the injury from habitual moderate use is not appreciable. The excessive use may certainly be accepted as very injurious, though it must be admitted that in many excessive users the injury is not clearly marked. The injury done by excessive use is, however confined almost exclusively to the consumer himself; the effect on society is rarely appreciable. It has been the most striking feature of this inquiry to find how little the effects of hemp drugs have obtruded themselves on observation. The large number of witnesses of all classes who professed never to have seen these effects, the vague statements made by many who professed to have observed them, the very few witnesses who could so recall a case so as to give any definite account of it, and the manner in which a large proportion of these cases broke down on the first attempt to examine them, are facts

In consideration
of the ascertained
effects of hemp

which combine to show most clearly how little injury society has hitherto sustained from hemp drugs.

The Commission faced a set of difficult tasks in estimating the incidence of consumption of Cannabis in India. In the first place, they gave up completely in trying to estimate the amount of bhang consumed. While the majority of bhang was thought to be made from the leaves of the wild hemp plant, there was considerable evidence of the plant being surreptitiously cultivated over wide areas and even failing that, there was recognition that the range of the truly wild plant was so extensive that no calculations were feasible. In addition to that, the Commission recognized bhang as being so innocuous, within its criteria for judgment, that there was really no point in pursuing this line of inquiry. On the innocuous nature of bhang even the dissenting members of the Commission agreed.

Ganja consumption presented a slightly less difficult problem because theoretically all ganja was sold subject to tax, and there were in many of the states fairly good reporting systems. Noting the economic incentive to produce ganja illicitly, thereby avoiding taxes and increasing profits, the Commission was aware that their dependence on official figures resulted in a substantial understatement. With this in mind, the Commission estimated using a normal per person, per-day consumption figure and extrapolating from the fact that the annual rate of recorded ganja sales ran around 125,000 lbs, that there were close to 400,000 ganja consumers in an India with a population of over 71 million souls.

This estimate, the Commission knew, represented only the regular consumers of ganja, and as mentioned probably underestimated that number greatly. But even after adding a correction factor which, incidentally, the Commission failed to do since its job was not speculation, we can see from our vantage point of today that the number of regular ganja users in India of the late 19th century probably represented no more than 5% of the adult population.

With reference to Charas, the Commission had to go on import figures and their knowledge of the general economic level of the population. A relatively small amount of Charas was being officially imported into India during this period, and it was quite expensive. Even illicit Charas, the Commission reasoned, was well beyond the economic means of the vast bulk of the population. They thus viewed the use of Charas as an almost exclusive property of the privileged classes and, in fact, stated that it was in this sector that the bulk of abuse of hemp drugs occurred. Since the evidence gathered by the Commission supported their view that the bhang, ganja and charas were used *and* preferred in that order, they didn't hassle themselves over much about the incidence of Charas, and were content to record official tax figures as their source of a very low estimate.

Of the Social and Religious Feeling on the Subject

In summing up, . . . the Commission would first remark that Charas, which is a comparatively new article of consumption, has not been shown to be in any way connected with religious observances. As regards Northern India, the Commission is of the opinion that the use of bhang is more or less common everywhere in connection with the social & religious customs of the people. As regards ganja, they find that there are certain classes in all parts, except the Punjab, who use the drug in connection with their social & religious observances. The Commission is also of opinion in regard to bhang that its use is considered essential in some religious observances by a large section of the community, and in regard to ganja that those who consider it essential are comparatively very few. The Commission has little doubt that interference with the use of hemp in connection with the customs & observances above referred to would be regarded by the consumers as an interference with long established usage and an encroachment on their religious liberty. And this feeling would, especially in the case of bhang, undoubtedly be shared to some extent by the people at large. Regarding Southern India, the same remarks apply with this reservation, that the difference between ganja & bhang as materials for smoking & drinking respectively is much less marked there, and the distinction between the two forms of the drug is much less clearly recognized, although by the term 'bhang' is generally meant the drug as used for drinking, and by 'ganja' the drug as used for smoking.

© Thor Todoruk

The Possibility of its Driving Consumers to . . . Other Stimulants or Narcotics Which May Be More Deleterious

India of the 1890's was a country & a people with incredibly varied & demonstrably longstanding experience with drugs. A comparison to contemporary America is not too far-fetched if you are willing to grant that our experience has been far more compressed & accelerated because of the nature of the times in which we live.

The citizen of India had access through his knowledge of the natural order to a wide variety of plant drugs which ranged from the benign to the frightful. Opium was, of course, well-known and widely used, though its proportional importance to the hemp drugs was miniscule. Morphine was the only known extrapolation of the opium series —heroin did not yet exist— and there was no call for morphine in Indian society. Tobacco was smoked by a small portion of the population and was still being recognized as a narcotic, though through assiduous marketing & advertising the American tobacco industry was already beginning to convince the world that their product was harmless. Liquor was considered harmful by most people from Doctor to peasant and was expensive to boot.

Within the rural apothecary there existed, however, ready access to a long list of natural & plant intoxicants far more dangerous than hemp. Those well-known to the rural Indian included datura seeds & leaves, arsenic, aconite, nux vomica, the roots of certain sorghums, the roots of certain varieties of rice, the juice of Callotropis, oleander root, strychnine, the seeds of black henbane, the skins of snakes & toads, various venoms, parts of the ailanturs tree, the Indian relative of Mullein, various fungi, Cayenne, the bout pepper, henbane, spurge, the juices, saps & gums of over 30 trees, several varieties of lilies, hellebore, and so on through a seemingly endless variety of plant intoxi-

97

cants & poisons. There exists within nature an infinite variety of substances which can intoxicate man, and such substances are more generally available than is imagined — certainly in India with its complex medicinal plant & herb systems these substances were common knowledge.

The Commission appreciated this fact. They also were aware that from among this infinite variety of readily available substances, only a few were in common use, and these only among a very limited group of people who were far gone into poisoning themselves.

The Commission, taking all of these factors into account, wrote:

A general review of the evidence relating to the question of prohibition of ganja & charas brings the Commission to the same conclusion as that which they have framed upon a consideration of the evidence on the ascertained effects alone. The weight of the evidence above abstracted is almost entirely against prohibition. Not only is such a measure unnecessary with reference to the effects, but it is abundantly proved that it is considered unnecessary or impossible by those most competent to form an opinion on general grounds of experience; that it would be strongly resented by religious mendicants, or would be regarded as an interference with religion, or would be likely to become a political danger; and that it might lead to the use of datura or other intoxicants worse than ganja. Apart from this, there is another consideration which has been urged in some quarters with a manifestation of strong feeling, and to which the Commission are disposed to attach some importance, viz, that to repress the hemp drugs in India and to leave alcohol alone would be misunderstood by a large number of people who believe, and apparently not without reason, that more harm is done in this country by the latter than by the former.

Failing prohibition, what should be the policy of the government in regard to the hemp drugs? On this point some important evidence has been recorded, and the Commission deems it to be within the scope of their duty to state in general terms their conclusions. In the first place, then, they are of opinion that in view of the harmful effects produced by excessive use, and in exceptional cases even by the moderate use, of the drugs, the action of the Government should be directed towards restraining the former and avoiding all enouragement to the latter. The object should be to prevent the consumers, as far as may be possible, from doing harm to themselves and to lessen the inducements to the formation of the habit which might lead to such harm. In aiming at this object, however, other considerations need to be kept in view. There is in the first place the question of illicit consumption. If the restriction imposed by government is counterbalanced by a corresponding increase in smuggling, no advantage is gained but, on the contrary, a moral wrong is done the community apart from the annoyance necessitated by such restrictions. Then, if there is a legitimate use of the hemp drugs, restrictions should not be such as to make the exercise of this use impossible. The Commission has formed the opinion that there is a legitimate use of the hemp drugs, and that it exists primarily among the poorest of the population. Again, if the restrictions lead to the use of more deleterious substances, or even drive the people from a habit the evil of which is known to another of which the evil may be greater, they are not longer justifiable. The policy of Government must be tempered by all these considerations, and the neglect of any one of them may lead to serious error.

The Policy Advocated is One of Control and Restriction...

In the Resolution which the Government of India adopted as its official reaction to the Report, the full outlines of this policy are presented. Here we will consider only a few examples of how this policy was carried out on the practical local level. The full text of this resolution is appended to this chapter for further reference.

Control over consumption implies control over source, and many of the provinces of British India had effective controls long before the Commission was called into being to study these matters. In most provinces the course of preference was to have a system of licensing & taxation, with comparatively severe restrictions on operating outside the system coupled with substantial rewards for operating within. There was, really, very little economic incentive for illicit traffic in hemp drugs with the possible exception of Charas.

The licensing of cultivators was the first point of control. Cultivators who applied for & received permission to grow Cannabis entered into a first contractual agreement with the government, an agreement which, while it gave the cultivator every latitude needed to pursue his profitable occupation, was primarily designed to facilitate government control & supervision. In addition, many farmers were also licensed as exclusive vendors, which greatly simplified matters for the government.

The economics of ganja cultivation are also fully discussed in the Report, and the example opposite is a typical expense breakdown for a one acre field of ganja with hired labor.

The only farmers who used hired labor in producing ganja under license were those who also retailed it, for the return from an acre of ganja is only about 400 pounds of superior quality, very clean stuff, and the wholesale price which a farmer could realize was about 4 rupees per 25 pounds, or 64 rupees an acre. If the farmer had retail outlets, however, his income from those same 400 pounds could rise well above 200 rupees.

When farmers dealt only with the wholesale end of the business they generally used only their own labor & that of their family, thus keeping the expenditure down around 20 rupees an acre, clearing over 44 rupees this way.

Even this latter income was extremely attractive, representing many times over the clear annual income of the Indian peasant of the late 19th century.

To deal with each of the provincial systems in force at the time of the Report would place an impossible burden on a chapter already overrun with lengthy citations. The systems outlined above, do, however, represent the general rule throughout the provinces. In discussing these systems in the overall, the Commission noted that . . .

The simplest method of dealing with the subject (of control) is to farm the monopoly of vend, leaving the lessee to make his own arrangements for a supply of the drugs & their sale to the public. This is the system, with some slight differences, which is in force in the North-Western Provinces, the Punjab, Madras, Bombay, & the minor administrations. It

Expenses for a one acre field: 'extremely attractive'

Item	Expenditure	
	Rupees	*Annas*
1. Rent	3	0
2. First ploughing, 8 days	6	0
3. Carting and spreading manure (Once every three years)	20	0
4. First bakharing, 4 days (Turning the Earth)	3	0
5. Second ploughing, 2 days	1	8
6. Second bakharing, 1 day (Turning the Earth)	0	12
7. Sowing, 1 day	1	0
8. Two seedings, 4 days	4	0
9. Five men with kolpas for five days (Kolpa-thinning device)	5	0
10. Four examinations, 32 men (Pulling males and abnormals)	8	0
11. Three waterings	4	0
12. Twelve men reaping	1	8
13. Two basket carriers from field to Khala (Khala-threshing floor)	0	8
14. Six men for 4 days for pressing	6	0
15. One cart from Khala to sheds	0	8
16. Six gunny bags	3	12
17. Labor for filling bags	0	12
18. One cart to Government storehouse	1	8
19. Tax at storehouse	0	6
20. Storage fees	0	12
Total	71	14

has the advantage of relieving the Government of all respon-
sibilities or interest in the matter beyond the disposal of the
farms. It secures a preventative agency of non-official kind
in dealing with illicit sale & smuggling; and if proper care is
taken to appoint respectable vendors to prevent combinations for the purpose of keeping down the price of farms,
and to license shops only when they are required by local
demand, such a system may appear to be successful & sufficient. But there are some serious objections to it. In the first
place, it has the disadvantage of exercising no control over
production & consumption. Large profits do not depend
upon the price being raised to the pitch necessary to check
excess sales; they are as easily realized by large sales at low
rates. Thus consumption may very probably be unduly stimulated. Secondly, the Government acquires no accurate information regarding the extent of the production, the sources
of supply, and the increase or decrease of the habit of using
the drugs. The Commission thinks it is the duty of the Government to acquire this information. Thirdly, the system leaves
the whole revenue & consequent check on consumption at the
mercy of competition, which is an unsafe regulator. And,
lastly, direct taxation has already been resorted to in some
cases with good results, whereas in provinces where only
the license system prevails control is insufficient & taxation
inadequate.

There are many obvious parallels to be drawn between
India of the 1890's & America of the 1970's, and there
are some significant differences. In both instances the
report of the Commission has bearing on rational discussion, but perhaps an even more valuable dimension
will be added by examining the report in relation to
America of the 1930's as well as the 1970's.

The British were dealing with an established
fact regarding Cannabis use, whereas the American
Government of the 1930's was satisfied that it was
dealing with a limited phenomenon, and its motivations
seem clear — to nip the Cannabis phenomenon in
the bud.

The British had a vested interest in assuming the
most rational stance, the American Government apparently felt that it could afford to swing indiscriminately.
There were not, after all, vast populations to be
offended.

The British were dealing with a country not their
own, and consequently the politicians & police were
somewhat more careful in one sense, and more liberated in another, than perhaps they would have been in
dealing with their own constituency. In America of
the 30's & the 70's the issue is one which directly affects
the political future of those in power.

The British were not dealing with a population
on whom they depended for disciplined, uniform,
production-oriented behavior. America of the 30's was
emerging from a great economic depression & the
powerful men of the nation wanted very much for every-
body to go back to producing wealth. And America
of the 70's very much needs the continuing & growing
desire of her citizens to keep their minds fixed on their
economic duties.

The British were dealing with an accomplished
fact of long standing, whereas the 30's America thought
that it was dealing with an infant phenomenon of an
incipient but readily thwarted drug culture. America
of the 70's, of course, dissipates this profound misconception of the national character.

The British were relatively free of competing drug
industries in India — hemp drugs were the preferred
stimulant & euphoriant. America has an enormously

profitable drug industry in tobacco, alcohol, the mood modifiers and, to stretch the point a bit, entertainment, the inevitable decline of which could hardly be offset by a booming ice cream trade.

The communications media phenomena of America — which would expose so many important people & concepts to the critical scrutiny of a populace high on Cannabis — are evidently intolerable to its present government & institutions. The British were not faced with so potentially cynical a population, nor were their leaders & concepts threatened even if their official poses were breached. The means for mass exposure did not exist in the largely illiterate, unelectrified, rural & urban peasant society.

But it is interesting that the gross differences in context between the world of the Report and the world of America today do not invalidate the substance or process of its conclusions. The differences, in fact, make urgent a recognition of the validity of the Report and its applicability to our society. All of us need very badly to recognize that we have participated in a 'serious error' in having acted so long in ignorance of this Commission's counsel.

The prevalence of the habit of using marijuana is great and growing; it diminishes only in proportion to those moving to other, more dangerous drugs, and not in proportion to persuasive speeches, scare propaganda & police action.

The social & perhaps even religious feeling on the subject is well established in the minds of millions of Americans, who while they do not always have the benefit of full understanding of the mystical nature of the plant, nevertheless have a strong sense of ethical proportions & personal values relating to their use of the drug.

But the phenomenon which most strongly suggests the need for our rulers to study closely this report of a Commission which deliberated half a world away is the parallel between the potential power of a five thousand year civilization to thwart its erstwhile master and the rising of an Atlantic subculture in this country. This subculture is so explosively primed with powerful drug perspectives *and* the technology of the

Use is great and growing — Cover of *Newsweek* July, 1967

101

times into which it has emerged, that it will either
become the new civilization or it will witness the destruction of the old.

It is ironic that hemp drugs are the axis of many
of the thrusts of this subculture. The lessons of history
would not have enlightened even the most lucid ana-
lysts thirty years ago. Who could have known the sym-
biosis that would be generated out of the meeting of
Cannabis with millions of young human minds facing
for the first time in history the threat of a total technological annihilation. A visible parting of the paths
is taking place. On the one hand lies a vision of a world
which has never been, yet one which the mind and
spirit of men have claimed to seek. On the other hand
is the prospect of the world which is developing projected on the future, with the majority of its detectable trends amplified, with its momentum hurtling it
irrevocably past the point where commitment to its
principles of repression & control can be revoked. The
irony of Cannabis' central role in the emergence of this
subculture is exquisite: the minds of a generation have
been opened in collective awareness of human beings
as we might have been while at the same time they have
been painfully sensitized to the mass movement of
human beings into the oblivion, however realized, of
whatever the machines we have conceived have in store
for us.

Appendix one
The Commission's Report: Question number 53

This analysis of witnesses' responses to Question
No. 53 on the Commission's standard inquiry agenda
is both interesting and conclusive. Question No. 53
was 'Does excessive indulgence in any of these drugs
incite to unpremeditated crime, violent or otherwise?
Do you know of any case in which it has led to temporary homicidal frenzy?'

When a witness before the Commission answered
in the affirmative, that witness was then questioned
at length to establish the basis for his knowledge. This
table reflects the Commission's findings as to the
nature of the evidence given.

Report of the Indian Hemp Drugs Commission, 1893-94

Analysis Made by the Commission of Cases Referred to by Witnesses in Answering Question No. 53

I. — Cases the records of which have not been called for.

Serial No.	Province	Name of witness	No. of Witness	Name of criminal	Nature of the crime	Reason for attributing the crime to hemp drugs
1	Bengal	Mr Williams	13	Not given	A Darbhanga sowar seems to have run amok in Calcutta. Witness was told he did not take liquor.	"My knowledge of the case was entirely hearsay."
2	Do.	Mr Taylor	36	Do.	When witness was passing through a Sonthal village in 1856 with some friends, a man attacked them with a sword. It was during the Sonthal rebellion.	The villagers and the man himself said he was intoxicated with *bhang*.
3	Do.	Abhilas Chandra Mukerjee	63	Do.	A lad in an altercation with his uncle killed him with a sword. This case was reported to witness by the District Superintendent, Police.	The lad was a *ganja*-smoker and the uncle used to remonstrate with him.
4	Do.	Nobin Chander Sen	39	Do.	A fakir committed murder.	No special reason given.
5	Do.	Govind Chandra Das	64	Radhai Haldar	A man killed his mother because she would not bring his son who had been cremated, but whom be believed to have been raised from the dead by Trinath.	The man is said to have smoked *ganja* at a "Trinath fair." But the case is very doubtful.
6	Do.	Nobo Gopal Bose	218	Not given	A Brahmachari sacrificed a human being.	The accused told his pleader he was intoxicated from *ganja*.
7	Do.	Nimai Charan Das	142	Do.	A Muhammadan fakir killed a disciple with his *dhow* for being late in bringing his smoke.	No reason given. The man had not had his *ganja* and was angry.
8	Assam	KC Sanyal	31	Not given	A man addicted to *ganja* was sitting talking with a friend and suddenly killed him.	He was addicted to *ganja*.

'he was intoxicated from ganja.'

'The U.S. Army has been directly
responsible for turning on more than a
quarter of million young Americans '

"THE JUNGLE OF
VIETNAM IS LITTER-
ED WITH MARIJUANA
ROACHES; THE
STREETS OF SAI-
GON ARE 'PAVED
WITH GOLD'. "

Vietnam — from
the cover of
Rolling Stone
November, 1968

Serial No.	Province	Name of witness	No. of Witness	Name of criminal	Nature of the crime	Reason for attributing the crime to hemp drugs
9	North-Western Provinces	Mr Robarts	32	Not given	A constable threw small stones at his comrades and threatened to shoot, but gave up his rifle quietly.	He was addicted to ganja.
10	Do.	Mr Partridge	20	Do.	A fakir in Srinagar chopped off a boy's head.	He was a consumer in considerable quantities and "fairly rational" when not under the influence of *charas*.
11	Do.	Munna Lal	123	Do.	A fakir threatened people on the street over 20 years ago.	The witness remembers it was *charas*.
12	Do.	Do.	123	Do.	2. A man was making a disturbance as witness passed by.	The people in the street said he was mad with *ganja* or *charas*.
13	Do.	Pandit Debi Parshad	204	Do.	A fakir threw idols into a well and also pushed in a man who remonstrated with him, fourteen years ago.	"He was an excessive consumer." He was sent to the asylum and remained there twelve years.
14	Do.	Mohant Keshoram Rai	242	Do.	Two men quarrelled four or five years ago.	
15	Do.	Do.	242	Lahri Baba	2. Killed a child for his ornaments 25 years ago when under the influence "of *bhang* with *dhatura* and arsenic in it."	No reason given in any of the three cases.
16	Do.	Do.	242	Not given	3. A teacher 40 years ago killed a student.	
17	Do.	Mr R Wall	233	Not given	A Gurkha soldier ran amok about 1879 at Naini Tal.	"It was ascribed by rumour to *ganja*-smoking."
18	Do.	Mr R Wall	233	Not given	2. A sepoy shot Lieutenant Coode at Benares in 1883.	"I cannot say whether it was a hemp case."
19	Punjab	Shekh Riaz Hossain	67	Not given	A fakir murdered a Tahsil chaprasi in Muzuffergarh.	He "was a constant consumer of *bhang* and did nothing else."
20	Do.	Mr Robinson	16	Do.	A man nearly killed a banya with whom he had had dealings.	He was "under the influence of some drug."

Serial No.	Province	Name of witness	No. of Witness	Name of criminal	Nature of the crime	Reason for attributing the crime to hemp drugs
21	Do.	Karm Elahi	44	Do.	A Sikh in Rawal Pindi throttled his nephew 8 or 9 months old.	He was "under excitement," and apparently insane, not under the influence of *bhang* at the time.
22	Do.	Colonel Hutchinson	4	Do.	A Gurkha belonging to the witness' then regiment ran amok. It was in the sixties. There was jealousy in the case.	No reason given. "It is too long ago to recollect details."
23	Do.	Mr Warburton	30	Do.	A police sergeant about 1874 became violent from the use of *bhang* and *charas*. Had he got a sword there would have been injury.	Witness' recollection. "He had been brooding over being passed over for promotion."
24	Central Provinces.	Hosen Khan	79	Not given	The witness' brother-in-law nearly killed his wife under the influence of *ganja*.	No special reason given.
25	Do.	Adhar Singh Gour	69	Do.	A confirmed smoker killed his own child.	The Sessions Court acquitted the man on account of insanity due to mental trouble.
26	Do.	Taradas Banerjee	70	Do.	A Sanyasi killed a Kapalik in the temple over 20 years ago.	He was a *ganja*-smoker, but witness cannot say he indulged that day.
27	Do.	Brijmohan Patnaik	24	Paltu	Tried to kill a woman under the influence of *ganja*.	No reason given. Witness does not know about provocation.
28	Do.	Dinanath, Rai Bahadur.	32	Not given	A Gond killed his wife because she would not give him water.	The man said he had done the deed under the effect of *ganja*.
29	Do.	Mr Naylor	30	Do.	A Banjara killed his wife and two members of the tanda 18 years ago.	The people of the tanda said so.
30	Do.	Do.	30	Do.	2. A zamindar 15 years ago killed his brother by whose death he succeeded to the estate.	His friends said so.
31	Do.	Prem Singh	57	Do.	"I have seen a boy, not used to ganja, on becoming intoxicated with it, kill his father."	Witness was present apparently.

106

Serial No.	Province	Name of witness	No. of Witness	Name of criminal	Nature of the crime	Reason for attributing the crime to hemp drugs
32	Do.	Mahomed Taki	33	Guppu Singh	Guppu wounded with a sword one of several constables who were drinking bhang with him 20 years ago.	The story is that he was drinking *bhang* at the time.
33	Do.	Do.	33	Not given	2. A Nat killed his wife 25 years ago.	The story is that he was drinking *bhang* at the time. "He subsequently became a lunatic and was sent to Jubbulpore."
34	Do.	Mr Pasley	34	Do.	One Sadhu killed another	No reason given.
35	Madras	Mr Simpson	67	Not given	A native officer shot his Subadar Major from jealousy about 1886.	Witness gives up this case. (N.B. — This case is quoted by witnesses Nos. 81 and 82.)
36	Madras	Mr Simpson (continued).	67	Not given	2. A barber cut the throat of his first wife and his own that they might die together, about 1883.	2. Witness is doubtful about this case.
37	Do.	Do.	Do.		3. A boy in mischief threw a stone over a purdah and killed a woman sleeping on the other side.	3. This is very doubtful: the people present said "the lad had thrown the stone in play."
38	Do.	Tyaswamy Pillay	109	Do.	A consumer was quarrelsome and used to attack his relatives and beat them.	The matter never came to Court. The man took liquor also.
39	Do.	Dr Lancaster	90	Do.	A sepoy in hospital at Nellore stabbed the orderly. He was "in a state of doubtful sanity" (*vide* Dr Pemberton's evidence).	He used *ganja*. He had ultimately to be sent to the asylum.
40	Do.	Dr Pemberton	98	Do.	A sepoy in Burma in 1881 ran amok. This witness also speaks to the Nellore case (No. 39 *supra*).	The witness had the man under obervation.
41	Do.	Dr Chatterjee	88	Do.	A sepoy ran amok in 1887 in Burma.	The discrepancies between Dr Chatterjee's written and oral examination show his recollection to be defective.

Serial No.	Province	Name of witness	No. of Witness	Name of criminal	Nature of the crime	Reason for attributing the crime to hemp drugs
42	Do.	Vasadeo Rajamani	128	Do.	A consumer tried to stab another man 23 years ago.	The man was a consumer.
43	Do.	Mahomed Murtaza	82	Do.	A sepoy shot a Jamadar without reason.	The men of his regiment said he was a great smoker.
44	Do.	BC Chatterjee	167	Do.	A man in Ganjam committed a murder.	"He was an immoderate smoker of *ganja*."
45	Do.	Revd. Mr Higgins	150	Do.	A Brahman beat his child and wept when he became sober.	The man made this excuse.
46	Do.	Very Rev. A Chelvum.	161	Do.	A sepoy was anxious 42 years ago to do violence, but could not control his limbs.	No reason given. Witness was then twelve years old.
47	Do.	Mr Merriman	28	Do.	A pensioned sepoy murdered his daughter-in-law and her brother and sister.	The man was a consumer.
48	Bombay	Mr Kennedy	54	Not given	A Biluch sepoy ran amok and shot some people.	Witness rather indicates that this was premeditated.
49	Do.	Mr Woodward	11	Do.	A man attacked and was shot by Mr Woodward, Collector of Nasik.	"It was commonly reported."
50	Do.	VR Katti	116	Do.	A Lingayat trader killed his brother by night.	He was a consumer.
51	Sind	Puribhdas Shewakram Advani.	29	Not given	A sepoy at Hyderabad ran amok several years ago	"It was believed." Mr Giles (Witness 2) also quotes this case doubtfully.
52	Do.	Rahmatala Khan	9	Do.	A drinker of bhang committed a murder in a scuffle about plucking berries.	The man was a consumer.
53	Do.	Mahomed Murid	11	Kowra Khokar	Kowra Khokar killed a companion at night.	"They were always quarrelling about opium and *bhang*."
54	Burma	Mr Mayne	24	Not given	A sepoy shot a Subadar-Major at Sagaing in 1888.	He was a consumer.
55	Do.	Do.	Do.	Do.	Another sepoy attempted to murder a Burmese girl.	Ditto.

Serial No.	Province	Name of witness	No. of Witness	Name of criminal	Nature of the crime	Reason for attributing the crime to hemp drugs
56	Berat	V Khot	30	Do.	A man ran amok in Mhow.	No reason given.
57	Berar	K A Baki	36	Not given	A bairagi murdered a woman while intoxicated.	No reason given.
58	Do.	Mr O'Grady	6	Ambrose	The servant assaulted the witness when he dismissed him.	The man made this excuse.

Report of the Indian Hemp Drugs Commission, 1893-94

II. — Cases in which the records were examined by the Commission.

Serial	Province	Name of witness	Witnesses	Name of criminal	Witness's view of the case.	Result of examining the records.
59	Bengal	Mr Ward	89	Not given	A smoker suddenly murdered a vendor because he would not supply him with more *ganja*.	In an altercation the vendor "first struck the accused with a split bamboo; and it was then that he wounded him with his knife," which he had in his hand as he had been eating fruit.
60	Do.	Do.	Do.	Isahak Shekh	2. A *ganja*-smoker cruelly treated his child. While under trial and on bail he hacked at his wife and father-in-law and killed another man who came to their rescue.	The man cruelly treated his child on trifling provocation. He determined to kill his wife for giving evidence against him, and killed a man who came to her rescue. There is no mention of *ganja*.
61	Do.	Dr Crombie	104	Kailash Chandra Mallik	"A Bengali Babu, as the result of a single debauch in an attack of *ganja* mania, slew seven of his nearest relatives in bed during the night, made a rapid recovery, and never again exhibited signs of insanity."	The Sessions Judge found that "for years prisoner has been peculiar in his behaviour. After his wife's death [six or seven years before this occurrence] he was quite mad for a month; and since his mother's death again he has been behaving like a man bereft of his reason." The murder was committed on the evening of his mother's *Shradh*; and the man's insane statements after the murder showed that he had

'He hacked at his wife and father-in-law and killed another man . . .

The further
adventures of
the Fabulous
Furry Freak
Brothers, by
Gilbert Shelton

Serial No.	Province	Name of witness	No. of Witness	Name of Criminal	Witness's view of the case	Result of examining the records
						the idea that the family were helpless without the mother.
62 to 64	Do.	Mr Marindin	16	Three cases	No particulars were given by witness; but he mentioned the cases as illustrating homicidal frenzy attributed to hemp drugs.	All three were cases of insanity. in the first case there is doubtful mention of hemp drugs. in the other two there is no mention of these drugs; but in one of them (the third case) there is mention of liquor.
65 & 66	Assam	Mr Dalrymple Clark	14	Two cases	The witness after consulting his subordinates examined the records of seven cases of this character and found two in which there was mention of *ganja*. He gave their names without details; and they were sent for.	In both cases the accused were *ganja*-smokers. But the record in each case indicates that the offences cannot be attributed to that drug. The one was a quarrel between some smokers. The other was a case of wife-branding.
67	Do.	Dr Mullane	19	Ramchandra Puri	In 1885 a religious mendicant murdered a guest in the middle of the night apparently while under the influence of *ganja*.	The record suggests the same view as the witness holds.
68		Do.	Do.	Jadu Murha	2. A man was charged with committing murder in the Dum Duma bazar under *ganja* delerium. The witness does not remember details.	2. This man wounded several people. He used to drink liquor and take opium. He never took *ganja*. The Judge found that he had not had any intoxicant.
69	Assam	Mr Moran	33	Lala Kamar	"I had a case of a man in my garden who cut off his wife's head whilst temporarily insane under the effects of the drug."	It is a striking fact that Mr Moran was examined at great length before the Magistrate and never mentioned *ganja*. The record is quite against the *ganja* theory. The man seems to have been addicted to liquor.
70	Do.	Mr McCabe	5	Not given	"A Nepalese under the excitement caused by *bhang* cut down an inoffensive person whom he had never met before and with whom he had no sort of quarrel.	The man was drunk at the time and committed the murder in a drunken fray of which the principal feature was that he demanded more drink.

Serial No.	Province	Name of witness	No. of Witness	Name of criminal	Witness's view of the case	Result of examining the records
71	Punjab	Mr Maconachie	8	Allah Baksh	In 1892 "a fakir excited with *bhang* made a furious attack on a companion with his club."	The man in a quarrel with his wife wounded her with an axe. Only one witness spoke to the use of *bhang*. Mr Maconachie himself tried the case.
72	Do.	Mr Dames	9	Kalu Khan, Khosa	"Kalu Khan stabbed a man with whom he had no previous quarrel while under the influence of *bhang*."	This is a very interesting case in connection with an effort on the part of the Punjab Government to make the Khosas give up all intoxicants.
73	Madras	Colonel Chrystie	65	Shekh Hussain	"A peon, having been fined four annas, got into a high state of irritation and went and smoked *bhang* in a *makkan* in Anantapur at noon. The *bhang* appears to have excited him to madness." He beat an old man to death and threatened others with a club [This case is quoted by several other Madras witnesses.]	This man's asylum history should be read as well as the judicial records. He is one of the 1892 cases. He was punished as stated for a crime committed (as was supposed) when he was intoxicated. But inquiry into his antecedents and his jail and asylum history show recurrent insanity, the outbreaks of which are quite independent of *ganja*.
74 to 76	Do.	Mr Stokes	10	Three cases	"The 1st class Inspector of Police, Tirupatur taluk, gives three instances of murder which he attributes to this cause."	There is really nothing to show that any of these cases was due to hemp drugs. They were cases of murder of a concubine in one case and a wife in the other two.
77	Do.	Mahomed Anwar Saheb	51	Kuppia	This man killed his child on Kartika Nakshatram day "to send the child to God." There was evidence that he was under the influence of *bhang*.	The High Court adopted this view of the case.
78	Bombay	Nanabhai Cowasjee	60	Not given	In 1885 certain Talavias committed a riot in Broach, in which Mr Prescott (District Superintendent of Police) was killed.	The present report of the Collector shows that this riot cannot be attributed to hemp drugs.

Serial No.	Province	Name of witness	No. of Witness	Name of criminal	Witness's view of the case	Result of examining the records
79	Do.	Mr Sinclair	6	Kunjandas	A servant entered his master's bed-room and attempted to throttle his master's wife. He was supposed to be under the influence of *bhang*.	The records bear out this view.
80	Do.	Do.	Do.	Not given	2. A Brahman was found in a temple with the broken image of a goddess. He was acquitted on the ground of insanity due to hemp drugs.	The man was acquitted for want of evidence that he had committed the offence at all. He had, moreover, been insane for twelve years, and his insanity was attributed to several causes other than hemp drugs.
81	Do.	Colonel Humfrey	51	Do.	A sepoy ran amok and (before the Sessions Court) pleaded that *bhang* had been given to him. "I do not think the *bhang* caused him to commit the crime. I think it was established that the man had taken *bhang*, and if he did take it the crime was committed within half an hour afterwards."	The High Court did not consider the taking of the *bhang* established. They held also that if taken, it was taken some hours before the offence; and they held that all his proceedings showed that he was not under the influence of the drug alleged to have been given to him, and that the offence was premeditated.

113

A user of Marihuana is a degenerate . . .
A California . . . poster from the Division of Narcotic Enforcement, 1935

Opposite: 'A police emergency squad eradicating a patch of the drug-producing plants from a vacant lot in Astoria, NY!' — *Popular Science Monthly*, 1936

Appendix two
The Commission's Report: The Resolution

Indian Hemp Drugs Commission

Government Of India
Finance And Commerce Department

[Resolution (*Excerpted*)]

[Calcutta, the 21st March, 1895]   ***330561**

Read:
Report of the Indian Hemp Drugs Commission.

Resolution:
The Report of the Hemp Drugs Commission,* which was received by the Government of India (in proof) on the 7th of August 1894, has been considered by the Governor General in Council.

This resolution is probably the most important single document connected with the Indian Hemp Drugs Commission Report, since it represents the culmination of several years' effort on the part of the Commission reflected in an official response by the convening government. Without such response the Report, for all its thorough research and rational consideration, could have been another filed and forgotten document, and the Government would have proceeded to act, as so many do, out of preconceived political notions unhindered by fact. In our remarkable times this bit of evidence of long-past coherence should serve as something to be cherished, a small proof that there is, somewhere, a God of things as they ought to be.

The Commission were appointed, under the orders of the Government of India contained in the Resolution quoted in paragraph I of the Report of the Commission, at the request of Her Majesty's Secretary of State for India, who, in answer to a question put in the House of Commons, had signified his willingness to have a Commission appointed to inquire into the cultivation of the hemp plant in Bengal, the preparation of drugs from it, the trade in those drugs, the effects of their consumption upon the social and moral condition of the people, and the desirability of prohibiting the growth of the plant and the sale of ganja and allied drugs. In view of ensuring that the inquiry should be thorough and complete, the Secretary of State was of opinion that it could hardly be confined to Bengal, but should extend to the whole of India, and that the Commission should ascertain to what extent the existence of the hemp plant all over India affects the practical difficulty of checking or stopping the consumption of ganja as distinguished from other narcotic drugs prepared from the hemp plant, and whether there is ground for the statement that bhang is less injurious than ganja to consumers.

2. The instructions given to the Commission are reproduced in paragraph 3 of the Report; it was left to the Commission to take up any other branch of the inquiry which in their opinion was likely to elucidate the subject and to aid the Government of India and the Secretary of State in deciding on the policy to be adopted in regard to hemp drugs. The Commission were directed to visit and take evidence in all or most of the provinces of India, but were informed that there were political objections to their holding sittings in Native States, although any information similar to that

required regarding British India, which could be obtained regarding Native States, should be included in the Report. This was the only restriction placed upon the scope of the Commission's inquiry, and the Governor General in Council is of opinion that the Commission have fully acted up to the instructions they received, and that the inquiry made has been as complete, full, and exhaustive as it was intended that it should be. The method of inquiry adopted by the Commission is described at length in paragraphs 4 to 16 of the Report. After distributing questions for reply by such persons as might be expected to possess information on the subject, the Commission made a tour of inquiry, lasting from the 22nd August to the 6th October 1893, and a second tour, devoted chiefly to the examination of witnesses, lasting from the 25th October 1893 till the 25th April 1894. From this last date till August 6th, the subject was discussed by the members of the Commission, and the report was drawn up.

Cultivation

3. The information obtained by the commission as to the existence, prevalence, and character of the spontaneous growth of the hemp plants shows that, except in a tract which may be generally defined as the area that lies within 40 or 50 miles of the foot of the Himalayas, the hemp plant does not grow wild, though there are two areas in which the spontaneous growth is of some importance. One of these areas is in the North-Western Provinces, and the second consists of the country between the Ganges and the Bhagirati on one side, and the Eastern Hill Tracts stretching down to Calcutta on the other. The plant grows wild throughout the Himalayas from Kashmir to the extreme east of Assam, though it probably disappears at a higher altitude than 10,000 feet. It is generally found in mountainous regions and in the lower slopes of the hills, where it probably springs from seeds carried down from the mountains. In the populous parts of the Sub-Himalayan Tracts and in the valleys of Assam the wild growth is kept up in a great measure by fresh importation of seed from the ganja and bhang which are consumed by the people, and this is true also, though in a limited degree, of the mountain and hill ranges. The plant is hardy when once established, but would probably not long survive unaided in the low country.

14. From the above summary of the Commission's Report on the extent of the cultivation of the hemp plant, it will be seen that cultivation is prohibited in Assam, the Feudatory States of the Central Provinces, Burma and the Civil and Military Station of Bangalore in Mysore. The culti-

vation, except under license, is forbidden in Bengal, the Central Provinces, Berar, Mysore, Coorg and in the Native States of Dholpur and Gwalior. The Governor General in Council is of opinion that there should be one system throughout all the provinces of India in which the cultivation of the hemp plant is permitted, and this policy should be that of forbidding all cultivation, except under license. Cultivation should also, so far as possible, be concentrated into selected areas in each province, which should be no larger than is absolutely necessary. The same system should, so far as may be, be introduced in the Native States.

Products

15. The narcotic products of the hemp plant are ganja, charas and bhang, and the definitions of these products as taken by the Commission from Dr Prain's report, and as used in their own report, are:

Ganja consists of the dried flowering tops of cultivated female hemp plants which have become coated with resin in consequence of having been unable to set seeds freely.

Charas is the named applied to the resinous matter which forms the active principle when collected separately.

Siddhi, bhang, subzi or patti are different names applied to the dry leaves of the hemp plants, whether male or female, and whether cultivated or uncultivated.

The name bhang is also applied to the drink prepared by infusion of these last.

The female plant properly is called ganja and the male plant bhang; and ganja, as above defined, is produced by the female plant only. Ganja under certain conditions can be prepared by infusion, as a drink similar to, and called by the name of, bhang. In some parts of the country the name bhang is applied to what is elsewhere called ganja. Charas is distinct from both ganja and bhang, though the name of charas is sometimes given to ganja. These differences of nomenclature give rise to considerable confusion in the replies given to the series of questions issued by the Commission, and have to be borne in mind in reading them; it was only at the later stage of proceedings that the distinctions were carefully observed.

16. It is, the governor General in Council considers, a well-established fact that the cultivation and preparation of the finest sort of ganja is a difficult process requiring skill and knowledge, whilst the drink known as bhang is easily prepared from the dried leaf of the plant. The majority of the witnesses examined state that ganja cannot be procured from the wild plants, and the Commission find that what is ordin-

'...the hemp plant does not grow wild, though... spontaneous growth is of some importance.'

117

Hemp
Commission
Report
An intimate
relation between
hemp drugs
and alcohol

arily accepted as ganja undoubtedly cannot be so obtained. Charas may be prepared to a small extent from the wild plant and from the spontaneous growth, but is almost all imported through the Punjab from Yarkand and Bokhara.

Consumption

17. The Commission in Chapter VII notice the trade and movement of the hemp drugs province by province, and in Chapter VIII they describe the extent of use and the manner and form in which hemp drugs are consumed. The Governor General in Council observes that in Bengal only 1 in 200 of the total population consume ganja, and not more than 1 in 20 of the consumers are classed as excessive. The yearly consumption of a moderate consumer is 35 tolas (9/10 lb avoirdupois), and the individual amount consumed by each consumer is, distributing the amount taken by immoderate users over the whole number of consumers, only 40 tolas. A maund of ganja on an average suffices 15,000 persons of the total population of Bengal for a year. In the North-Western Provinces one maund of ganja suffices for 10,000 persons only, if the population of the Meerut, Rohilkhand and Kumaon Divisions, in which the drug is not used, be omitted from the calculation. In the Central Provinces 1 in 160 of the population consume ganja. Ganja is used principally for smoking, and so is charas. Bhang is used principally for drinking, and it is not used regularly like ganja or charas; it forms a refreshing drink in the hot weather; it is easily procurable, and it is difficult to furnish any statistics as to the extent of its use. Ganja is usually mixed with tobacco and sometimes with spices of various kinds, and occasionally, too, ganja is mixed with the seeds of the dhatura, opium, nux vomica, kanher root, hemp seeds, the root of the jowar plant (Sorghum), the root of rice, the juice of the madar, the skins and poison of snakes, and lastly with cantharides. Bhang too is mixed with other ingredients and sometimes with alcohol. Ganja and bhang are also eaten as well as drunk, and there is a considerable consumption of sweetmeats made with ganja, bhang and sometimes charas. Hemp is also sometimes compounded into cakes.

18. Confining attention to the more important provinces, it appears that the use of ganja is not on the increase in Bengal, notwithstanding that the population increased by 7½ per cent between 1881 and 1891, and that liquor is much dearer than ganja in Bengal. In the North-Western Provinces the hemp drug revenue has increased from 4 to 7 lakhs, and it may be assumed that the use of the drug has increased. It must be remembered that the population has increased

in the North-Western Provinces by five millions in the last twenty years, so that the increased consumption is in a measure accounted for. There is, moreover, an intimate relation between hemp drugs and alcohol; when alcohol is dear, the use of hemp drugs increases, and when alcohol is cheap, the use of hemp drugs decreases. Now, during recent years, hemp drugs have not grown dearer whilst the price of alcohol has been raised.

In the Punjab the use of charas, which in this province takes the place of ganja, is on the increase, though the figures are open to some doubt, as the increase may be due partly to improved registration and to the increase of the population. In the Central Provinces the evidence points to an increased use of ganja. In Madras ganja is both cheap and inferior, and it is used much less than in Bengal or Bombay; the use is no doubt increasing. In Bombay little reliance can be placed on the figures of retail sale, and there is no satisfactory basis on which an opinion can be formed. As regards the minor provinces, the evidence is conflicting. It is found that there is little evidence of excessive use of hemp drugs in the Army.

19. On a review of the whole evidence the Governor General in Council is not convinced that there is anything to show that the use of hemp drugs is increasing in a greater ratio than can be accounted for by the growth of the population and by improved administration and means of information. As to the use of bhang, the information is so imperfect that no opinion can be formed whether it is increasing or not.

20. The use of hemp drugs by religious devotees and ascetics and its employment in religious ceremonies was one of the subjects to which the special attention of the Commission was directed. Paragraph 450 of the Report, in which their conclusions are summed up, may well be quoted at length:

450: In summing up their conclusions on this chapter, the Commission would first remark that charas, which is a comparatively new article of consumption, has not been shown to be in any way connected with religious observance. As regards Northern India, the Commission are of opinion that the use of bhang is more or less common everywhere in connection with the social and religious customs of the people. As regards ganja, they find that there are certain classes in all parts, except the Punjab, who use the drug in connection with their social and religious observances. The Commission are also of opinion in regard to bhang that its use is considered essential in some religious observances by a large section of the community, and in regard to ganja that those who consider it essential are comparatively very few. The Commission have little doubt that interference with the use of hemp in connection with the customs and observances above referred to would be regarded by the consumers as an interference with long-established usage and as an encroachment upon their religious liberty. And this feeling would, especially in the case of bhang, undoubtedly be shared to some extent by the people at large. Regarding Southern India, the same remarks apply, with this reservation, that the difference between ganja and bhang as materials for smoking and drinking respectively is much less marked there, and the distinction between the two forms of the drug is much less clearly recognised, although by the term 'bhang' is generally meant the drug as used for drinking, and by 'ganja' the drug is used for smoking.

21. His Excellency in Council is prepared to accept the conclusions of the Commission upon this point. In this connection the following paragraph from Raja Soshi Sikareshwar Ray's dissent is worthy of attention:

Although I am fully convinced of the injurious effects of ganja and the benefit which will be derived by its total prohibition, I think I would not be justified in advocating a sudden prohibition, having regard to the dissatisfaction which it may likely cause to a class of people known as sanyasis, bairagis, and fakirs, whose facilities for giving trouble are very great owing to their peculiar position and habits of life. I do not think, however, that this dissatisfaction of certain classes of people on account of the prohibitory measure in itself is likely to cause any serious annoyance to Government, but this, when added to other similar causes of dissatisfaction, might bring about discontent. It is scarcely necessary to point out the nature of the influence which these sanyasis and fakirs still exercise over a vast number of people who have not received English education.

It should, however, be mentioned that the use of hemp drugs in connection with religious or social observances is confined to Hindus, and in no way affects the Mohamedans, as the Mohamedan religion condemns such practices (paragraph 437 of the Report).

Effects

22. Turning next to the effects of the use of hemp drugs, the Commission have divided their report into three heads — Physical, Mental, and Moral, and they have prefaced their remarks on these three heads by certain general observations. The main difficulty in dealing with this subject is the remarkable want of definite information on matters relating to hemp drugs. The subject has not hitherto attracted special atten-

tion, but it is, nevertheless, very noteworthy that there should be so very little accurate information available. Vague impressions exist, but they are not founded on close or recorded observation. And in many cases even professional witnesses, who had given fairly definite answers to some of the questions circulated by the Commission, turned out, when subjected to oral examination, to be speaking from general impressions, and not from facts that had come before them in their professional experience.

23. The Commission justly found upon this an argument that if the effects of ganja were such, or so common, as they have often been alleged to be, much more would be known about them. It is impossible to imagine any vagueness or indefiniteness in the information that would be available to a Commission of enquiry into the extent and effect of the habit of alcohol consumption in England; and the fact that so many differing opinions are held, and so little precise information is generally possessed, with regard to ganja, makes it evident that it cannot be the cause either of much mischief to the individual or of much harm to the public.

24. The subject of bhang may be disposed of in a word. It is a harmless and refreshing drink, used as such, especially during the hot weather, by the best classes of native society. Even the two members of the Commission who advocate prohibitory measures with respect to ganja object to interference with bhang, and even to its being subjected to taxation.

25. As regards the effect of the evidence relating to ganja, there is great difficulty in distinguishing with any precision when the witnesses are referring to moderate use, and when they are referring to excessive use. To say that excessive use causes harm to the smoker of ganja, is merely to say that there is a point, just as there is with the most harmless articles of consumption, where consumption becomes harmful, and therefore excessive. The real question is to what extent among the smokers of ganja the consumption of it is pushed to the point where it causes harm. And even in this respect further difficulties arise; for injurious effects, when they occur, often arise, not from the smoking of ganja pure and simple, but from the habit of smoking it mixed with other ingredients. As remarked by Raja Soshi Sikareshwar Ray in his dissent:

At present we have not sufficient means to ascertain how far the injury caused to the consumers of the drug is due to the pure drug itself, and how far to the other poisonous substances that are occasionally mixed with it.

Of these the most injurious is dhatura, and the opinion

'Bhang ... is a harmless and refreshing drink ...'

119

Hemp
Commission
Report
There are no
marked mental,
physical or moral
ill-effects . . .

that the consumers of hemp drugs, and especially, though not exclusively, excessive consumers, would take to dhatura if hemp drugs were denied them, is, as the Commission point out, entitled to much weight. There is a medicinal use of hemp drugs, and moderate consumers would feel a sense of deprivation if they were unable to obtain what they regard as a beneficial stimulant. This deprivation would be chiefly felt by the poorer classes, who are, as a rule, admittedly moderate consumers; for those who, according to many witnesses, suffer harm from hemp drugs are persons who lead sedentary or idle lives, or, in other words, the richer classes.

26. Ganja is held by a proportion of seven to five of the witnesses to be harmless if taken in moderation; but charas is a more potent form of the product, and is generally considered to be more injurious. On the whole, if moderation and excess in the use of drugs are distinguished, which is a thing that the witnesses examined have, as just remarked, found it very hard to do, the weight of evidence is that the moderate use of hemp drugs is not injurious. This conclusion of the Commission the Governor General in Council feels bound to accept. It is also found that the habit of using hemp drugs is easier to break off than the habit of using alcohol or opium. It is a very striking fact that of the small minority of witnesses who compare the effects of alcohol and hemp drugs, a majority of nine to one declare alcohol to be more injurious than hemp drugs. There is a significant remark made by Khan Bahadur Kadir Dad Gul Khan, CIE, Sind Witness No 4, on this point. He says:

All classes of the people, from the most influential spiritual leader to the lowest beggar, will say that the British Government, while not interfering or prohibiting the use of alcohol in their own country, are stopping them here from the use of less intoxicating drugs, which they have been using from time immemorial, and which is also religiously respected.

Paragraphs 496, 497, and 498 of the Report are too long to be quoted *in extenso* in this Resolution, but they will well repay perusal. They indicate, in a general way, the manner in which the witnesses in many cases, and the public generally, have formed opinions or impressions on matters relating to ganja consumption, which, when brought to the test of examination, prove to go beyond any of the ascertained facts. As a rule, the presumption based upon the evidence is, as has been already said, that the moderate use of hemp drugs does not cause injury, though exceptional cases do arise in which this rule does not hold good.

27. As to the physical effects of the use of hemp drugs, the Commission consider that the moderate use of ganja and charas is not appreciably harmful.

28. The question of the mental effects produced by hemp drugs has been examined by the Commission with great care. The popular impression that hemp drugs are a fruitful source of insanity is very strong, but nothing can be more remarkable than the complete break-down of the evidence on which it is based. Popular prejudice has over and over again caused cases of insanity to be ascribed to ganja which have had no connection whatever with it; and then statistics based on this prejudice are quoted as confirming or establishing the prejudice itself. Of 222 cases of insanity ascribed to hemp drugs in the lunatic asylum statements of 1892, only 98 are found, on careful enquiry by the Commissioners, to have any connection with them. The result is that of the whole number of cases admitted to lunatic asylums in that year, only 7.3 per cent can be ascribed to hemp drugs, and if cases in which hemp drugs have been only one of several possible causes are omitted, the percentage falls to 4.5. Of course some cases in which the cause of insanity is entered as 'unknown' may be due to hemp drugs, though the Commission put forward the view that there is little difficulty in ascertaining the existence of the hemp drug habit, and therefore do not reckon cases in which the cause of insanity is returned as 'unknown' as cases in which the cause may be referred to the use of hemp drugs. But even if the percentage of cases in which the use of hemp drugs may be reasonably taken as one of the causes of the insanity be reckoned on the total admissions to asylums, and not only on the cases in which the cause of insanity is recorded as 'known,' still the percentage would be only 12.6. Moreover, the duration of insanity in hemp drugs cases is shorter than in cases of insanity due to other causes, and temporary intoxication has been frequently confounded with insanity in the case of consumers of hemp drugs. Whilst allowing that hemp drugs do cause insanity, the Governor General in Council finds that they cause insanity in far fewer cases than has hitherto been popularly understood, and that the insanity so caused is usually of a temporary character and is of shorter duration than insanity which is due to other causes.

29. The moral effects of the use of hemp drugs and the connection between hemp drugs and crime next come under discussion.

Out of 700 witnesses 600 say that moderate consumers are not offensive to their neighbours, and the Governor General in Council accepts the conclusion of the Commission that moderate consumers are not offensive as a rule, and indeed are not distinguishable from total abstainers.

As to the connection of hemp drugs with crime, the excessive use of hemp drugs may bring the consumer to poverty and so lead him to dishonest practices, and cases have been known in which excessive use of hemp drugs has induced to violent crime. There are, however, the Governor General in Council considers, no such marked ill-effects, physical, mental or moral, attendant on the use of hemp drugs as there were popularly believed to be before the present inquiry was made.

Policy of Government

30. Having now reviewed the information collected by the Commission, the Governor General in Council will proceed to consider the recommendations made by the Commission before passing orders upon them.

31. The remarks of the Commission on the general principles which should govern sumptuary laws and their application of India are as follows:

553. The question of prohibiting the growth of the hemp plant and the sale of ganja and allied drugs is one which stands in the forefront of the present inquiry. It has been remarked by a well-known historian that 'no laws are of any service which are above the working level of public morality, and the deeper they are carried down into life, the larger become the opportunities of evasion.' If these words are true as applied to England under a feudal system, they are much more true in the present day as applied to British India. The Government of this country has not grown out of the forces contained within it, but has been superimposed upon them, and the paternal system of government which may have been suitable in England during the sixteenth century, and in the initial development of some Indian provinces during the period immediately following their annexation, becomes purely visionary when public opinion is in process of formation and the needs of the people are year by year finding more ready expression. Occasionally, no doubt, the Legislature in India has anticipated a standard of morality not universally accepted by the people, as in the case of laws relating to infanticide or the burning of Hindu widows; but these measures were passed under an overwhelming sense of the necessity of correcting popular notions of morality in matters coming well within the sphere of Government, and in the assurance that in the course of time they could not fail to secure the assent of all intelligent members of the community.

In the chapter of Mill's Political Economy which treats of the non-interference principle, a distinction is made between two kinds of intervention by the Government — the one authoritative interference, and the other giving advice or promulgating information. And the following remarks are made regarding the former: 'It is evident, even at first sight, that the authoritative form of Government intervention has a much more limited sphere of legitimate action than the other. It requires a much stronger necessity to justify it in any case, while there are large departments of human life from which it must be unreservedly and imperiously excluded. Whatever theory we adopt respecting the foundation of the social union, and under whatever political institution we live, there is a circle around every individual human being which no Government, be it that of one, or of few, or of the many, ought to be permitted to overstep: there is a part of the life of every person who has come to years of discretion within which the individuality of that person ought to reign uncontrolled either by any other individual or by the public collectively. That there is, or ought to be, some space in human existence thus entrenched around no one who professes the smallest regard to human freedom or dignity will call in question: the point to be determined is where the limit should be placed; how large a province of human life this reserved territory should include. I apprehend that it ought to include all that part which concerns only the life, whether inward or outward, of the individual, and does not affect the interests of others, or affects them only through the moral influence of example.

With respect to the domain of the inward consciousness, the thoughts and feelings, and as much of external conduct as is personal only, involving no consequences, none at least of a painful or injurious kind, to other people, I hold that it is allowable in all, and in the more thoughtful and cultivated often a duty, to assert and promulgate with all the force they are capable of their opinion of what is good or bad, admirable or contemptible, but not to compel others to conform to that opinion, whether the force used is that of extra-legal coercion, or exerts itself by means of the law. Even in those portions of conduct which do not affect the interests of others, the onus of making out a case always lies on the defenders of legal prohibitions. It is not merely a constructive or presumptive injury to others which will justify the interference of law with individual freedom. To be prevented from what one is inclined to, or from acting contrary to one's own judgment of what is desirable, is not only always irksome, but always tends, *pro tanto*, to starve the

'. . . not to compel others to conform to that opinion . . .'

Hemp
Commission
Report
'Not prepared
to prohibit the
use of bhang?

development of some portion of the bodily or mental faculties, either sensitive or active; and unless the conscience of the individual goes freely with the legal restraint, it partakes, either in a great or in a small degree, of the degradation of slavery. Scarcely any degree of utility short of absolute necessity will justify a prohibitory regulation, unless it can also be made to recommend itself to the general conscience; unless persons of ordinary good intentions either believe already, or can be induced to believe, that the thing prohibited is a thing which they ought not to wish to do.' These remarks have been given at length, because the Commission believe that they contain a clear exposition of the principles which should guide them in deciding whether the prohibition of the hemp drugs should be authoritatively enforced by Government.

Without feeling himself called upon to pronounce an opinion on all the psychological and moral considerations raised in the previous quotation, the Governor General in Council observes that in framing laws on sumptuary matters, Government ought to be careful to keep touch with public opinion and ought not to interfere in matters affecting the conscience of individuals, in which the exercise of individual freedom is not harmful to the public. In connection with such sumptuary matters it is also generally accepted that acts which are in themselves injurious to nobody except the doers of them should not be made penal, and also that it is not expedient to make prohibitions which cannot be enforced.

Question of Prohibition

33. It is true that in the Resolution of the Government of India, Finance Department, No. 3773, dated the 17th December 1873, it was said of hemp:

There can be no doubt that its habitual use does tend to produce insanity. The total number of cases of insanity is small even in proportion to the number of ganja-smokers; but the cases of insanity produced by the excessive use of drugs or spirits, by far the largest number must be attributed to the abuse of hemp.

The enquiries of the present Commission cast grave doubts upon this conclusion, but it is accepted as the result of the inquiry that hemp drugs do cause insanity, and it is shown in paragraph 524 of the Report that the percentage of known cases of insanity which are due to hemp drugs, including mixed cases, is for 1892 7.3 per cent of the total admissions to lunatic asylums, whilst the percentage due to alcohol is 4.4 per cent, so that hemp is a more potent cause of insanity than alcohol in India. The total number of cases

of insanity due to hemp is, however, so small with reference to the whole population — the actual admissions to asylums are only about 1 for every 2¼ millions of population — that the Governor General in Council is not of opinion that the prohibition of the use of hemp is necessary because of its tendency to produce insanity.

34. In considering the question of prohibiting the use of hemp for reasons other than its tendency to cause insanity, the several preparations of hemp will be considered separately.

With regard to bhang, the Commissioners say:

564: The effects of the hemp drugs have been treated in Chapters X to XIII of the Report; and as the first result of these conclusions, the Commission are prepared to state that the suppression of the use of bhang would be totally unjustifiable. It is established to their satisfaction that this use is very ancient, and that it has some religious sanction among a large body of Hindus; that it enters into their social customs; that it is almost without exception harmless in moderation, and perhaps in some cases beneficial; that the abuse of it is not so harmful as the abuse of alcohol; that its suppression, involving the extirpation of the wild hemp plant, would in some tracts be a matter of great difficulty; that such a measure would be extremely unpopular, and would give rise to widespread discontent; and, finally, that, if successfully accomplished, it would lead to the use of more hurtful stimulants. The Commission deem it unnecessary to traverse the evidence further than has been done in the preceding chapters of this Report in support of these propositions. It is almost unanimous in regard to them. The utmost that is necessary in regard to this product is that it should be brought under more effective control, and this matter will be dealt with further on. But absolute prohibition is, in the opinion of the Commission, entirely out of the question.

The Governor General in Council is entirely in agreement, and is not prepared to prohibit the use of bhang.

35. The question of prohibiting the use of ganja and charas may be considered together, as their effects are similar, though charas is the more potent drug.

First, as regards the mere question of practicability. Charas is an imported drug, and its import could be easily prohibited, but to prohibit it would paralyse the trade with Yarkand, the importation of charas being the means by which Yarkand makes payment for its consumption of Indian products. Ganja is cultivated in Bengal, the Central Provinces, Madras, Bombay, and Berar. In Bengal and the Central

10. HEMP, BHANG. *Cannabis sativa* L. (Fig. 131, *a*). A native annual herb of central and western Asia is one of the best fiber-yielding plants. It is cultivated and allowed to run wild in many countries. In the continental United States, a Federal permit is required for its cultivation, as it also yields a deadly drug; in Hawaii, it is outlawed, hence is rare. The plant is bushy, rough, strong-smelling, 3 to 15 feet high, hollow-stemmed, and bears many alternate, thin, palmate leaves, with long petioles and with three to seven narrow, toothed leaflets. Male and female flowers are separate, usually on different plants, the male in long, loose clusters, the female in dense, short clusters. Male plants bear stronger fiber, which is in best condition when the plant is in full flower. The fiber is from the stem bark, and is 3 to 9 feet long, durable, somewhat lignified and therefore not so flexible as flax. The uses are many: for rope, twine, mats, sails, bags, paper, and oakum. Seeds yield oil for soap, paint, varnish, and lamp oil. Flowering tops of female plants, the leaves, seeds, and resin contain the narcotic drug marihuana, or hashish, which when smoked in "reefers," chewed, or drunk affects users seriously, sometimes causing them to run amok. However, the drug has long been used beneficially as medicine.

In the Gardens of Hawaii, 1930's; 'yields a deadly drug'

FIGURE 131.—a, Hemp (*Cannabis sativa*), leaves and fruit; b, artillery plant (*Pilea microphylla*), plant and enlarged leaf; c, pellionia (*Pellionia daveauana*); d, ramie (*Boehmeria nivea*), branch bearing male and female flowers; e, mamaki (*Pipturus albidus*), leaves and fruit.

Hemp
Commission
Report
'The prohibition
of ganja is an
interference
with liberty . .

Provinces the cultivation is under complete control, and the control of the cultivation is possible everywhere. It does not, however, the Commissioners think, follow that it would be possible to prevent cultivation altogether. It would be necessary to induce the Native States to prohibit cultivation, which would be difficult, and, even if this were done, it would be necessary to suppress illicit cultivation. This would, though not impossible, be a matter of difficulty, for ganja of an inferior kind can be manufactured from the spontaneous or casual growth, which is found near human habitations in many parts of India, and its suppression would require the entertainment of a large preventive force and considerable interference with individuals. Moreover, there would be a great risk of oppression on the part of preventive officers.

Summing up the evidence, it is found that of 575 witnesses who have expressed a decided opinion on the subject of prohibition, only 99 advocate it (paragraph 569 of the Report). Amongst no class of witnesses is there a preponderance of opinion in favour of total prohibition.

36. On the question of policy, the general conclusions of the Commission are contained in paragraph 585 of their Report:

585: A general review of the evidence relating to the question of prohibition of ganja and charas brings the Commission to the same conclusion as that which they have framed upon a consideration of the evidence on the ascertained effects alone. The weight of the evidence above abstracted is almost entirely against prohibition. Not only is such a measure unnecessary with reference to the effects, but it is abundantly proved that it is considered unnecessary or impossible by those most competent to form an opinion on general grounds of experience; that it would be strongly resented by religious mendicants, or would be regarded as an interference with religion, or would be likely to become a political danger; and that it might lead to the use of dhatura or other intoxicants worse than ganja. Apart from all this, there is another consideration which has been urged in some quarters with a manifestation of strong feeling, and to which the Commission are disposed to attach some importance, *viz*, that to repress the hemp drugs in India and to leave alcohol alone would be misunderstood by a large number of persons who believe, and apparently not without reason, that more harm is done in this country by the latter than by the former. The conclusion of the Commission regarding bhang has been given in paragraph 564. Under all the circumstances they now unhesitatingly give their verdict against such a violent measure as total prohibition in respect of any of the hemp

Allen Ginsberg,
Moratorium Day,
San Francisco,
April, 1970,
accepting the
sacrament.
Photograph:
Annie Leibovitz

drugs.

37. The prohibition of ganja is an interference with liberty which the Government of India is not justified in undertaking, except upon evidence which clearly establishes the fact that the harm permitted by non-prohibition is great and manifest. Not only is this not the case, but the evidence has rendered it abundantly manifest that those who have hitherto recommended the prohibition of ganja have done so under an erroneous, or at least a greatly exaggerated, impression as to its real effects. To a million people in India, ganja affords a harmless pleasure, and in some cases even a beneficial stimulant. It would, in the opinion of the Governor General in Council, amount to oppression to take active measures to suppress it, on the mere ground that it is possible to quote isolated instances in which individuals have received injury from its use. Nor can the Government commit themselves to so unequal a measure as the suppression of the use of ganja (which is the form in which the poor man uses the drug) and the permission of the use of bhang (which is the milder form in which the better situated classes enjoy it). There seems to the Governor General in Council no argument in favour of the prohibition of ganja which would not equally apply to the enforcement, by State Agency, of total abstinence from intoxicating or stimulating liquors and drugs throughout India — a proposal which is not within the range of practical politics.

Dissents

38. This seems the proper place to notice the dissents of two members of the Commission, Raja Soshi Sikareshwar Ray and Lala Nihal Chand, which refer mostly to the question of prohibition.

39. The former sums up his opinion on the evidence in the following paragraph:

Consideration of all these leads me to come to a conclusion which is not quite in agreement with that of my colleagues. I believe that the injurious effects of the hemp drugs are greater and their use more harmful than one would naturally suppose to be the case after reading the concluding portion of Chapter XIII of our Report, although I think I should say that the facts elicited by our inquiry do not go to support the extreme opinion held by some well-intentioned people that these drugs in all their forms and in every case are highly pernicious in their effects. We have seen in almost all parts of India people connected with temples and *maths* who are quite healthy, strong, and stout, who excessively indulge in bhang. Instances were not rare in which habitual

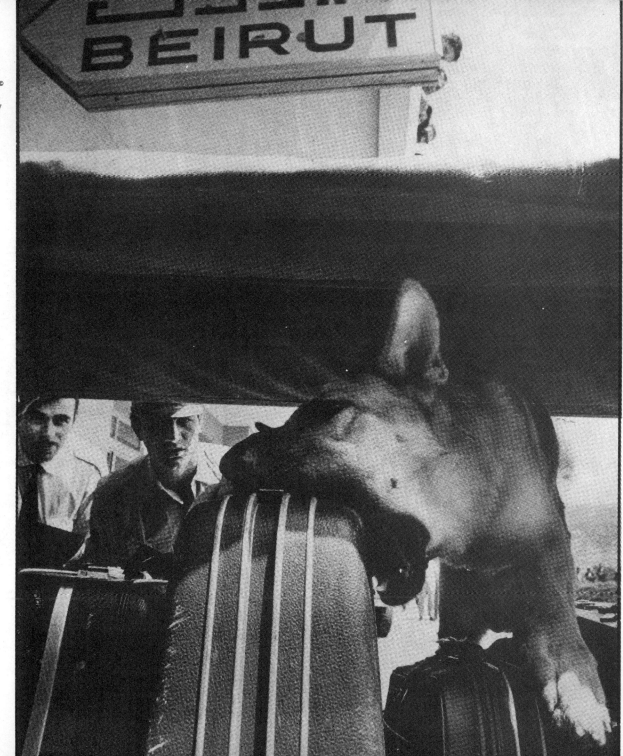

BEIRUT

ganja-smokers were seen to be quite healthy and strong. It is among the very poor and the mendicant classes that shocking instances of human wrecks caused by over-indulgence in hemp drugs can be found. The general opinion that I have been able to form is that ganja and charas are no doubt injurious in their action on the constitution of certain people, specially those who are weak and underfed, even when they are taken in comparatively moderate doses, and only for a short time. When they are consumed in excess and continuously for a long time, their effects are undoubtedly most ruinous. It should be remembered that it is the men of the poorest class generally, who cannot afford to pay for the luxury of spirituous drinks, who take to the use of ganja. It is also a fact that men who are naturally weak, and who suffer from some sort of bodily or mental indisposition or discomfort, to obtain temporary relief generally indulge in ganja, at first in medicinal doses, and then gradually turn to be excessive consumers of the drug. This accounts for the fact why so large a number of the consumers of the drugs are often found to be in a most deplorable condition. On the whole, therefore, I am inclined to believe that the prohibition of the use of ganja and charas would be a source of benefit to the people.

40. He goes on to discuss the practical difficulties in the way of prohibition, and comes to the conclusion that the prohibition should, for practical reasons, be attained gradually and not immediately. After referring to a political phase of the question in a paragraph already quoted under paragraph 21 above, he says:

There are other grounds besides the one mentioned above which lead me to recommend gradual prohibition. If, instead of adopting a sudden prohibitory measure, the Government adopt a gradual one, it will get time to institute further inquiries, should it be considered advisable, with a view to ascertain the exact physiological action of ganja. If it be found possible to refine the drug and make it less injurious by diminishing its narcotic effect, the question would then arise whether, like opium, it would not be advisable to make a Government monopoly of the drug. If, however, on moral or other grounds, this course does not commend itself to Government, it would be a question for further consideration whether the cultivation and manufacture of ganja might not be concentrated at one place under direct Government supervision.

Another great advantage to be derived by the adoption of this course is, if after further consideration and investigation, as suggested above, the Government decides for total prohibition, that nothing would be more easy than to give effect to such a measure.

41. With reference to this the Governor General in Council must observe that, even accepting to the full the Raja's estimate of the effect of the evidence as to the injurious nature of ganja, and its possible confirmation by future enquiries, he cannot consider that prohibition would become the duty of Government, or would even be justifiable. There are many matters in which adults must be allowed to judge for themselves and to use their own discretion, and the mere fact that some of them would be benefited, morally or physically, by abstention from any particular indulgence, does not warrant the Government in making that indulgence penal. For it is beyond a doubt that it is only by attaching to the cultivation, or sale of hemp drugs, the penalties of the criminal law, that prohibition could be made effective.

42. The dissent of Lala Nihal Chand takes somewhat different ground; he has made a laborious numerical analysis of the evidence, and practically comes to the conclusion that evidence is so various in character that the conclusions as to fact arrived at by his colleagues ought not to be accepted. The vagueness of the witnesses' answers and the absence of definite information as to facts is a characteristic to which the Commission have called attention; they tried to remedy it as far as possible by making a second tour of India, and calling the witnesses before them for cross-examination upon their written replies. Lala Nihal Chand was unfortunately unable, by reason of bad health, to be present on more than 5 days out of the 86 on which these cross-examinations were recorded, and it is not surprising that he should be more impressed with the discrepancies and differences in the evidence, and less confident of the establishment of any conclusions upon the basis of it, than the other members of the Commission.

43. The Lala's dissent was drawn up after the dispersal of the Commission, and his opinions were not submitted to, or discussed by, his colleagues; but it is quite clear that his estimate of the value and tendency of the evidence of particular witnesses differs from that of the rest of the Commission. It is not improbable that this difference arises, in a large measure, from the want of precision, and the tendency to state opinions and impressions rather than facts, which characterized the first collection of evidence. The Governor General in Council, however, has thought it due to the dissentient to make a careful examination of the evidence regarding which this difference of opinion exists, so as to arrive independently at an estimate of its value. A summary

of that examination is appended to this Resolution, and the conclusion at which the Governor General in Council has arrived is that the evidence has been correctly analysed and its effect correctly set forth by the Commission in the body of their report.

For this reason the Government of India, after duly considering the dissent of Lala Nihal Chand, do not find in it any reason to reject the conclusions which the Commission have reached as to the general effect of the evidence.

44. But again, even admitting to the full the arguments of the Lala as to the inconclusiveness of the evidence, the practical result must be that which the Commission have recommended. The question is whether the cultivation and sale of ganja products are to be taxed (and taxed as heavily as possible), or whether they are to be prohibited under a penalty. The prohibition of the use of ganja is, in the opinion of the Governor General in Council, an interference with individual liberty which requires for its justification the strongest and clearest evidence of the noxious character of the drug, both as it affects private persons and as it affects the public generally; it cannot be based upon evidence of which the most that can be said is that ganja is not proved to be harmful. The penalizing of cultivation and sale involves,

to the public generally, an amount of interference, and only too probably an amount of oppression and harassment, which it would require not merely vague possibilities, but the strongest grounds of evident public advantage, to justify.

45. The Lala refers in his dissent to the decision of the majority of the Commission not to append to their report the replies given to their printed circular of questions by the Commanding Officers and Medical Officers of Native Regiments, and by the witnesses who gave information as to Native States. The Commission have in their report stated the general effect of this evidence (see paragraphs 11 and 12); but as the subjects referred to were, by the express orders of the Government in one case, and by considerations of military administration in the other, placed outside the limits of the Commission's enquiry, they were unable to carry their investigations beyond the preliminary stage, or to supplement them either by local inquiries or by oral examination of witnesses; and it appears from the Commission's proceedings of 5th to 9th June, when the question of the treatment of this evidence was before them, that they felt themselves unable to found very largely upon evidence which they had not submitted to these tests. For political reasons the Government of India do not consider themselves at liberty

to publish the evidence relating to Native States; and that relating to the Army, as it contains particulars and details of a confidential character, can be published only after the elimination of names and regimental numbers. Under these circumstances, the Governor General in Council considers that the Commission were right in abstaining from appending the evidence as part of a report intended for ultimate publication. It has, however, been separately received by the Government.

Conclusion

68. In conclusion, the Governor General in Council desires to thank the President, Mr. Mackworth Young, and the members of the Commission for the exhaustive inquiry they have made. The investigation has been a laborious one, but it has been very complete, and the manner in which the Commission have pursued, to definite conclusions, the various matters arising out of the evidence brought before them, leaves nothing to be desired. The general ignorance on the subject of hemp drugs will, it is trusted, now be dissipated by the attention which the investigation of the Commission has directed to the subject. The want of uniformity in the excise administration of hemp drugs which has been found by the Commission to exist, will, no doubt, in due time be set right, and this most valuable result is of itself sufficient to justify the appointment of the Commission. The Report of the Commission has shown how little foundation there is for many of the popular beliefs and impressions which have prevailed in regard to the preparations made from the hemp plant and the effect of the use of hemp drugs upon their consumers, and the information which has been brought together on the subject in the Report of the Commission is of great interest and value, not only to Government and its officers, but also to the general public.

69. The acknowledgments of the Government are especially due to the three unofficial gentlemen, Raja Soshi Sikareshwar Ray, Kunwar Harnam Sigh, and Lala Nihal Chand, who at great expenditure of time and comfort, and, in one case at least, at some risk to health, took part in the investigations of the Commission. The inability of the Governor General in Council to agree with two of these gentlemen, in the points on which they dissent from the views of their colleagues, does not diminish his appreciation of the care and labour they have bestowed on the task entrusted to them.

Order: Ordered, that a copy of this Resolution and of the Report be forwarded to all Local Governments and Administrations and to the Agent to the Governor General in Baluchistan.

Ordered also, that copies of the Resolution be forwarded to the President and Members of the Commission.

Ordered further, that the Resolution be published in the *Gazette of India*.

Stephen Jacob,
Offg. Secretary to the Government of India   129

'The investigation has been a laborious one . . .'

Prototype of present-day 'Junkie House' showing a group of 'stoned' subjects, the archaic 'Barrel-fix', etc, with spotter outside to warn of police raid. — from *Fuzz Against Junk* by Akbar del Piombo, © 1960

It seems more important to acquire tools to banish dragons...
Photograph: Ted Porter

130

From the perspective of the 70's, it's easy to build fantastic mythologies about the infiltration of marijuana into the contemporary American consciousness. Likewise, it's tempting to look for a uniqueness in marijuana's progress through the society which reflects the character of the drug. But in fact the greater part of marijuana's impact on contemporary life was generated by the same sort of mundane forces & needs which lie behind so many of our institutions. This is particularly true of the way in which marijuana gained its current legal status, which status has been responsible for a major portion of marijuana's force in current affairs.

Marijuana, in one form or another, has been around the USA for a long time. The most common format for its use in the 18th & 19th centuries was as a fluid extract in patent medicines, though there was a widespread appreciation of its utility as smoking material among rural folks in the south & southwest. In the first few decades of the twentieth century smoking spread quietly along the central river systems and into the northern industrial centers. Relatively isolated cities in the west became centers of mild activity about this same period, but no particular disturbance followed in the wake of this expansion. The focus of anti-drug agitation in the late teens & early twenties centered on the opiates and on alcohol. Marijuana was not deemed a relevant issue.

The national preoccupation with prohibition, enforcing it, profiting from it, and circumventing it — led to many profound shifts in institutional power structures in America. Perhaps the most significant shift for future generations was the emergence of a federal police power with the specific mission of enforcing moral decisions.

Many people found a new set of heroes among the federal agents, who obliged by playing the diverting role of mediacop for the folks in the hinterlands. But

132

while Eliot Ness was doing his thing out front, the gray men of the supporting federal police bureaus had to face the fact that heroes have no job security. And neither do their managers. An additional problem for the gray men was that the end of prohibition was calculated in its inception. So even if the heroes lived they would survive only in quaint memory. Hardly the stuff of which bureaucratic power bases are made.

But how could such an unimaginative bureaucracy as the federal anti-alcohol police forces come up with a winner like marijuana, the ideal American evil, on their first shot? Most likely marijuana was frequently mentioned in investigative reports as a minor, relatively uninteresting aspect of the criminal & ethnic subcultures with whom the federal police dealt. Someone simply took the time to inquire into its character. Guilt or evil by association is a time-honored methodology, and the person who either took this initiative himself or who stole the idea from some underling was Harry Anslinger.

Harry Anslinger was placed in charge of the Treasury Department's finger-in-the-dike operation to halt liquor smuggling in 1926. In 1926, not by coincidence, the first anti-marijuana stories began to appear in mass-circulation newspapers, and the yellow press had a lot of fun trying out marijuana's front-page possibilities. The first successful anti-marijuana campaign in the country was waged by the morning & evening papers of New Orleans. While the editors of these papers did hedge their bets with the sure-fire winner of racism, the central point of their stories was that all them niggers had found a new way to get at your (white) kids, and the secret weapon they used was stuff called muggles.

Whether or not the Treasury Department simulated these first scare stories is a moot point. What did happen is that as a result of the anti-muggles drive, local legislation was passed swiftly in New Orleans. Interestingly enough, it was legislation which equated marijuana, in terms of penalties, with rape & murder, the two crimes most feared & fantasized by whites in their non-relations with blacks.

Moreover, Harry Anslinger & the anti-alcohol

Marijuana—Assassin of Youth

H. J. Anslinger
U. S. Commissioner of Narcotics

A Harry Anslinger special on the evils of marijuana — murder, suicide, rape, depravities & perversions . . . ! First published by *The American Magazine*, 1937

NOT LONG AGO the body of a young girl lay crushed on the sidewalk after a plunge from a Chicago apartment window. Everyone called it suicide, but actually it was murder. The killer was a narcotic known to America as marijuana, and to history as hashish. Used in the form of cigarettes, it is comparatively new to the United States and as dangerous as a coiled rattlesnake.

How many murders, suicides, robberies and maniacal deeds it causes each year, especially among the young, can only be conjectured. In numerous communities it thrives almost unmolested, largely because of official ignorance of its effects.

Marijuana is the unknown quantity among narcotics. No one knows, when he smokes it, whether he will become a philosopher, a joyous reveler, a mad insensate, or a murderer.

The young girl's story is typical. She had heard the whisper which has gone the rounds of American youth about a new thrill, a cigarette with a "real kick" which gave wonderful reactions and no harmful aftereffects. With some friends she experimented at an evening smoking party.

The results were weird. Some of the party went into paroxysms of laughter; others of mediocre musical ability became almost expert; the piano dinned constantly. Still others found themselves discussing weighty problems with remarkable clarity. The girl danced without fatigue throughout a night of inexplicable exhilaration.

Other parties followed. Finally there came a gathering at a time when the girl was behind in her studies and greatly worried. Suddenly, as she was smoking, she thought of a solution to her school problems. Without hesitancy she walked to a window and leaped to her death. Thus madly can marijuana "solve" one's difficulties. It gives few warnings of what it intends to do to the human brain.

Last year a young marijuana addict was hanged in Baltimore for criminal assault on a ten-year-old girl. In Chicago, two marijuana-smoking boys murdered a policeman. In Florida, police found a youth staggering about in a human slaughterhouse. With an ax he had killed his father, mother, two brothers, and a sister. He had no recollection of having committed this multiple crime. Ordinarily a sane, rather quiet young man, he had become crazed from smoking marijuana. In at least two dozen comparatively recent cases of murder or degenerate sex attacks, marijuana proved to be a contributing cause.

In Ohio a gang of seven addicts, all less than 20, were caught after a series of 38 holdups. The boys' story was typical of conditions in many cities. One of them said they had first learned about "reefers" in high school, buying the cigarettes at hamburger stands, and from peddlers who hung around the school. He told of "booth joints" where you could get a cigarette and a sandwich for a quarter, and of the shabby apartments of women who provided the cigarettes and rooms where boys and girls might smoke them.

His recollection of the crimes he had committed was hazy. "When you get to 'floating,' it's hard to keep track of things. If I had killed somebody on one of those jobs, I'd never have known it. Sometimes it was over before I realized that I'd even been out of my room."

It is the useless destruction of youth which is so heartbreaking to all of us who labor in the field of narcotic suppression. The drug acts as an almost overpowering

police bureaus, without authorization and exceeding
their statutory authority, began circularizing sympa-
thetic newspapers with reprints of such stories. As
anti-marijuana press campaigns spread, more & more
local legislation was enacted to protect the citizenry.
By the time that prohibition drew to a close, an awareness of the new drug menace had been generated
among the people, and the Treasury in 1930 responded
to this awareness by creating a special Bureau of Narcotics. Harry Anslinger was appointed as Commissioner. The reprinting of newspaper articles on the
dangers of marijuana increased in tempo almost
immediately. For whereas the public was sufficiently
aroused to the dangers of marijuana, the new Bureau
had been given jurisdiction only over recognized narcotics, the opiate drugs & cocaine. Marijuana had not yet
been elevated to this status.

    With a commendable sense of tidiness, the
Narcotics Bureau under Anslinger moved through the
thirties reprinting articles here, giving out insider
interviews there, all aimed toward the elevation of
marijuana into a narcotic. This seems to have been
motivated by the fact that there were not enough
people who were into cocaine or the opiates to give the
Bureau the kind of business it needed to expand its
influence & budget. It was the same sort of game which
Hoover played with the communist menace in the
forties & fifties, and with crime in the streets in the
sixties, to expand his FBI operation. But the tactics of
the Narcotics Bureau, while superficially crude, dis-
played a subtle understanding of the workings of the
federal system which is the hallmark of talented bureaucrats in search of power & security. Rather than expose
their backsides by lobbying directly in Congress for
anti-marijuana legislation — an approach which could be
interpreted as a power grab by their jealous competitors among the federal agencies — the Narcotics Bureau
simply stimulated the growth of a tangled web of local-
level anti-marijuana legislation, and then, about 1935,
began pointing out the need for unifying legislation on
the federal level. Within two years the Bureau was
home free; the Marijuana Tax Stamp Act of 1937, a
piece of unifying legislation if there ever was one, was
passed virtually unopposed by the Congress.

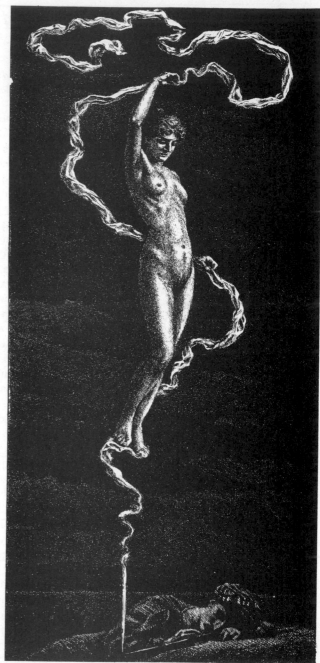

HASCHISCH

One of the most interesting areas of the marijuana controversy in the United States over the past forty years has been the interaction between officialdom & the scientific community. There has been an increasingly interdependent relationship between the two forces, due largely to the ever stronger controls which officials are able to exert over scientists through manipulation of public funding for research projects.

The central fact bearing on marijuana research in America has been that marijuana is illegal — something which citizens are not supposed to use, have access to or, in reality, know much about. Prohibition is a pretty cut & dried process, not requiring those who supported passage of the law or those who now enforce it to have reference to any body of scientific fact or opinion. It is not a unique circumstance that this particular law was conceived, passed & upheld through a joint exercise of moral judgment & deep ignorance. There are, in fact, a good many laws which serve this society that have sprung from similar origins.

To insure that there are not many citizens who might be able to find support for a bias in favor of personal use of marijuana, or for agitation for relaxation or abolition of legal sanctions, there seems to be an official desire that only information which supports their position be made available. Happily, there are still provisions in this country which encourage the free flow of information to a degree. Officials realize that in this arena they must compete for credibility. At this point scientists are needed; cooperative scientists.

There is an old saw, to which most of us have been exposed at one time or another, that through statistics you can prove anything you want. This premise holds in so far as the audience is ignorant of the valid use of statistics. An even more subtle modifier of truth, though, is that in science you can achieve any results you wish by paying careful attention to methodology, and while the public is gradually becoming aware that they must question statistics, and how to go about it, very few citizens know or care enough to question methodology.

For several generations of Americans the Government served as an unquestioned source of

Marijuana inflames the erotic impulses and leads to revolting sex crimes . . . one girl, known for her quietness and modesty, suddenly threw all caution to the wind. She began staying out late at nights. — the *Daily Mirror*, UK, 1929

Illustration: © R. Crumb

135

factual truth; not that there wasn't the traditional agreement that politicians are crooks, etc, but there was a wide spread conviction that the Government as an institution, and particularly those portions of the Government charged with perpetuating freedom and justice, would not out-and-out lie to the people. This trust was undoubtedly buttressed by an implicit faith that it is difficult to lie in public about something as factual as scientific evidence. For thirty years, then, as the government periodically pronounced marijuana an unmitigated evil, and as the only real dissent from this position seemed to come from alien spirits who had somehow infiltrated the periphery of solid middle-class American life, there was little motivation for the citizenry to question the facts. Surely, the Government has examined all available evidence before coming to its decision.

Within the past ten years, however, a growing number of citizens have been searching for facts on marijuana convinced, some by personal experience, that there must be more evidence on a several thousand year-old phenomenon than was being reflected in the propaganda of the Government. Serious students of the drug culture began digging through scientific journals & publications from other countries and, despite the apparent scarcity of such literature on the shelves of American libraries, began to find a great body of evidence which refuted the calculated hysteria of the enforcers.

The times they were a-changing, & the Government, while a bit slow, recognized that a new approach was needed. What was needed, it turns out, was 'more research,' one of the oldest ploys in the scientific & federal world for milking the public cow. We are presently in the middle of a spate of 'more research' on marijuana, some of which is ludicrous, some of which is sinister.

One of the favorite games scientists & officials play is 'replication.' This means doing something which has already been done over again to see if anything has changed. There are valid uses for replicative studies, but consider the following cases.

The National Institute of Mental Health has a wide variety of projects among which are several designed to isolate factors affecting potency in Cannabis. After several years of 'research' and several large annual grants, the Director of one of its major projects had the nerve to announce in 1970 with a straight face that, while 'potheads' have known for some time that wild grass was inferior to Acapulco Gold, his team had discovered that it wasn't climate or soil conditions which accounted for potency but that 'it's not where the plants are grown, but where their parents come from that counts'. After several years & lots of money this succinct observation might even stand as a scientific milestone, were it not for the fact that in 1942, in this country, it was positively established by the Carnegie Institute that marijuana strains showing polyploidy (inherited from Mom & Dad Cannabis) were more potent than their diploid brethren; were it not for the fact that in several places in the testimony before the Indian Hemp Commission in 1893 the selection of seeds for genetic properties affecting potency was fully discussed; and were it not for the fact that the inheritance factor was recognized in 300 BC by the compiler of a Sanskrit materia medica.

Such tomfoolery is not confined to the federal level. In one recent instance, the Governor of a midwestern state proudly announced a large grant to one of his state's universities so that its scientists could discover some ecologically sound, biological enemy of Cannabis which they would turn loose to roam the countryside, destroying the wild weed as it rambled. The amount mentioned for the grant was quite large; and many people will receive substantial paychecks over the lengthy period of the project. They will, no doubt, announce success sometime in the future, near the end of the grant period. The only real problem with this expenditure is that there already exists a body of scientific literature on precisely this subject, and five such biological agents are already identified. We do not, naturally, wish to say what these agents are, or where reference to them may be found; only to wonder at the marvelous ingenuity of those who dreamt up the project. At least we can be sure that midwestern weed will be safe until research funds for this project run

The danger in illegalizing marijuana . . . is that you make criminals out of the most intelligent, sensitive people in the country.— Allen Ginsberg. Photograph: Robert Altman

137

out & bureaucrats demand results.

So much for the ludicrous — I suppose that these fellows are simply following the time-honored injunction to watch out for old number one, and America has seen so much of this perverted sort of 'research' that we are all no doubt immune to the point where further absurdity fails even to bring a chuckle.

Far more serious is the major research effort aimed at proving that marijuana is harmful & dangerous. This effort is being pursued largely through NIMH, but is not limited to that august institution alone. We will not go into comparative evidence at this point, but rather discuss some of the methodology & premises on which much of this research is based.

There are several major areas of marijuana research presently under way in this country & abroad, under our direction & encouragement. These areas are:

(1) to determine the active intoxicating principals in marijuana;

(2) to determine its effects, physiological and psychological on humans;

(3) to determine the link between marijuana and other drugs.

The history of research into the intoxicating constituents of Cannabis goes back over a hundred years, and needs only the most cursory outline. A good case can be made that the first attempt at analysis of Cannabis constituents was by the ancient Chinese & Indian philosophers and religious healers. They isolated the source of Cannabis activity in the leaves & flowers, and went to great lengths to describe the organic relationship between man's mind and the drug in nonmolecular terms. With the advent of Western science, in particular chemistry, men began to realize that they could isolate & describe Cannabis' causal agents through their unique molecular structures. Early experiments by British, French & German scientists were aimed at finding the substances which carried the active ingredient. Those substances were variously described as red oils, honey, viscous fluids, resins, and so on. The tools for breaking these substances down into their molecular components were not applied until the early 1940's in the US, when a long series of articles ran in the Journal of the American Chemical Society, describing the work of teams of scientists here & overseas in isolating the active ingredients.

But where the early investigators had succeeded in isolating natural exudations of the plant which gave experimental results similar to those produced by the whole plant, this second string of experiments with their finer discriminations appeared to be getting further away from mimicking the effects of organic marijuana. This failure was ascribed to the fact that the active principle was very elusive. Further research was obviously needed. Working with instruments of ever greater precision scientists in several countries continued their search for the key to marijuana's many properties. From the early 1940's it has been known that Cannabis is loaded with a group of complex molecules, isomers of tetrahydrocannabinol, and research has concentrated on this group as the most likely location of the Cannabis genii. Very recently there have been claims that two isomers THC, particularly 1- $\triangle$ '-trans-THC, are the psychomimetically active constituents of Cannabis, and in 1965 two Israeli scientists reported success in synthesizing $\triangle$ '-THC.

These latter discoveries have evoked a great deal of enthusiasm among official scientists, particularly at NIMH. They believe that with further refinement of the process of synthesisation & identification of the active compounds that they will be able to meet one of the basic requirements of drug research — consistency in the dosage administered experimentally.

The truth, as ever, is not so simple. It may begin with an understanding of the nature of drugs, an understanding embracing both pharmacology (the NIMH approach) and some drug science yet unnamed in the West, a science concerned with whole relationships. For a brief clue as to the nature of this science, consider the herb doctor of primitive cultures. To arrive at an expected result (the desired effect) he may mix together many different items, some organic, some inert. He may employ parts of many plants, parts of animals, insects, a variety of earths, stones, metals, salts, acids, & a generous dose of faith-inspiring ritual. What he does *not* do is to build apparatus to isolate the

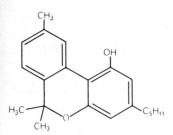

CANNABINOL

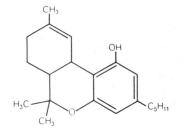

Δ¹-TRANS-TETRAHYDROCANNABINOL

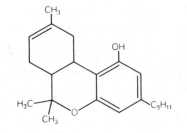

Δ⁶-TRANS-TETRAHYDROCANNABINOL

A few of the active constituents of Cannabis drugs. The delta-1 form (middle in top row) is believed to be the primary active component . . . *Scientific American*, December, 1969

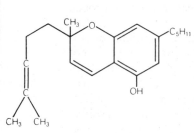

CANNABICHROMENE

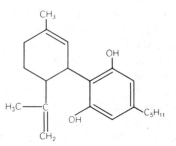

CANNABIDIOL

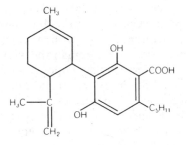

CANNABIDIOLIC ACID

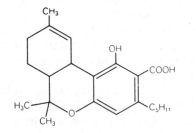

Δ¹-TRANS-TETRAHYDROCANNABINOLIC ACID

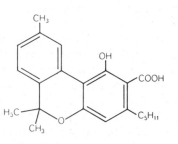

CANNABINOLIC ACID

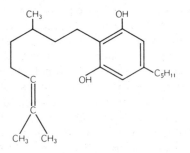

CANNABIGEROL

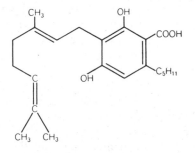

CANNABIGEROLIC ACID

139

one substance which will produce the one effect he
wants. Without going overboard in ascribing motivation to our witch-doctor, let's adopt an inferential position to try to understand the basis of his actions.

He knows, as does Western science, that when a
human organism ingests what can be broadly desig-
nated a natural drug, that the organism has set in
motion a chain of internal physiological & psychological events which will terminate in one or more
hopefully predictable results. The results are, however,
a product of the sum total of interactions. Each of the
multiple molecular compounds in the organic products
interact with each other, with the complexities of the
organic system of the human and with the psychological entities dependent upon that system, and all of
this is modified by external conditions such as setting,
by preconditions such as susceptibility, and by internal
conditions such as anticipation. No one would argue
that each of these interactions is equally relevant to the
process; there are key interactions, and by definition
key interactants, in any complex series of events. The
absurdity of the approach which attempts to isolate the
active principle in marijuana lies not so much in attributing a major role to one or more identifiable molecular entities, which is very likely true although no such
case has been adequately made. It lies in believing or
pretending that once you have isolated such substances
you can then produce experimental results with them
that will provide generalizations of the effects of the
intricate, complex whole plant and the state in which
it is normally used. A further step toward absurdity is,
of course, the pretension that a synthetic *approximation* of the major constituent, which doesn't even
possess the saving grace of perhaps having minute
amounts of some of the lesser natural products cling-
ing to its molecular walls, can be used to produce experimental results which will validly demonstrate
the evils of Cannabis in whole cloth.

Yet this is precisely the direction in which NIMH
and practically the whole scientific community in the
US has chosen to move with respect to Cannabis. It is
well to keep in mind that when the results of current
research are announced, whatever is said, whether pro

or con about Cannabis, will likely be concerned with
the results obtained from the administration of 1- △
trans-tetrahydrocannabinol, not from the *smoking of
a joint*.

One of the major flaws in current research, then,
is that the agent employed in many of the experiments
to determine effects of Cannabis is not Cannabis —
it is an unproved, synthetically derived approximation
of what is *thought* to be one of the active principles of
the plant. The next area where methodological questions arise is in the experimenter's approach to, and
choice of, subjects.

A classic problem of marijuana, not to say all
drugs, research is in deciding whether or not the subjects are to be human or other animals. If the lot falls
to humans, a swarm of irritating problems arises. Moral
& legal implications must be dealt with, the former requiring that the researcher search his soul as to the pro-
priety of introducing subjects, naive & experienced,
to a drug held in broad disrepute, and the latter necessi-
tating lengthy & often humiliating concessionary agree-
ments with the guardians of public & private virtue.
Serious researchers invariably report that, at some
phase in arranging for legal immunity for themselves &
their subjects, they are forcefully reminded that scientific investigation into some areas of truth requires
monitoring by the police.

If such conditions are acceptable to the investi-
gator, he is then faced with problems inherent in the
nature of human beings. Since marijuana activity is
pretty much idiosyncratic, he must pay careful attention
to the personality & personal histories of his subjects,
selecting for homogeneity. But then, of course, his
experimental results could hardly be generalized to the
infinite variety of human personalities & histories. If
the scientists can resolve this problem (usually by
entering a *cavaet emptor* somewhere in his report) he
must then consider the set of his subjects. These sets
vary too, and the careful approach to controlling this
variation is to use rigid selection procedures to determine attitudes toward marijuana, coupled with a rigor-
ously uniform setting in which marijuana is administered. The experimental results so obtained of course,

POLICE DEPARTMENT
ADMINISTRATION BUREAU

Is Marijuana an aphrodisiac? It depends on who you're with when you're high. — Richard Neville, *Playpower*. Photograph: Baron Wolman

would be generalizable only if all people who used dope were carefully selected & prepared, wired for sound, placed in a clinical setting for their experience, and questioned about how they felt periodically as their high progressed. If this hurdle is passed, the scientist faces another—he needs to have a control group as well as an experimental group, or else he will have no way of knowing which if any of the observable effects can be attributed to marijuana. The control group has to be administered something other than marijuana, but they have to think it's marijuana. The problem here is that, to date, no suitable placebo has been found, particularly since the control group must include experienced as well as naive subjects.

After resolving all of these problems (no one yet has, by the way) the experimenter must decide on the route of administration of marijuana. Many experimenters object to having the subject smoke marijuana because: (1) dosage will vary and (2) technique is a very important determinant of effects. But then, if you don't pass out joints, how do you administer the drug? Injection & ingestion are the only way; at least no one yet has suggested suppositories. But the problem arising here is that smoking is the common method of using marijuana; smoking undoubtedly alters the chemical conditions under which marijuana passes into the body; the effects produced by swallowing marijuana are often quite different from those produced by smoking; and the gastro-intestinal tracts & metabolic processes of individuals are as idiosyncratic as their respective heads.

In the face of all these problems, many experimenters have turned to animals other than humans to use as subjects. One longtime favorite has been the pussycat, though why the cat should be chosen as an example of base-line stability must remain a mystery to anyone who has seen a kitten leaping into the air at the approach of a ghost, or an otherwise staid old tabby suddenly freaking over a ratty wad of twine. Early experimenters favored cats because they were plentiful and their defenders were less vocal than those who supported the inalienable right of hounds to recline undisturbed by their master's chair in front of the fire.

Not that other animals were not tried & found wanting; O'Shaughnessy, an inveterate experimenter with Cannabis' effects on animals, dosed Noah's entire contingent two by two. In one of his little noted papers he made a point which, while well-taken, is so far overlooked in today's experiments as to throw the whole process of animal experimentation into doubt. His experiments 'tended to demonstrate that while carnivorous animals & fish, dogs, cats, swine, vultures, crows & adjutants invariably & speedily exhibited the intoxicating influence of (Cannabis), the graminivorous such as the horse, deer, monkey, goat, sheep & cow experienced but trivial effects from any dose we administered.'

Where, then, would this leave vegetarian humans?

Other experimenters have noted a similar lack of effect in our graminivorous cousins. Victor Robinson reported early in this century on some of his experimental results, thus:

I gave a rabbit a gram & a half of fluid extract of Cannabis. No sooner did I release the animal than it began to nibble a commonplace vegetable, indifferent to the circumstance that it had been baptised with the most precious opiate (*sic*) of the Orient. For four hours I watched this member of the genus Lepus, but no physical effects could be observed, while the mild expression in its gentle eyes induced me to conclude that all mental manifestations were lacking to such a degree that the bunny still worshipped the rather material trinity of crackers, carrots, & cabbages.

Undaunted scientist Robinson proceeded to replicate his experimental results:

Few creatures have so slight a hold on life as the pretty guinea pig—which does not come from Guinea and is not a pig. A blow of the hand, a bit of moisture, a breath of cold, and then squealing is done. But they do not mind Cannabis. I chose a fine fellow, anesthetized his glossy back with ethyl chloride, and then by means of a hypodermic syringe injected 100 minims of the powerful fluid extract into his circulation. There were no results. After the lapse of some hours the generous cavy so far forgot the incident as to pull some sweet pea pods from my hand.

In the appendices to the Indian Hemp Commission Report extensive experimentation with animals is reported. They resemble in every way current research with animals, with the possible exception that they appear to be more thorough. It is worthwhile to note, in both of these reports, that no particular attempt is made to argue from the data procured from animals to the results expected in humans.

This is certainly not the case in current studies. Evidently these 19th century scientists recognized that they were dealing with a drug whose effects could be attributed only partly to straight physiological activity and even that activity was relatively idiosyncratic. We only wish that science today had advanced to that same point of rationality. It should be clear that experimentation with animals provides no real clues to the effects of Cannabis on human beings short of demonstrating that it is nearly impossible to kill a living organism with Cannabis in any form, however strong. To seek more sophisticated levels of discrimination through experimentation with animals is absurd. Of course, if that part of the scientific community which is employed by the government wishes to violate the canons of rationality to produce evidence of the evil nature of Cannabis (applause, applause), nothing will stop them from doing so. Except perhaps the laughter of intelligent men who have no wish to relate their experience to that of a doped pussycat.

The last major research area which commands the attention of contemporary scientists & officials is the link between the use of marijuana and the admittedly more severe drugs. This concern is reflected in the statements of high public officials, high on ignorance and power, to the effect that 'We have got to get proof that it (marijuana) does create this (psychological) dependency'. (John Mitchell, AG, circa 1970).

Why do we got to get proof that marijuana moves people to severe drug problems? Because if it doesn't we would have to ask what does? Because if we can prove that it does, we can then stop the use of it? Because we can't be wrong after all these forty years, the experiences of millions of people over centuries notwithstanding? Because we want our populace dependent on other, more controllable things? Because psychological dependency is such a rare phenomenon that is is markedly deviant when it occurs? How do we, after all, make the fact that America in the 1970's is probably the most drug & power spaced society the world has ever known, comfortably consistent with our Boy Scout mottos?

Arguments which pander to the enforcer's doctrines are as absurd as arguments which take them seriously. Why should we debate whether or not marijuana is beneficial, benign or desirable? It serves no purpose to try to prove that Cannabis is not what its opponents imply and should therefore be legalized. The same hangups which prevent anyone from scientifically demonstrating beyond reasonable doubt that the weed is harmful prevent someone else from proving

143

Marijuana in
America
Drastic changes
would have to
be worked out

that it is not. It is the wondrous nature of Cannabis that it is what it is to each person — he alone determines the uses to which it is put, he alone improves or suffers as a consequence. And if it is true that Cannabis is out of place in contemporary American society, it is because of the collective failure of Americans to make a society where men can function as free & creative, healthy citizens.

This last argument is not intended to be the last word. If it can be proved by legitimate means to reasonable men that the use of Cannabis is dangerous, undoubtedly many such reasonable men would eschew use of the drug. Doubtless many people who are possessed of less than adequate rationality would need to be reached by less than rational means. But it is certain, if one has any faith at all in democratic processes & the inherent preference of people for good over evil, that if people were convinced through an appeal to their intelligence that Cannabis was an evil they would exercise their independent decision making powers accordingly.

That such proof will never be seems a foregone conclusion — too much has been done on Cannabis, too much experience lived & recorded on all sides of the issue for any government's scientists to arrive at valid conclusions through legitimate methods demonstrate inherent evil in the drug.

There remains only one avenue open to a courageous government & scientific community — to prove that Cannabis is dangerous in context. To do this the scientific community would have to examine, analyze & indict contemporary American society as a society whose private & collective morals, values, life-styles, institutions & aspirations were so unstable that Cannabis brought forth and perpetuated an intolerable threat. Surely no government which reached such conclusions would then seek to maintain what it had just condemned as weak & unstable, threatened so easily by a mild drug. Drastic changes would have to be worked out.

This, of course, will not happen in our society, because there is not honesty enough, nor hope. We are hanging on without creative effort; surviving until we die. The furor over marijuana is symptomatic, not definitive. We will not seek the flaw in our character, when we once long ago might have; we will seek instead to prove that it is the marijuana which corrupts. It is probably right & proper that we identify the use of drugs as a major threat to our existence, not because drugs themselves threaten, but because of what their use has become in the context of our society. But is it reasonable to assume that we will ever rid ourselves, or even reduce the overall use of drugs, so long as we are what we are. Our economy depends on drug use — wealthy people know that drug companies are the safest, most depression-proof stocks to buy; government & industry encourage incredibly varied usage of drugs & other sorts of chemical props; and each of us knows in his heart that some drug or other is an indispensable aspect of our role as an economic man. Our social interactions depend on drugs, on some form of chemical

'Our economy depends on drug use...'
An extract from a Love Comic of the 70's
©Lust Comix

145

manipulation before, during & after the important
moments of social intercourse in our lives. In all but the
most contemplative spiritual endeavors drugs play a
central role.

All societies turn to drugs very early in their existence, because all people, with few exceptions, enjoy
& need the effects of drugs upon their minds, emotions
& physical selves. The need for chemical high is particularly strong in people who have no access to the
emotional & intellectual euphorias of power, prestige,
achievement, enlightenment, all of the privileges which
are normally reserved by special classes of people. The
need is there, too, when there is stress & despair not to
be overcome, but faced as a constant fact of life.

In the ideal process of investigation mentioned
earlier, where scientists set out to discover in what ways
the context of America today made certain drugs
dangerous, they might inquire into the nature of the
drive to be high. They might then discover what seems
to be the real link between marijuana & the hard drugs —
a cost-analysis process which is subtle, quite conscious,
objective, & devastatingly accurate.

The major point in this cost-analysis process is that
marijuana is an expensive high. In cases of moderate
or occasional usage, or where usage is for reasons other
than primarily intoxication, the cost-benefits ratio of
marijuana is not intrusive. But where a person wants &
needs a high, and is trying to achieve that high through
expenditure of limited funds, marijuana is rapidly seen
as unsatisfactory because of its expense, its relative
inconvenience, the relatively great dangers posed by
possession and use, and, finally, the limited nature of
the obtainable high.

Soldiers, politicians & weapons-makers are
constantly at pains to portray themselves as costs-
benefits conscious (who hasn't heard of 'More bang
for a buck?'). The middle classes are constantly on the
lookout for 'deals' whereby they can get more of their
material desires fulfilled with a less-than-usual expenditure of their mortgaged future. Poor people apply the
same principles for sheer survival. Merchandizers hold
sales to appeal to precisely these aspects of the consumers' consciousness.

In all of these cases costs are recognized as more
than cash expenditures; taking into account all sorts of
expenditures which are inherent in acquiring a given
set of benefits: time, effort, cash & a host of intangibles.

This same process holds true for a person who is
shopping around for a high. Alcohol, tobacco (remember your first cigarette?) & marijuana are the most
accessible highs in our society, so quite naturally most
people start there.

Alcohol is pretty much of a dead-end. There are no
further variations on the theme, no other forms of that
particular drug genre to explore — except of course the
economic progression from hooch to 12-year-old
scotch, from Ripple to Chateau Lafite-Rothschild.
Costs-benefits analysis of alcohol is only tangentially
predicated on the intoxicating qualities, though given
a choice between 80 and 100 proof for the same price,
someone whose primary goal is not prestige or discrim-
inating taste will always choose the stronger.

Tobacco — same thing. Pretty much of a dead-end
drug series. People usually choose their favorite from
among the contenders in the field and stick with it.
Of course, when money is tight, you buy the cheapest
possible tobacco in cans and roll your own.

Marijuana is a different matter, largely because it
is a different genre of drug from the two above. It is
psycho-active, not a depressant yet permissive of
escape from pressure, not a hallucinogen yet allowing
the mind to deal with reality on different terms. For the
person who wants an occasional or even frequent high
but whose high terminates in a pretty much satisfactory
reality, the cost-benefits balance is in favor of marijuana. When it's over, it's over. There is no impairment
of the faculties. You can stay in touch with normalcy if
you wish, or take a short vacation. But for someone who
wants a high which is not over all that soon; who doesn't
mind trading impairment for a more profound high,
since being unimpaired carries no particular advantage for him; who has no interest in normalcy but
rather, would prefer to trade his normalcy for just
about anything else — the cost-benefits of marijuana
don't balance out.

Even in such cases, marijuana would probably

'It is interesting to note that while the drugs appear now to be frequently used for precisely the same purposes and in the same manner as was recommended centuries ago, many uses of these drugs by native doctors are in accord with their application in modern European therapeutics.'
— *Indian Hemp Drugs Commissions Report, Ch. X*

Photographs from the Mexico Border, 1970; Jack Scheaffer. 'Not all grass that passes into their hands is reported.'

147

The Amazing Spiderman What you've been waiting for! This one's got it ALL! *Marvel Comics,* published by © Magazine Management Co, Inc, May, 1971

Photograph:
Arthur Rosato

149

Marijuana in
America
There is a hooker
in the deal,
naturally

remain the preferred drug most of the time were it not for two factors in the analysis: the actual cost per unit of high and the risk per unit of high inherent in marijuana use. Were marijuana cheap enough & available in sufficient strength, even people with severe needs for long-term profound and extra-normal highs would usually find it preferable to opiates, barbituates, amphetamines & other common drug series. If marijuana use did not impose such risks as it docs in this country, then the risk factor would not be so great a part of the equation and the drug of preference would be marijuana.

But neither of these two conditions holds. After an initial set of experiences with marijuana, people who need a substantially greater high reach a point which they view in exactly the same way as economists view a process which has reached a point of diminishing returns. The search for alternatives with greater cost-benefits begins.

The point at which diminishing returns sets in is controlled by the combination of all factors in the cost-benefits equation. The more severe the laws, the lower the point and the sooner reached. The more successfully access to marijuana is prevented, the lower the point & the sooner reached. And the search for alternatives begins. All the principles of supply & demand in the drug market apply as they do in the consumer goods market. There are, in fact, a host of competitive products made available to people who have reached the point where brand loyalty has become too expensive & risky, products which offer (on the surface) more high for less cash and less risk.

At the risk of redundancy, let me point out again that the move from marijuana to something else is not the move of preference in most cases. Rather, it is the move of someone who has been shoved out of one market and into another by external conditions which directly prey upon & manipulate his internal state. And this push comes not from competitive products unless they are given the opportunity by dissatisfaction of the consumer with his drug of choice. Such dissatisfaction can rarely be induced by persuasion — if a person can get all the high he wants at very little cost & very little

risk, is it likely he will change to something else which offers no better?

There is a hooker in the deal, naturally. Once the consumer has switched from marijuana to another drug in order to satisfy his needs, he becomes, in most cases, addicted. Physiological addiction is the advertising man's ideal of brand loyalty. And not only will the customer not stop buying your product, he will be highly suggestible. He will buy increasing quantities. He will sample your other lines. He will prefer your product to other products which don't even compete — food, material goods, entertainment.

There are drug series, of course, which do not fit this analysis, and when a person who uses marijuana also uses, say, mescaline or acid it is probably not so much because cost-analysis has moved him there — he still smokes dope too — rather it is more like a person who prefers good wine, but also likes imported beer, English gin & well-aged scotch whiskey.

So when scientists & officials begin to talk of increasing research budgets to discover the link

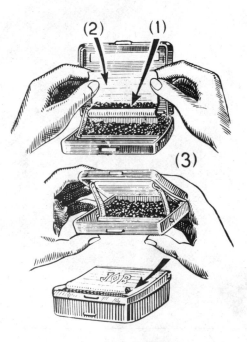

between marijuana & heroin, seconal & methedrine, they are either abysmally ignorant or viciously cynical. They, themselves, are the link. They control through conspiracy, sprung from diverse personal & public motives, the primary factor in the cost-benefits analysis of the person who needs a deep, constant & blinding high to absent himself from his own circle of hell. It's not a matter of arguing whether or not the addict chose to use drugs — of course he did, he had to, in response to his need. But rarely does a man choose his needs on that level. Such needs are created for him by the milieu in which he is born & in which he lives.

To look elsewhere for the link between marijuana and other drugs would be folly.

Each day the news media bring to us new accounts of this study or that which has something to say about marijuana. Most of these studies are not considered newsworthy enough for reprinting in substantial detail; they are usually characterized by the spokesman for the institution, by the researcher himself, or by the government, with a brief summary of the findings &

offhand recitation of supporting prior studies. Almost all such research is riddled with methodological errors— and this should not be taken as perfectionistic, finicky quarrel with basic solid research. Either the truth is respected sufficiently to be sought through legitimate methods, or there is not respect for truth. Scientific truths, after all, are only in jest reported as being validated by the Lord; in serious moments it is admitted that any truth is only as valid as the logical foundations upon which it rests and the bricks and mortar of these foundations are assumptions & methods. It seems more important to acquire the tools to banish dragons than to roam around analyzing their droppings, and that former approach, for better or worse, is what has been attempted in this book.

Choice of needs?

Marijuana is an illegal plant and the trouble with nature is . . . The Furry Freak Brothers, by Gilbert Sheldon

'But rarely does a man choose his needs'
Illustration:
Alan Aldridge,
OZ Magazine,
October, 1968

Acapulco Gold!

We thought through a lot of alternative ways of dealing with all this information on the natural aspects of grass & its cultivation. If parts of this section sound like heavy biological rap, it's because science is a life trip as well as a machine trip, and can be full of understanding.

Growing grass is easy enough. You can just plant seeds and let them grow or not, on their own. But grass is a plant in very delicate balance with its environment, for all its apparent strength. As with people, whether or not a plant merely survives is not a real issue. Harmony & balance should be created between the vital forces in the plant and the beneficial aspects of the environment, if its life is to have high quality.

We'll talk about two things in the course of this long chapter — how to grow grass, and why grass grows. In the interests of keeping the verbiage down, we'll stress the mechanics when an understanding of the process involved is valuable. Because of this approach, we may not always cover every aspect of your possible unique situation as a cultivator. In cases where problems arise that you aren't able to handle by applying the information in the book, we've tagged an extensive bibliography onto the end. While some of this stuff may seem pretty esoteric and hard to find, most of the articles & books should be available through a large university library, particularly one of the land-grant schools. If this approach doesn't help you either, write to us and we'll try to help.

Since we won't be dealing with the pharmacy or psychology of Cannabis and its use, and since we won't be going into any sort of supposed inside look at the drug scene, we'll use this introduction to give a brief description of the drugs derived from Cannabis, and to talk briefly about a few of the more destructive myths which continue to circulate about grass.

According to tradition, hemp (Cannabis Sativa) was cultivated in China as long ago as 2800 BC.

Illustration: from the works of Dioscorides, 1st century AD.

154

Although the Chinese grow hemp *(ma)* mainly for the sake of the fiber, they utilize all parts of the plant for medicine. The flowers *(ma-p'o)* are used in treating open wounds; the seed coat *(ma-len)* and its adhering resin is used to stimulate the nervous system; the seeds themselves *(ma-jen)* are used to counteract inflammations & skin irritation, are considered tonic (mentally or morally invigorating — Webster's 2nd definition), a restorative of good health, laxative & diuretic, and excellent for worming babies & animals. The oil *(ma-yu)* is used as a hair tonic and to counteract sulphur poisoning; the fresh juice of the leaves is used for treating scorpion bites and the ash obtained after burning the plant is used in sky rockets.

The resin which is associated with the intoxicating qualities of the plant is brown and shows no crystalline structure, and burns with a bright flame, leaving no ash. If the water is slowly distilled out, the resin yields an amber-colored volatile oil which has a warm aromatic taste and smells like hemp.

The drug derived from Cannabis was used in Europe to treat mania, hysteria, delirium tremens, hydrophobia, tetanus, & cholera. (There must have been some very happy but very dead folks in Europe over the several hundred years when these remedies were popular). The drug has a powerful & peculiar odor, is practically tasteless, and is sold in a variety of forms known respectively as ganja *(Kan-cha)*, ganjah *(K'ou-Kan)* or guaza *(K'ou-ch'a);* as charas, churrus, kirs, or momeea; as bhang *(yon-tu-ma)*, siddhi *(yeh-ma-yen-ts'ao);* and as hashish *(ta-ma)*.

Ganja consists of the young flowering tops & shoots of the female plant which, along with the resin, are pressed or rolled into a sticky mass which is dark green to green-brown in color, has an agreeable aroma, & a characteristic taste. It is prepared from cultivated plants in the central provinces of India; the cultivation, manufacture, & sale being regulated by law. Ganja is commonly sold in the form of flat or round cakes and is smoked like opium, usually after being mixed with tobacco. Ganja yields a dark green powder which fizzes in dilute hydrochloric acid, and a tincture of ganja in alcohol is bright green. The loose resinous

Sino-Japanese ideogram for Medicine:-- ⾋ means 'grass', and the body of the character means 'pleasure'.

Stylised Japanese: 'Hemp'

Script: When all things are hushed, suddenly a bird's song arouses a deep sense of stillness. When all the flowers are departed, suddenly a single flower is seen, and we feel the infinity of life.

155

particles which fall out when ganja is being pressed into cakes are known as chur.

Charas, produced principally in Kashmir & Afghanistan, consists of the resinous excretion of the leaves, flowering tops, twigs, & fruits of cultivated plants. It is obtained by rubbing the top of the ripe plant between the hands and then scraping off the adhering resin & dust. It is also collected by men, either naked or clad in leather, who run through the fields on hot afternoons, the resin thus adhering to their sweating bodies or leather aprons, from which it is scraped by collectors at row's end, prior to the dash back among the plants — a mad relay race at high noon through the glare of the snowfields up in the Hindu Kush.

The resinous mass of charas is pounded & kneaded until a gray-white powder is formed, which is then made into cakes for sale in the markets. The highest quality charas comes in thin sheets, which should be almost transparent, and which, because they look so much like mica, have no doubt crossed many borders in the company of earnest-looking rock collector types. Charas more commonly comes in dark brown resinous lumps which when examined under magnification show a crystalline structure. Charas is stronger and thus more expensive than ganja, but is often adulterated, particularly with linseed oil.

Bhang is made of the older, more mature leaves of *wild* plants in Madras, the Punjab, & the Northwest provinces of India. It is weaker than & inferior to ganja & charas, and is used in most of India to make sweets called majum. Its most common use, however, is in the preparation of a green intoxicating beverage known locally as hashish. Hashish is created by crushing & boiling the mixture down considerably until it is of a syrupy consistency. It is then strained through a cloth much like cheese cloth, with the vegetable-butter mixture pressed into cakes, and the liquor being drunk.

Myths — Fact and Fiction

Let's talk briefly about some of the myths about grass, and the reality which confronts them.

Acapulco Gold, Panama Red & other strains of grass are reputed to be particularly potent because of a fortuitous combination of climate & soils. Actually, soil has nothing to do with potency, except that it contributes to the plant's health, and certain mineral deficiencies do cut down on resin potency (see page 171). Climate has a similar relationship with potency. It is the genetic properties of grass which determine potency, and these genetic properties vary from strain to strain, but can be easily manipulated by cultivators.

Another myth holds that male plants are useless for drugs. This just ain't so, and we go into the explanation on page 160.

Myth number three says that high potency grass can only be grown in certain places in the world, when the truth is that it can be grown anywhere indoors, and in most places outdoors.

There are a couple of downright destructive myths in circulation about some aspects of growing grass. One of these is that the more nitrogen you throw in, the better; but the fact is that an overdose of nitrogen in early life will kill the plants, and too much nitrogen at maturity cuts potency way down by limiting resin secretion. Another myth is that infra-red light is beneficial to Cannabis, when in reality it starves the plants of energy, causing them to stretch out in an agony toward the light source. Another myth is that soil in which grass is to be grown should be very alkaline. This will kill most plants and weaken the rest, and we go into soils extensively later on. Another is that Cannabis doesn't need much water, the less the better; while in truth Cannabis needs a great deal of water — it's just that it can't stand over-wet soil. Then there is a bit about needing high temperatures and some say even high humidity, which has led a lot of people to build sweat-boxes in their closets & bathrooms. Grass doesn't really need temperatures over 75° F, and as for high humidity, it can cause an accumulation of plant poisons which kill it in short order.

Rather than rambling, we'll deal with most of

In truth,
Cannabis needs a
great deal of
water . . .
Photograph by
Barry Bratten

these myths & others in the relevant parts of this chapter and go into detail on the whys & wherefores. But isn't it a shame that so many such myths have been in circulation for so long? Makes one wonder how come. We've been careful in checking out the information in this book from all possible angles, and we know that most of the errors in the original sources have been uncovered & eliminated, but some may remain.

Overview of the Plant

Cannabis Sativa is a hearty weed which grows well under extreme environmental conditions. It is probably a native of Central Asia, and has been the object of intense interest for several thousand years of human history. It is a multi-purpose, high-order plant which yields a versatile & useful fiber from the stem; a subtle, aromatic & nourishing oil from the fruit, and a valuable & exciting resin from the leaves.

One of the principal reasons that Cannabis occupies a distinctive niche in the plant kingdom is because of its unusual & almost unique sexual character. Cannabis is dioecious; that is, the male & female organs are normally manifested on separate plants. Each sex exhibits a host of specific behavioral & vegetative variations through a wide range of environmental conditions. The normal sex ratio is about 1:1, give or take a few points either way, but under abnormal conditions, the ratio can go as high as 9.5:1 female. Then again, when the environment becomes really threatening, Cannabis is capable of switching to a predomin-

The female
and the male

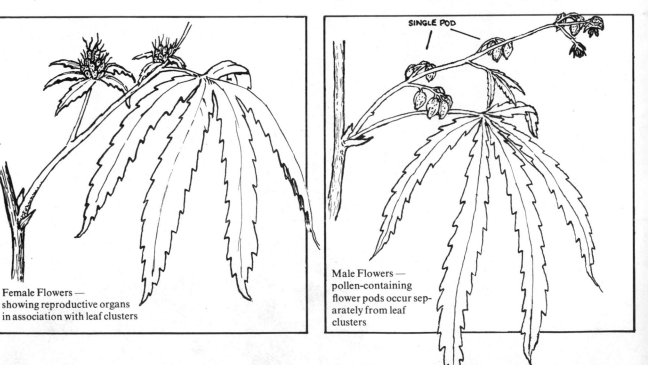

SINGLE POD

Female Flowers —
showing reproductive organs
in association with leaf clusters

Male Flowers —
pollen-containing
flower pods occur sep-
arately from leaf
clusters

antly bisexual or hermaphroditic state. Changes such as these may be thought of as the plant's ability to manifest a survival drive under conditions which cut off the possibility of normal reproductive activity. It may be helpful to retain this image when you consider manipulating the sexual state of your plants, because you will be intervening in some potent life forces and such activity should be undertaken only with sympathy & understanding. The mechanics of manipulating sex are deceptively simple, and we'll run them down for you in detail further on.

To begin with, many folks have a lot of awfully vague ideas about the difference in appearance between male & female Cannabis. While appearance, particularly before the sex organs are formed, is not a conclusive indication of gender, it can be very helpful in making first estimates of the sexual composition of your crop.

After about the third week of normal growth, some plants will be taller than others. These taller plants will also be more skinny, have fewer leaves, and the branches bearing the leaves will be spaced out along the stem more than in short plants. They will be a bit more pale, and by about the sixth week a little tuft of leaves will have developed at the top, giving the appearance of a shoddy crewcut. These plants have dominant male tendencies.

Females, on the other hand, will tend to be squat, rounded in profile (the middle eastern ideal), darker green, more leafy. Their branches will be spaced closer together on the stem, and the stem will be getting thick when she is about in middle life.

Both male & female plants will have certain features which are characteristic of Cannabis. The leaves have serrated edges, and are shaped like tapered spearheads. There are from five to eleven leaves to a bunch, and the most common clusters contain either seven or nine leaves. The leaves are dark green on top, light green-yellow on the bottom, and have fine downy hairs along the lower surface.

The stem of Cannabis is fluted & hexagonal, with a large, normally hollow central pitch cavity. Internodes — places where branches diverge from the stem — occur every five to ten inches along the stem in a normal plant. The mature stem is very tough, particularly near the base where it becomes solidified. Stems can reach a height of 25 feet under certain conditions, and become several inches thick.

The root system consists of a main tap root, normally eleven to fourteen inches long, with a layer of very fine lateral roots which spread out through the subsurface soil a distance of five to seven inches. These lateral roots occur even more markedly in rich organic soils.

Where adequate elbow room is given the growing plants, they may become extremely bushy, with complex branching and lush foliage; but where they are crowded together, the plants may have only a little top knot of leaves. Crowded conditions favor development of males — other things being equal — and adequate space favors development of females.

It will be important to remember, whenever you are dealing with sex-related phenomena in Cannabis, that each plant bears within itself the capability to be either a male or female, whatever its apparent identity at the moment. Cannabis hangs onto its sexual role very strongly under some circumstances, and readily abandons gender under others. Too much messing around can ruin a crop as surely as hostile forces in the environment; and as long as you're going to grow grass, you might as well do so with an appreciation of what's involved.

At any rate, let's go on and deal with some of the sexual distinctions which this fascinating plant exhibits.

159

The Male Cannabis

The slender male plants, while less potent and thus a bit less desirable than the female, have many features which should be of great interest.

The male flowers develop in small, drooping pouches like scrota which are attached near the forks of branches & down near the stem of the plant. These flowers are very rarely associated with the leaf clusters; but when they are, they occur in bunches of three, as contrasted with their normal single state. The male flowers have no petals as such, though the sepals enclosing the pod are often taken for petals. There are five of these enclosing lobes, and they are usually greenish-yellow, occasionally with a red tinge. After the flower opens, five little stamens pop apart and dangle what are called anthers from gossamer threads. It is the anthers which are responsible for dispensing pollen when fertilization time draws nigh, so it's pretty easy to gauge the divine moment by noting whether or not the anthers are swollen & eager-looking. You will be able to tell when the anthers become fully extended. Their surfaces will begin to show little white pollen grains about twelve hours before pollen dispersal. Another sign is that the tiny hairs on the undersides of the leaves will become swollen about their bases due to an accumulation of calcium oxalate crystals.

The males produce less chlorophyll than the females, thus they are able to thrive on less intense light. In line with the survival drive of Cannabis, we will see later that one of the effects of cutting down on the energy levels or photoperiods of your plants will be an increase in the number of male plants.

Males also produce a lower level of auxins in the tissue fluids. Auxins are generally thought to be plant growth stimulators vital to vigor & leafiness. Associated with the male's tissue fluids, one finds a slightly acid ph factor (acidity-alkalinity). This distinction also contributes to the plant's overall survival capability, and the tissue fluids of the plant can adapt to the acidity. Female Cannabis is, by contrast, slightly alkaline in the tissue fluids.

Many writers have picked up on a piece of mis-
information which holds male plants to be useless for drug purposes. It is substantially true that males have a much lower potency than females, but that is not the reason that they are pulled up & destroyed by professional growers. They are pulled primarily because if the male is allowed to go to maturity & pollenate the female, she will lose considerable potency because much of her energy will then be turned to nourishing the fertilized seed. What might be gained, then, in terms of overall bulk at harvest time by keeping the male plants will be lost in per-unit potency of female plants. So it becomes a trade-off situation where you have the option of lots of leaves (both male & female plants harvested) with lowered potency per unit of yield, or less yield (destroy the males and keep only females) with a higher per-unit potency. It is up to the individual cultivator to make the decision.

Male plants follow a uniform pattern in blooming and it is a truly symphonic process. The first flower will pop open before sunrise, and this will be located about two-thirds of the way up the plant, nestled against the stem. As the sun rises, blooming begins to radiate from this initial flower outward, progressing at a controlled rate in all directions until the flowers nearest the periphery and on the top-most tuft are reached. Between the seventh & the twelfth hour, the final flower will appear and the process will stop, with all blooms open and in readiness. At the first breeze, a blue-white cloud of pollen will be released, to drift downwind across the field where the females wait with their pistles poking through the tip of their pods to snag the life-giving dust. It is an act of creative energy, and drains the male of life from that moment on.

Soon after pollen release, the male plants begin to lose their green color & waxy texture. They show signs of death near the base at first, but soon their sheen will decay completely, to be replaced with a green-white tinge over the whole plant. The leaves on the lower portions will shrivel, the plant will give off a dry rustle and release its last puffs of pollen if shaken by the wind or a passing creature.

And the life cycle of the male will be complete in the twelfth week of its existence.

The male (left) and the female (right)

161

The Female Cannabis

Females outlive the males by three to five weeks, and this in part reflects their greater health & vigor during life, and in part is tied to their life cycle, which is more complicated than that of the male.

The female flower is not as obviously complex as the male, but it goes through a greater variety of changes and is the nexus of the reproductive drive in Cannabis. Female flowers look even less like conventional blossoms than do the males. The flower is structurally very simple, consisting of a downy pistle surrounded by specialized leaves with overlapping edges which form a little pod or cup, open and pointed at the top where the tip of the pistle, and its two stylar branches, poke out to snag the life dust. This pistle is the ovary of the female Cannabis, and it looks like an oval, slightly flattened termite egg when you peel back a few of the protective leaves and take a peek.

The pod containing the pistle does not open at blossom time, and thus it is pretty hard to follow the development processes of your plants without exposing them to trauma. These flowers lie in close association with the leaf clusters and never occur by themselves. Although the female flowers spring up in pairs originally, one of the pair will normally abort at fertilization, which is another example of the marvellous backup systems which nature devises to assist in fulfilling the life drive. The surviving flowers are packed more or less tightly together, and these leaf/flower clusters often reach an impressive size, particularly near the tops of mature females.

Female plants produce large amounts of chlorophyll and seem to be more consistent producers of the plant auxins so necessary to vitality and leafiness in most plants. The tissue fluids of females can be either neutral or slightly alkaline, and this in part accounts for the difference in drug potency which is commonly believed to be characteristic of Cannabis males and females. It has been well established, however, that drug potency in Cannabis is only partly sex-determined, so the attribution of different levels of drug potency to sex differences alone is clearly wrong. Other things

being equal, it does appear, however that the unmodified female plant is more effectively utilized for marijuana. Other things are rarely, if ever, equal and it appears that even plants with modified sexual characteristics are associated with their original sexual identity. The implications of this fact will become clear in our discussions of sex modification on pages 190 & 204; but for the moment, it is sufficient to say that if a plant starts out to be a male, even if it is later switched to a female, it will never attain the leafiness and vigor of a true female. The reverse holds as well, naturally.

Largely because of their greater leaf mass, but also because of their more vigorous water uptake, female plants will outweigh male plants 2:1 at maturity. They will generally have more leaves per cluster, and more clusters of leaves than male. Because of these heavier vegetative characteristics, the female will have greater energy requirements than the male, and will exert a greater draw upon soil nutrients.

All the time the males are reaching maturity and preparing to release pollen, the females are coming into their fertile period and the flowers are undergoing developmental changes which will prepare them for sustaining the reproductive act. The pods are spreading apart slightly so that the pistle with its stylar branches can protrude. The leaf clusters show a marked drooping, so as not to interfere with the circulation of pollen-bearing breezes. Water intake, which has peaked & is declining slightly, increases once again. Sunlight or light energy becomes critical. Temperature variation can have negative effects on the exposed sex organs. Nutrient requirements undergo some alteration, with calcium & potassium salts constituting the equivalent of ice cream & pickles. The female plant is preparing for her role. After this point is reached —somewhere in the tenth to the twelfth week under normal conditions—there is no going back. Attempts to modify sex after this point are against the natural grain, and will fail, or else will result in offspring so warped that the results are the equivalent of failure.

Following the act of pollenation, as previously noted, one of each pair of female flowers will abort.

The surviving member is then free to draw upon the sustaining fluids of the plant for energy, and the seed begins to develop.

If good seed is desired from the female, she should be left alone for at least two weeks after blossoming, or else the seed will be immature. Even if it manages to germinate, it will produce feeble plants. Leaving the female in the ground past flowering, however, tends to decrease the drug potency of the plant, as much of its energy turns to producing viable seed. The decision as to when to harvest, therefore, becomes a crucial one. For maximum potency, the female plant should be harvested before the stalk begins to pale and lose its waxy texture; for maximum seed viability, it should be left until the leaves have dropped off and the seeds rattle in their pods. Somewhere in between — in completely normal circumstances about ten days after female florescence — seems to be a happy compromise. Of course, the seed requirements of individual cultivators will vary, and many of the possibilities which will be suggested for modifying the growing plant may have already ruined the next generation, so many factors need to be considered.

Sex Abnormalities

The marvelous survival drives & mechanisms of Cannabis manifest themselves in sex anomalies under conditions hostile to normal growth & development, conditions which threaten life, limb, & offspring.

If such sex anomalies occur on your plants, even though in all other respects they appear normal and even healthy, you can be sure that they are being threatened by some oversight on your part which has led to environmental chaos which is being reflected in the sexual state of the plant.

A. Maleness in the under-developed pod of the female
B. Normal female flower, (cut-away pod)
C. Predominantly female flower, with male projection
D. Female showing maleness by developing stamens
E. Male flower with female stigmas

163

Soil, Water, Nutrition and Environment

A great deal of the misinformation floating around about the soil & water requirements of grass is the direct result of people not bothering to research carefully what they are in a rush to put on the market to exploit a general interest in the subject of marijuana. This is especially unfortunate because a lot of carefully compiled information is available, particularly in the agricultural journals of the first few decades of this century. We'll try to synthesize the best of this information here, and count on the bibliography to point the way for folks who want to do more extensive research on their own.

General Soil Principles

The soil which is to be used should be of as uniform quality as possible. The importance of this fact becomes apparent when you begin to modify certain characteristics of your crop, particularly with indoor growing, and are counting on a consistent sort of outcome. Non-uniform soil quality can jeopardize even the most sophisticated experimental efforts. For indoor work, this means that all soils used should be thoroughly mixed, and for outdoor planting it means you should stick to areas where the soil has been deposited in uniform depth from the same general source.

Uniformity of the soil also is desirable if you contemplate reusing it. Cannabis soaks up a great deal of the nutrients in any soil, and when you re-fertilize you want to be certain that you aren't going to burn some of your plants and starve others because the nutrient level wasn't even to begin with. We have calculated that Cannabis absorbs the equivalent of 1500 kilos of fertilizer for every 100 kilos of fiber obtained from the mature plant. Since fiber yield is about 6.5% of the weight of the mature plant, this means that Cannabis absorbs around one kilo of nutrient per kilo of vegetable mass. This gives an idea of the importance of adequate nutrition.

In a mature plant, the proportions of plant products break down in the following way:

Loss in drying	+/-30%
Leaves, roots & tops	+/-25%
Extraneous stem material	+/-15%
Sticks	+/-15%
Seed & Miscellaneous	+/-10%
Fiber	+/- 5%

This means that one can count on leaves & flowers to constitute from ten to twenty percent of the harvested weight of a crop.

Types of Outdoor Soil

Outdoor soils suited to growing good quality grass should be a rich loam, interlaced with fine sand and low in clay content. Soils having their origin in sedimentary rock are generally considered to be the best bet for stability & nutrition.

This does not mean that folks living in areas where the soil is sandy or poor in nutrients need to get upset because with proper thought & preparation, Cannabis will thrive in most soils. The truly limiting factor is the compaction of the soil, related to clay content. Such soils will resist generation of the fine lateral root system by which Cannabis picks up nutrients, and are generally poor in available organic nutrients. Most disastrously, they promote pooling of water around the roots of the plants, something which Cannabis cannot tolerate.

A simple test will give you an idea of how much clay is present. The soil should be rich & easily crumbled —a few handfuls selected at random from the field should give the cultivator a pretty good idea as to compactness. The soil should ball together when squeezed in the hands, but crumble easily into fine particles. Soil which compacts too easily and which will not crumble under light pressure (applied by pressing lightly on the ball of soil) is too wet, has too much clay, or has other problems rendering successful cultivation unlikely.

The rich topsoil described above must be suffi-

THE PRINCE OF ILLUSION

A good supply
of humus . . .
Photographs:
Peter D'Agostino

ciently loose in texture to permit root system development at least two feet down. A good supply of humus
(decayed organic matter) is a big help because it not
only provides nutrients, but also helps retain & spread
out moisture. Cannabis requires substantial amounts of
water compared to other crops but, as just mentioned,
will not tolerate standing water about its root system.
For outdoor soils, the water table should be at least
three and not over six feet below the surface.

If you are forced to plant your crop in poor soil
due to lack of alternatives, you can help your plants
toward health & happiness by working an organic fertilizer into the soil at least a week before you plant. We'll
deal with specifics of fertilizers shortly.

Another alternative is to look for a field where a
crop of clover, beans, or some other nitrogen-fixing
plant is growing; and, if such an area is available, turn
under a plot of such vegetation several months before
planting your Cannabis.

The Outdoor Environment

Certain areas are to be avoided unless there is
absolutely no alternative. Soils which contain any concentration of salt should be bypassed. If Cannabis is
planted in such areas it will grow (if at all) very short,
high on cellulose, very poor on leaves, with low starch
& sugar content, and give an extremely poor grade of
resin.

Soils which are downwind or downstream from
tobacco or tomato fields should be avoided, also, as
these plants harbor molds & parasites which are very
destructive to Cannabis.

Equally bad are areas with poor drainage, or areas
which are likely to be swamped for even short periods.
Care should be taken to locate an area which receives
at least eight hours of sunlight a day, and which is not
exposed to high humidity situations (like fog) in association with temperatures below 50° F.

The soil should be loose enough to support the
penetration of growing roots, yet not so loose at to
provide an unstable base for the plants in a strong wind.
You should check the kind of plant growth that occurs
naturally in the area. There is no real need to worry
about ground-level weeds, because Cannabis will over-
shadow them quickly. The thing to look for is their
general health. If they appear poorly nourished, and if
it looks as though this is due to a leached soil, then you
will probably want to look around for a better area. A
lot of animal trails through the area could mean that the
seedlings will be placed in unnecessary jeopardy. You
will also want to check on the depth of the topsoil. If
the weeds don't seem to be able to penetrate more than
a few inches down, the soil is not going to support your
plants very well.

166

Planting Outdoors

The best crop will be carefully planted, using a seed drill. If you don't plan to return to weed and thin the growing crop, then you should use only one seed per hole. If you plan to return in a week or two, you can buy a little insurance if your seed is untested, by using two or three seeds every other hole. The best bet, obviously, is to test the germinating powers of the seed before going into the field. (See chapter on seeds)

Just about any method of sowing that results in the seed being covered by a half inch or more of decent soil will produce some plants. Of course, the more prepared the cultivator, and the more methodical, the better will be the yield of his labors.

Assuming a somewhat systematic approach is your bag, the first thing you'll want to do, after finding the appropriate location for your plot, is to determine whether or not any sort of nutrition supplement is going to be needed. If you are using land which also supports other kinds of crops, you may be in luck. Hemp is best grown in rotation with non-exhaustive crops such as wheat or with crops which yield a high return to the soil such as beans or peas — one pound of dry beanstalks contains as much available nitrogen as five pounds of manure. Assuming that your land is not seriously depleted, the following approach works well in most cases.

In the early fall of the year, manure should be worked into the selected plot with a hoe, and beans or another legumenous crop should be planted. After two to two and a half months, the beanstalks should be turned under, and the surface compacted somewhat. Just tramping around in heavy boots is adequate. The plot may then be left for the winter. In the early spring the plot should be weeded, dressed with a potent organic fertilizer such as manure or chicken crap, and will then be ready for planting Cannabis when the weather turns.

Indoor Soils

Indoor growers can profit from a greater ability to regulate soil quality, consequently there is no nutritive reason why superior quality Cannabis cannot be grown indoors.

The indoor cultivator has two choices — he can locate, dig & transport high quality loam or he can buy commercial nursery soils. The latter, if certain minimum standards are met, are inexpensive & work well.

Commercial soil for the cultivation of Cannabis should:

(1) be neutral to slightly alkaline;

(2) have substantial humus content — about 15 percent will do nicely (if desired, one can buy soil with low organic content and supplement both humus and nutrient content of this basic soil with a variety of the organic fertilizers to be reviewed later in this chapter);

(3) contain at least 15 percent fine sand; and

(4) be sterilized using heat rather than chemically sterilized.

One of the most pervasive myths about Cannabis is that harsh soils promote resin production, and rich soils inhibit resin production. The underlying rationale for this myth seems to be that the plant tries to protect itself from a harsh environment by throwing out resin. In reality, soil quality has little or nothing to do with resin production. Factors which do regulate resin production are discussed throughout this chapter. What poor soil *will* do is cut down on the health & vitality of the growing plant and result in skimpy plants at maturity.

Indoor soils should hold moisture but not allow pooling of water. To test for this quality, poke a small hole a few inches deep in freshly watered soil. If, after a few minutes, standing water appears at the bottom of the hole, the soil is probably too compact (if you haven't gone too heavy on the water). A pint per cubic foot shouldn't produce pooling in the hole. The same crumbly quality is required of indoor soils as outdoor soils and the same test will do.

Assuming that most indoor growers will be putting the soil in some sort of container, let's review a few general principles of soil depth, compaction & drainage which hold here as they do for outdoor soils.

Soil depth should be at least 12", the more the better after this. Each plant should have at least 15" distance between it and either the sides of the container or another plant's root system. There should be some provision for adequate drainage, otherwise the soil will (1) become highly saline and (2) become water logged. Either condition is fatal to Cannabis.

Indoor soils will salt up rapidly when chemical potash & nitrogen fertilizers are being used, but will eventually increase in acidity no matter what fertilizers are used, or even if none are added at all. For this reason, it is best to change soil each time new plants are to be grown. When this is not possible, the soil should be thoroughly spaded after the top several inches are scraped off and thrown away. This is extremely important — it gets rid of most of the harmful salts which may have been formed or deposited.

In areas where high mineral content water is used for irrigating the plants, this operation is essential. The soil should be allowed to dry thoroughly, and irradiation with ultra-violet can help destroy any micro-organisms which exist. (New bacteria will, of course, be reintroduced by successive fertilizing). This dried soil should now be thoroughly mixed & subjected to the same tests as the original soil for compactness, moisture retention, and crumbly quality. It may be necessary to add humus once again.

When fertilizers are to be added to an indoor soil, they should be added to the entire lot of soil at the same time and should be thoroughly mixed in. The mixture should then be allowed to stand for a least a week before it is used. This is true of both chemical & organic fertilizers because you have no way of knowing how much of what kind of nutrient is involved, thus you take serious chances on burning plants by not waiting for organic decay to proceed for a week. Organic fertilizers should be added to the soil only before planting — they should never be added to the soil, even in small amounts, once the plants are growing. Chemical fertilizers, such as soluble nitrogen can, on the other hand, be added in small amounts during the growth cycle without harmful side effects.

One of the most beneficial agents an indoor grower can use is the common worm. Indoor soils compact severely with repeated watering. Introducing a few earthworms into the prepared soil will aid immeasurably in root development and nutrition uptake of the plants, increasing the vegetation appreciably. Worms are also a good testing device — by and large they react negatively to many of the same things that plants do — too much water, overdoses of chemical fertilizers, highly compact soil, etc. If worms thrive in the beds, the chances are good that plants will.

The Indoor Environment

It's depressing to contemplate how many good plants have been ruined by lack of attention to the indoor environment.

Get yourself some earth worms

A critical factor in the photosynthetic process is the ability of a plant to rid itself of the poisons it manufactures in the course of the organic conversions it goes through. These processes depend upon a steady flow of water; from the soil, through the root cells, transported up the stem, passed through the leaf tissues & discharged into the air as water vapor. The escape velocity of the water vapor molecules from the stoma is very low, consequently discharged water vapor tends to hang around the leaf surfaces, preventing further discharge, until it is swept away by breezes.

These little hemispheres of water vapor form a deadly shell which can suffocate Cannabis, which depends on a high volume of water passing through its tissues, very quickly. Indoor growers should take great care to provide for constant input of fresh, unsaturated air and for exhaust of saturated air.

Another common source of death & destruction among indoor Cannabis plants is tobacco smoke. It is with a heavy heart, my fellow Americans, that I announce the smoking lamp is not lighted during grass cultivation. If smokers are using the same air supply which the plants must breathe, you must try to filter the air somehow or take great risks with the plants' survival up until the third week, and their health beyond that.

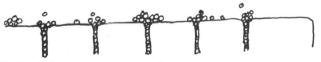

Poison-laden water vapor cannot be discharged without adequate ventilation

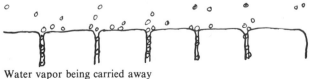

Water vapor being carried away

Leaf cross-section showing pores   169

Water Requirements for Cannabis

We've already reviewed the overall soil moisture characteristics which will affect Cannabis. All that remains is to look at the pattern of water uptake. These patterns are important, particularly for the indoor grower, because they give clues as to the critical growth stages where deprivation of water will have very negative effects.

Key points to keep in mind when inspecting this chart are:

(1) Air & soil temperatures will be equal (Columns A & D) under normal indoor conditions. Bottom heating will produce the differences noted in Columns B & C. (See pages 177 & 184.)

(2) The figures given are per plant, per week.

(3) The water uptake figures are given in milliliters, which are equivalent to 1/1000 of a liter; thus, 500 ml=1/2 liter (or 1/2 quart) of water, & so forth.

(4) The figures given for the wild strain represent the *minimum* requirements for a healthy plant. The figures for the commercial strain, grown for fiber, represent about the maximum a plant can handle.

Chart 1:
Water
requirements

Week	(A) Air=75°F Soil=75°F		(B) Air=75°F Soil=60°F		(C) Air=60°F Soil=75°F		(D) Air=60°F Soil=60°F	
	Wild	Commercial	Wild	Commercial	Wild	Commercial	Wild	Commercial
1	60	210	50	175	80	150	70	60
2	70	200	40	100	80	190	45	100
3	130	290	85	105	85	190	50	120
4	125	380	65	240	105	260	65	180
5	160	650	105	420	110	380	90	240
6	155	560	115	420	125	430	120	260
7	175	730	80	470	170	530	100	430
8	140	650	100	490	200	610	135	430
9	175	730	120	540	140	540	70	530
10	140	850	120	530	155	840	100	670
11	150	850	60	560	90	650	75	450
12	160	670	105	470	125	600	100	420
13	150	770	110	470	90	620	45	480
14	160	750	105	510	105	600	50	510

Enzymes and Sex

The action of environmental factors in altering sexual expression & vegetative development in Cannabis should not be considered in isolation from some of the plant mechanisms which interact with environment to produce the changes we've been discussing.

Enzymes play an important role in sex expression. The enzymes adrase (male) and gynase (female) are produced, and how much of each is utilized by the plant seems to be determined by environmental factors, in particular the photoperiod. While both enzymes are produced in every hemp plant, hermaphroditism is rare under normal conditions because the male enzyme has a self-inhibitory quality.

The complex interaction of environment & enzyme may be viewed as a trade-off situation. If environmental conditions are strongly in favor of production of the male-associated andrase, its self-inhibitory powers come into play so that the female-associated enzyme can influence sexual development at least to the point where the plant will be hermaphroditic. This seems to be a self-preservation & reproductivity-retention mechanism, for without it, only male plants would be produced under radical environmental conditions and the plants would not be able to propagate.

Under conditions highly conducive to the production of the female-associated gynase, a process occurs which has the same outcome from the plant's point of view — the plants retain the ability to propagate by becoming hermaphroditic.

Under normal conditions, of course, Cannabis has no need to protect itself by going through these genetic gyrations and in the ordinary course of events the cultivator will not have to worry about manipulation of sex in his plants. If, however, the cultivator is interested in producing a high ratio of females to males, deviating from the normal 1:1 relationship, then an awareness of what is happening — the plant's survival capability is being challenged — should make the cultivator more sensitive to changes in his plants. Most important, the cultivator should not try for high 9:1 or 9.5:1 female ratios unless willing to pay the price of hermaphroditic plants with potential genetic defects in future generations and highly variable drug potency.

Deficiency Signs

There are a few good clues which your plants will give you if they are being starved of any of the really essential nutrients. The following discussion should be useful as a guide, but before acting upon leaf analysis, it is highly advisable to check for soil acidity, which can produce many of the below symptoms by limiting nitrification and promoting excess uptake of toxic salts. Use litmus paper to test for acidity, and simply follow the directions on the package. Litmus paper can be easily obtained at many drug stores and always at chemical supply houses & nurseries.

Nitrogen Deficiency:

This is the most common problem which users of natural soils will encounter. Nitrogen is absolutely essential for the production of many life-sustaining organic materials in Cannabis, particularly chlorophyll.

Cannabis shows a nitrogen deficiency by a yellowing of the older leaves. The young leaves will remain green, except in severe cases, because in the face of starvation the older leaves give up their nitrogen for the young, and the plant sends whatever nitrogen it can draw from the soil to the youngest leaves first.

Use of organic fertilizers like manure or chicken dung, plus plowing in some nitrogen-fixing plants like beans, will assure that you won't have this problem. Chemical remedies include nitrochalk or nitrate of soda.

Phosphorus Deficiency:

Phosphorus is another essential element for plant health, and its function appears closely linked with nitrogen. It is needed for the plant's metabolism of sugar, from which much of its energy is derived.

The mature leaves of Cannabis will show phosphorus deficiency first, and they will appear a dark, dull green, curled up a bit at the edges. The undersides of the leaves, particularly close to the veins, may show a purple tint. Commercially available triple or super-phosphate will remedy this ailment.

Calcium Deficiency:

While calcium is an absolutely necessary mineral, it is used by Cannabis only in minute quantities.

The symptoms of calcium starvation are difficult to detect — they consist of an inhibition of buds which are in the process of becoming leaf clusters, and a wilting of the tips of the fine lateral roots. Most cultivators of Cannabis won't have to worry if their soil is of sedimentary origin. Commercial remedies for calcium deficiencies are readily available, or you can work in bone meal & chicken feathers (but not in large quantities) to soil you suspect of being calcium deficient.

Magnesium Deficiency:

Magnesium is an integral part of the chlorophyll in all green plants, and serves in other important ways as an activator mechanism.

Symptoms occur first on older leaves, and consist of a yellowing of the tissues around the veins of the leaf. The leaves will develop a general 'varicose vein' look very quickly, and the yellowing will then spread over the whole leaf.

Many of the magnesium sulphur compounds available in commercial fertilizers can correct this condition; agricultural epsom salts will be the most easily available.

Iron Deficiency:

Cannabis requires only trace amounts of this element, though it is an essential link in the photosynthetic process, as well as in respiration.

Deficiency symptoms look the same as those for magnesium deficiency, but they occur on the younger leaves first. Most plant foods contain enough of this trace element to assure no problems with your grass.

Potassium Deficiency:

Relatively large amounts of potassium are needed by Cannabis at certain growth stages, because this element functions as an activator of essential metabolic activities.

Again, the older leaves will show deficiency signs first. There will be a slight yellowing of the leaves initially, followed rapidly by dark spots and the edges of the leaves becoming a bronze-gray. Application of

sulfate & muriate of potash will help remedy any such problems.

Sulphur Deficiency:

This deficiency is not common, because most soils have plenty of sulfate.

The symptoms usually occur first in the younger leaves, as opposed to the normal pattern for Cannabis, and amount to a slight general yellowing. This condition soon spreads to the rest of the plant. Any commercial sulfate dressing will work well if you have a sulphur problem.

Boron Deficiency:

This element is necessary for the development of strong stem tissues in Cannabis, and there is usually enough in the soil to prevent problems.

The symptoms are a bit difficult to detect unless they are of a critical nature. They include a swelling of the stem near the base, and the stem will crack open and be very dry & rotten-appearing on the inside.

Again, most plant foods have enough borate in them to prevent this sort of problem.

Chlorine Deficiency:

This disease can be confused with many others, because the symptoms are a general yellowing of the leaves, and a gradual turn in color to bronze or bronze-orange. The one sure indicator is if the tips of the lateral root system become swollen, and if they are much shorter than the normal 5" to 7" radial spread just beneath the soil surface.

This is a very uncommon problem, and will not occur at all if any care is taken in seeing that the major nutrients have been supplied, as the chloride ion is associated with many of the major nutrient compounds.

Zinc Deficiency:

This disease will begin to show along about the fifth week in Cannabis, and will result in very small leaves which are wrinkled around the edges and which are faintly yellow along the veins. The distance between nodes on the stem will also be greater than you would expect on a normal plant, in some cases only the top knot of leaves will be viable.

Any plant food containing zinc compounds will

Nepal, 1971.
Photograph:
Norman Kulkin.

Nepal 1971

do the trick if the problem is caught in time.

Molybdenum Deficiency:

Many soils lack the trace amount of this element which is essential for Cannabis in nitrogen fixation.

Symptoms are a yellowing of the sections of the leaves between the major veins, and this yellowing occurs first on those leaves near the middle of the plant, progressing rapidly to the younger leaves at the extremities. The younger leaves will, in addition, become severely distorted and twisted. The yellowing may not occur if you have been using ammoniacal nitrogen fertilizers, but the twisted young leaves will be a giveaway sign.

Be sure to use a plant food containing a trace amount of this essential element.

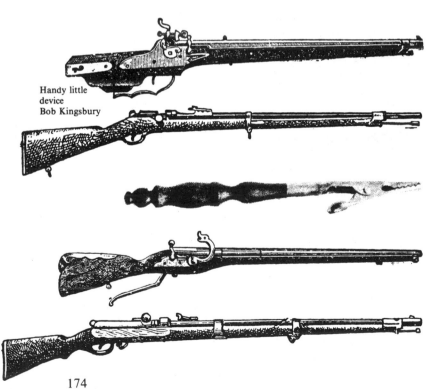

Handy little
device
Bob Kingsbury

Some Chemical Fertilizers

The use of chemicals instead of organic fertilizers has several advantages under specific conditions. Chemical quantities can be regulated rather closely with established plant requirements. The problem with grass is that very little research has been done on its requirements, with the exception of a great little article by Sister Mary Etienne Tibeau in 1933. Sister Mary writes of her work with her plants with the systematic vision of a fascinated researcher. Her work concentrates particularly on the nutrients required to produce the largest & thickest leaves and the greatest amounts of resin. Sister Mary is every grower's spiritual mother superior.

Luckily for those of you who are not dead set on total organic cultivation, the mineral requirements of hops are very similar to those of Cannabis, and its reaction to nutrient deficiencies are equally similar. Consequently, if you are able to convince the friendly neighborhood flowerman that you have a sick hops vine in your backyard, he may be able to point out a commercial prescription cure. If you don't live in a place where hops are familiar plants, you can refer to the remedies outlined above, and ask for a commercial product which is similar.

Even if your plants aren't putting out sickness vibrations, you might want to consider supplementing their straight soil & organic diet. If you do, the following charts may be helpful in choosing a commercial product; or if you are skilled in basement chemistry, you may want to try to brew up a batch of your own nutrient solution.

There are four basic solutions of metallic salts which occur in one form or another in many chemical and chemical-organic fertilizers, or which can be easily put together in a home lab. These solutions are designed specifically for use with Cannabis on an experimental basis. Once you make one of these solutions you should include the solution as a part of your regular watering procedure — the idea is that one 7 liter batch of solution will last about 7 weeks if you use a liter a week in watering your plants, (see charts two & three).

Effects of the Use of Supplemental Solutions
of Essential Salts on Cannabis Sativa

Foliage & Resin

1 Production of very large leaves stimulated; calcium oxalate crystals are heavily concentrated; resin production is inhibited if a potassium overdose occurs after the tenth week. Sex ratio 7:3 females. Potassium is very essential in the early stages of life, but has substantial negative effects at maturity if too great a concentration is continued.

2 Foliage is more sparse than with high potassium dosage; older leaves wilt readily. A magnesium shortage will inhibit or prevent resin production. Sex ratio 6:4 males. Magnesium is vital to overall health but conservative supplementation is advisable.

3 Healthy plants are produced with somewhat smaller leaves than with the other supplements; foliage is not very thick or abundant; high calcium salt concentration inhibits resin production. Sex ratio 7:3 males. Overdose of calcium in early life will stunt growth but an adequate supply is essential in the sixth to ninth weeks.

4 Foliage is abundant, healthy, dark green and leaves are thick; excess nitrogen promotes water loss and can cause wilting; nitrogen deficit at maturity stimulates resin production. Sex ratio as high as 9:1 females. Excess nitrogen will cause plants to grow fast in seedling stage and to appear healthy, but they will die off at the time of sex differentiation.

Stature & Growth

1 Potassium yields greatest height; stem is large and thick, very low on fiber, woody and brittle; leaves are thick, healthy, dark green; growth cycle is shortened by about a week.

2 Magnesium concentrations give good height; stems will be fibrous and hollow, somewhat woody, not as strong as with calcium supplements; leaves will be healthy but pale-green in color and will brown or wilt around the edges and tips.

3 Very strong and fibrous stem which is desirable where heavy winds are common; plants do not grow high; color is dark green and flowers are swollen.

4 Plants will be short, squat and very leafy. Nitrogen should *not* be cut back until after the sixth week.

Four Basic Supplemental Solutions of the Essential Salts

Formula 1

High Potassium	Ratio (Parts)*
KNO_3	2
KH_2PO_4	2
KCL	2.5
$MgSO_4$	1
$Ca(NO_3)_2$	4
K_2SO_4	4.5

Formula 2

High Magnesium	Ratio (Parts)*
KNO_3	1
KH_2PO_4	1
$Ca(NO_3)_2$	4
$MgCl_2$	3
$MgSO_4$	4

Formula 3

High Calcium	Ratio (Parts)*
$Ca(NO_3)_2$	15
KH_2PO_4	1
$CaCl_2$	11
$MgSO_4$	1
KNO_3	1

Formula 4

High Nitrogen	Ratio (Parts)*
KNO_3	1
NH_4NO_3	17
$Ca(NO_3)_2$	4
KH_2PO_4	1
$MgSO_4$	2

*Parts are expressed in Grams per 7 liters of Solution

Bottom Heating Effects

In the next section we will talk about bottom heating, the process of raising soil temperature above that of the surrounding air; but since this is an environmental manipulation, we'll present this chart here (4). Before you go through the expense & effort of using this procedure on your plants, be sure to refer back to this chart to get an idea of the relative advantages & disadvantages.

	AIR = 60° F	AIR = 75° F
Soil 60° F	**A** Lowest water needs; appx. 40% less than (D). Lowest rate of nutrient uptake occurs between weeks 5 & 7 in the growth cycle. Mean number of leaves on mature plants equal to (D), but female plants are more sparse. Leaf area is substantial; color & thickness good. Use of a 16-hour exposure to light daily at this soil-air temperature level produces mainly female plants. Height at maturity is low compared to (B) & (D).	**B** Water needs are substantial. Lowest rate of nutrient uptake occurs in the twelfth week. Lowest mean number of leaves per plant for both males & females. Leaf area is very low, and leaf thickness is considerably less than under all other temp/air conditions. A 15 to 20 hour light exposure will produce a sex ratio of 6:4 females. Height of mature plants substantial.
Soil 75° F	**C** Water needs are substantial. Lowest rate of nutrient uptake occurs in the third week. Mean number of leaves per plant is the greatest, but females have fewer leaves per plant than the females in (D). A 15 to 20 hour daily exposure will produce predominantly female plants. Height at maturity is low; a squat, bushy plant results.	**D** The greatest water needs occur under these conditions. Lowest rate of nutrient uptake occurs in the fifth to seventh weeks. Mean number of leaves per plant is less than (C), but females have 40% more leaves per plant than (C). A 16 hour photoperiod produces a 1:1 sex ratio, less than under other conditions, but normal for Cannabis.

Chart 4

Seeds, Seedlings Germination & Transplantation

When you consider the amount of time and energy that goes into preparing for cultivation, whether you plan on a large-scale operation or just a couple of plants grown in some little nook, it doesn't make a lot of sense to take a cavalier approach to seed selection. This is particularly true when it is so simple to assume yourself that the seed you're using is of good quality.

The Good Seed

External appearance will give you a good set of clues to the seed's state of health. Viable seed will be well fleshed out and not be all crinkled up. It will be bright gray, gray-green, or gray-brown and will appear glossy if rubbed between the palms of your hands. Good seed will usually be heavy enough to sink in a pan of pure water. Occasionally a good seed will not appear gray, but it will prove itself by weight, fleshy appearance.

The constituents of Cannabis seed break down thusly:

Constituent:	%
Fatty Oils	19.1
Resin	1.6
Saccharin	1.6
Gum Extract	9.0
Albumen	24.7
Woody Fiber	13.3
Loss	.7

This table demonstrates, incidentally, how wasteful it is to smoke or otherwise consume Cannabis seed, which contains only 1.6% resin by weight, an exceedingly small amount.

To test further for seed quality, several methods are suggested. It's a good idea to carry testing beyond a glance at the seed's appearance, because a number of internal conditions affect their germinating ability and these are not always detectable by appearance and the water test.

Crack open several seeds selected at random from the batch which will be used. If they have a musty, oily taste, they are pretty old and may well have gone bad. Another test is simply to germinate a group of ten seeds and count up those which fail to sprout. This will give you a rough estimate, by percentage, of what you can expect overall. Anything above 50% is pretty good for a bunch of seeds acquired at random on the streets of North America these days. Considering the traumas which most grass goes through before it reaches the domestic market, it's a wonder that any seeds remain viable. We'll cover this subject in detail later on.

If you have cracked open a few seeds and note that the insides are black, then fermentation has set in and there is no chance that they will germinate. Conversely, if they are pale & dusty on the inside, they are overage and will produce feeble plants at best.

Another test is to drop a few seeds onto a red-hot iron. If they burst with a noticeable crack, they were good seeds. In Thrace, seeds were thrown upon red-hot stones, and 'their perfumed vapor, so obtained, used

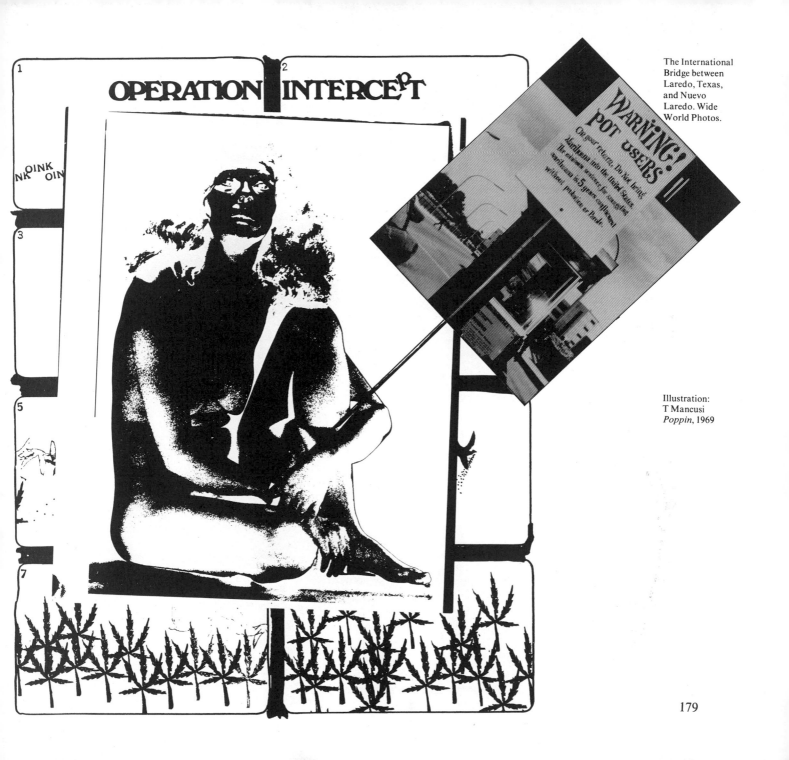

OPERATION INTERCEPT

The International Bridge between Laredo, Texas, and Nuevo Laredo. Wide World Photos.

Illustration:
T Mancusi
Poppin, 1969

179

for a fume bath which excited from those enjoying it, cries of exultation.' A great idea for your backyard sauna, if you are a profligate sort of soul.

Incidentally, Cannabis seeds are considered excellent bird food, because they are fattening & stimulate egg production, so be very careful with those brownie recipes.

Seeds can provide an important clue for those who are breaking the law by purchasing lids. Since the optimum time for harvesting grass for drug potency is at, or shortly after, female flowering, the greater proportion of seeds in such a plant will be immature. Conversely, if all the seeds in the lid appear to be ripe; that is, bright gray, the chances are good that not only was the plant overage when she was harvested, but she had also probably been pollinated, which will have lowered her effectiveness as a drug. And, of course, if there are very few seeds at all in the proffered lid, the chances are increased that you are being offered leaves from a male plant. At any rate, it would pay to be very suspicious of any grass which doesn't have a ratio of immature (white) to mature (gray) seeds of at least 2:1.

Preparation of Seeds

Once you are fairly sure of the vitality of your seeds, you should go through a couple of pre-planting steps.

You should soak your seeds overnight in a starting bath of distilled water. Actually, any pure water will do, but if you are city-bound, you would do well to invest in a bottle of store-bought water to avoid the chemicals & crap which might damage the swelling embryo beyond saving.

You can, if you wish, give the seeds a little boost by using additives in the soaking solution. Very little research has been done on the effects of using plant growth stimulants on Cannabis seeds in the starting solution. One standard additive which is available through nurseries contains ammoniacal nitrogen, nitrate nitrogen, phosphoric acid & soluble potash. Use of such compounds is more or less at your own risk; be sure to look at the fertilizer information in the previous chapter first.

Additives

There are a couple of general points covering the use of additives with particular significance for Cannabis, if you decide you want to experiment a little.

(1) Most growth regulators & stimulants in the pregermination and germination stages require that temperature and moisture levels be held constant, usually between 65° & 75° F, and 30-50% relative humidity.

(2) Commercial preparations are manufactured to cover a wide range of plant response levels, and therefore aren't necessarily good for one specific plant. It seems more sensible to design your own growth stimulator, even if it is simply adding little soluble nitrogen, than to waste money on commercial products.

(3) Most plants seem to benefit from application of growth stimulants at later stages in their growth cycle. Cannabis Sativa is no exception. Limiting stimulation to a carefully controlled environment and perhaps some nutrients seems to be the best policy at the pre-germination stage.

(4) If you think that your seeds have had a rough time in transit, you should be particularly careful in using stimulants at the early stages of life. Let the plants try to make it on their own, rather than forcing them to exceed capacity in a weakened state.

(5) Particularly after applying stimulants through the starting solution, (but this precaution applies generally) one should exercise care in handling the seeds because they are going to be swollen and tender. Sterilized tweezers are the best instruments for handling the seeds in transfer from the starting solution to the germination beds. The seeds should be picked up with the lightest possible touch, and should be picked up by the sides of the seed rather than the ends. To put pressure on the ends might damage the embryo root permanently.

(6) The seed should be placed in the earth with the pointed end up because as the primary tap root emerges from the pointed end, the natural tendency is to make a turn & grow downward. If it has to twist & turn in order to seek its proper direction, two negative

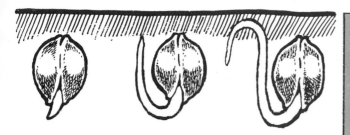

Seed improperly positioned — the pointed end is down. Tap root makes natural bend out of the seed, but then has to reverse itself. Vital seed energy is lost.

effects will result.

First, a great deal of energy stored in the seed which should be going for root extension will be expended in root positioning, resulting in a lowered energy level at this critical growth stage. Second, the plant has to exert a great deal of force, after the tap root is extended, in lifting its head, enclosed by the two halves of the seed pod, above the soil and in forcing the pod off its back so that it can spread out its two embryo leaves to begin the photosynthetic process. Carelessness on your part can exhaust any but the most hearty seedling at this stage, resulting in feeble plant in later life.

(7) Seed should be placed about 1/2" to 3/4" under the soil surface. As it develops, it should not have to expend large amounts of energy pushing through the soil because it will need the energy later on to stand erect & throw off the seed coat.

181

Stages of Seedling Growth

The germinating Cannabis seeds go through several distinct stages, and it may prove worthwhile to pull one or two sprouts each day to check on development according to the following time table. If the seeds do not develop approximately in the sequence and at the time indicated, something is wrong. You may save yourself weeks of work, a substantial electric bill, and some disappointment by checking on these growth stages.

Stage 1: Upon germination, the primary root emerges from the stylar end of the seed (the pointed end). The seed is split in half, but the halves remain together protecting the emergent leaves. This primary tap root undergoes rapid growth.

Stage 2: After approximately 48 hours from germination, the tap root should be around 1-1/2 inches long. Root growth normally slows at this point.

Stage 3: After from 72 to 96 hours, a fine lateral root system should begin developing just below the soil surface. At this point, the seedling will begin to force itself above the soil surface and to exert pressure to throw off the seed coat.

Stage 4: The seedling stem begins to stand erect during the fifth day, and the seed coat falls away or remains at the soil surface. The embryo leaves are slightly oval in shape and are not serrated. They should be yellow-green at this point, and have a moist, waxy appearance.

Stage 5: The stem of the seedling below the embryo leaves lengthens steadily from the fifth to about the tenth day. The first leaf node where the embryo leaves are attached should be 1" to 1-1/2" above the soil surface. During this period the first pair of foliage leaves will appear. This first pair will be simple leaves, slightly oval, and will show serrations. They only last a short time, and the second & third pairs should appear by the twelfth day.

Stage 6: The embryo leaves, which have functioned as photosynthetic and food storage organs for the first few weeks, yellow and fall away during the early part of the third week.

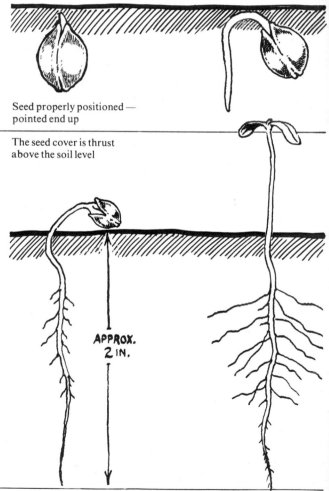

Seed properly positioned —
pointed end up

The seed cover is thrust above the soil level

APPROX.
2 IN.

Stage 5 growth; tenth day. '...fascinated with the news that marijuana grows in Sausalito's main street planter boxes...'—*Herb Caen*, 1971
Photograph: Vincent Maggiora

Germinating Beds

To assure maximum survival of Cannabis seedlings during & after germination, care should be exercised in selecting the medium and the environment for germination.

The most effective medium for germinating young Cannabis is fertile soil. The soil should be a mixture of rich humus & fine sand (spagnum moss and aquarium sand will do nicely). The soil should not be acid; in fact, a ph reading of 7.5 to 8.0 would be just about right. A simple litmus test should indicate when the balance is adequate. The soil can be supplemented with a soluble nitrogen fertilizer in a solution strength of about 5%. An alternate method is to work animal manure into the germinating bed soil; a small amount is adequate. In either case, enrichment should take place 5-7 days before planting or use as a germinating bed.

Moisture content in germinating soil is a critical factor. The surface of the germinating soil should be almost dry, and the subsurface soil not so moist that it adheres to the finger. Testing for good moisture is much like testing gingerbread to see if it is done — as long as any soil sticks to a pencil thrust to the bottom, it is too moist. Care should be taken, however, to see that the germination beds are kept within a range of moisture, neither too wet nor too dry. If too wet, the seeds are likely to rot & ferment; and if too dry, they are apt to sprout weakly, if at all.

Several authors state that germination can be accomplished in many mediums — even wet paper towels — but there is substantial evidence that subjecting seedlings to transplant shock twice in their early growth stages is as harmful as would the case be if germination takes place in a non-nutritive & impermanent medium.

Temperature plays an important role in assisting germination. While Cannabis is capable of sprouting & surviving at root temperatures as low as 46° F, an ideal range should start at 65° F and run upwards of 80° F. Many researchers have found that maintaining soil temperatures slightly higher than air temperature in seedling stages promotes rapid growth. This procedure, called bottom heating, is somewhat tricky and not at all necessary for healthy, vital plants; but if you insist on nothing but the best for your little charges, you can invest in the necessary equipment (expensive) which nurseries will probably be able to find for you. An alternative is to strip an electric blanket of its heating wires and lay them out beneath your germinating boxes. Needless to say, care must be taken to avoid shorts & shocks.

If heating devices fail during germination; or, if outdoors, a chill occurs and the seedlings wither & turn yellow, all hope is not lost. Regeneration of apparently dead seedlings is fairly common, and you should wait at least a week before starting all over. The exception to this rule will be when there has been a heavy frost, in which case there just isn't much hope.

Germinating Equipment

Almost any container imagination can devise will do for a germinating box, as long as it meets certain size & depth requirements. Coffee cans, plastic basins, window boxes, jars, bathtubs, etc, all have been used for indoor germination. Outdoor germination most often occurs in a hothouse or quasi-hothouse situation, with plastic film laid over the furrows or a plastic or glass enclosure surrounding the seedlings.

A few tricks to remember which might make germination a good deal more simple & reliable process for the Cannabis grower:

If the seedlings are to be transplanted at any point, it will be helpful to germinate them in containers making transfer to the planting soil easy & nontraumatic. Germinating the seeds in ice-cube trays or similar devices allows easy transfer of the seedlings in their original soil. The ball of soil can either be popped out at transplant time; or each depression in the tray can be lined with foil or plastic before the germinating soil is added, making transplantation a matter of lifting out the ball of soil intact and placing it in the receiving soil equally undisturbed. The foil or plastic film can be removed easily prior to placing the seedling in its new home.

Paper cups are good germinating containers too, because you can cut them away and leave a well-shaped ball of soil. But be sure to use one big enough to not cramp the roots of the germinating seedling—at least a 12 ounce cup.

Whatever the construction of the germinating box, it must (1) insulate well & retain heat; (2) allow for adequate ventilation for respiration; (3) provide adequate drainage; (4) allow space for initial root growth & development. Either glass or plastic film will do for insulation & light, and ventilation is easily provided for. Drainage is necessary, or water will tend to pool at the lowest levels of the beds, producing an over-moist environment for the roots of the plant.

Preparation for Transplanting

A substantial exposure to risk comes during transplanting for the Cannabis seedlings, but there are a series of steps which can be taken to minimize the danger & promote healthy adaptation.

A primary consideration is the receiving soil. It should be as similar to that used in germination & sprouting as possible. It must be fertile, neutral or slightly alkaline, loose & friable, moisture-retentive at the sub-surface levels, well-drained, spaded to a depth of at least 12″, and reasonably clean of weeds & mold. A few earthworms introduced into the transplant soil would be very beneficial.

It is at this point that a number of critical differentiations occur in the plant's environment which determine in large part whether its ultimate usefulness will be for its fiber or for its resin.

One of the most important determinants is the crowding which young plants experience. A general rule may be stated; for fiber, the closer together the

The further apart the better

Custom-built hashish pipe, by Pan, Berkeley, 1971. Photograph: Annie Leibovitz

185

better, and for resin the further apart the better. Plants which are crowded closer than 12-14 inches from one another will produce, other things being equal, rather good fiber & rather sparse leaves. Cultivators after the leaves, rather than the fiber, have to work largely by inference on spacing, but several sources indicate that plants should be spaced at least a foot away from any other if leaves are desired; two-foot spacing would be even better.

The seedling sprouts should be exposed to at least eight hours of sunlight or its equivalent before and after transplanting. While the specific lighting requirements of Cannabis are discussed further on, it is most important at this early stage that lighting be consistent. Reducing the amount of lighting the sprouts receive immediately after transplanting seems to speed development of the mature plant by about one week. This reduced period of lighting, the lower limit of which is seven hours per day, should be discontinued after the fourth to sixth day of seedling growth and the plants put on the light regimen which you have decided to follow through their lifetime.

When the time comes for transplantation, you should have all your equipment at hand, and have the germination beds close to the transplant beds so that there will be minimum exposure.

Use Green Safelight

It is really a good idea to perform the transplant under green light of low intensity. If no green light is available, a green filter will do. The green light is the cultivator's equivalent of the photographer's darkroom red. It allows him to see well without danger to the plants, because green light is the least active part of the spectrum for photosynthetic processes in plants, and tends to shut down the major metabolic processes which, if active during transplant, will put a great strain on the seedling.

In a more general sense, any time you perform any operations which entail exposure of the delicate tissues of your plants to light, use green light and you cut your radiation damage risks to almost zero. This is particularly important if you leave the seeds in the starting

bath too long and the embryo root has begun to emerge. Seeds in this condition should be gently, but swiftly, placed in earth in the proper 'heads-up' position described earlier.

Transplanting the Seedling

One of the most traumatic experiences which seedlings can undergo is to be transplanted. This is true of Cannabis even though it is a hearty plant in later life. In cases where the cultivator takes the outdoor hit-or-miss route there will be no worry about transplantation; indoor cultivators, careful outdoor cultivators, and experimenters will all want to germinate their plants under a controlled set of conditions.

Several steps can be taken to assure maximum transplantation survival.

The soil which is to receive the seedlings should be completely ready; that is, there should be no need to disturb it for a week after the seedlings are planted. It should be fertile, friable & thoroughly spaded. Earthworms should have been introduced at least two days prior to transplant, or their introduction should be delayed several days after transplant.

Transfer should take place under a pale green light, and the place should not be subject to drafts or temperature variation.

All instruments should have been sterilized, and sterile cotton gloves should be worn, if possible. If not, washing your hands with soap which removes surface oils on the skin should help prevent damage to the seedlings.

Where at all possible, the receptor soil should closely approximate the donor soil.

Over use of fertilizers at this stage is not recommended, but several commercial preparations for stimulating transplant setting are readily available and work well when directions are followed.

If possible, the seedling should be lifted with a ball of the original soil surrounding the roots, and this placed in a hole in the prepared growing bed. When lifting the seedling, it is best if the ball of soil can be lifted without the necessity for touching the plant in any way. If the plant must be handled, it is best to grasp it lightly right near the soil level, supporting the plant's weight from above and that of the soil from below. Exposed roots and the upper stem & embryo leaves of the seedlings should not be handled.

Seedlings should be placed in an upright position in the receptor beds with their leaves oriented to the principal light source. Phototropic (light-seeking) movement in newly transplanted seedlings can be detrimental to good secure rooting. The hole should be deep enough to allow the young root to extend to full length as it probably will be somewhat cramped from the germinating beds. The root should not be mashed down into a shallow hole, or the plant will not be able to summon energy enough to establish itself. The soil should be gently built up around the seedling to a level equivalent to that of the germinating bed. Piling dirt too high up the stem can be harmful.

The soil in the transplant beds should be dry enough so that when you add water after the trans-

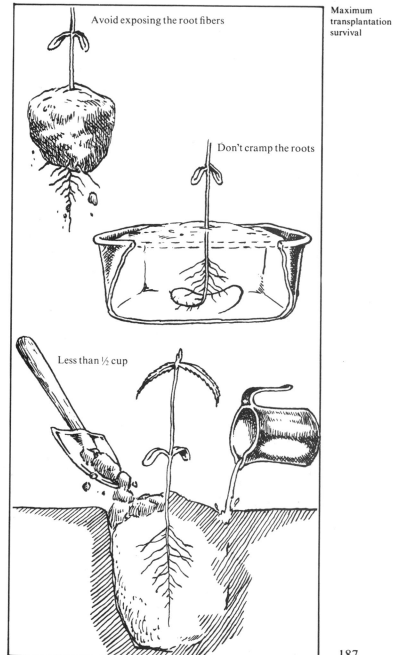

Avoid exposing the root fibers

Don't cramp the roots

Less than ½ cup

plant is finished, it will be absorbed rather than pooling around the roots. Adding water helps the transplanted seedling by, in effect, bonding the ball of original soil to the new soil, and makes root penetration of the new soil much easier. A teaspoon of water at room temperature will be enough for a transplanted seedling on the first day, provided the soil is fertile and contains enough moist humus to begin with.

If any form of treatment is undertaken before transplanting is completed — such as Colchicine treatment described elsewhere — special care should be taken to protect the roots either with moist cotton or filter paper, or with a plastic film wrapped gently around the ball of soil to preserve moisture & compactness.

All plants undergo transplant shock; some seem to die and eventually recover, and some die; but the majority of plants transplanted correctly will survive & thrive with no apparent bad effects. If some of the transplanted seedlings yellow, droop, and even appear to die, leaving them alone is the best policy, after checking to see that the bending over has not exposed the delicate white flesh of the root.

With proper precautions & adequate soil, moisture & lighting conditions, the cultivator indoors should expect at least a 75% survival rate for transplants while outdoor transplants will have a lower survival rate in a less controlled environment.

Cannabis is a
very tough
plant...
Photograph:
Jim Ball

Seed Storage

While Cannabis is a very tough plant, one whose seeds retain their power to germinate under a wide range of conditions, there is no sense in taking unnecessary chances with next year's crop if some simple precautions will give you the necessary protection.

The chief villain in the destruction of Cannabis seeds is moisture, whether atmospheric or surface film. Assuming dry conditions, Cannabis will not be injured by temperatures up to 98.6°, regardless of whether or not they are exposed to air. If the temperature in the storage vessel rises above this level for even short periods of time, however, the vitality of the seeds will decrease markedly, and prolonged exposure to temperatures over 100° will kill all but the most hearty & *lucky* seeds.

If the atmosphere where you live, or where you are going to be storing your seeds, is appreciably humid, this upper limit is lowered to 86° F. So if you have no way of keeping the seeds absolutely dry, at least don't allow higher temperatures than this.

The general rule may be stated: as moisture becomes a factor in storage, temperature becomes a factor, and seed vitality loss is directly related to both.

You will come as close as possible to a set of ideal conditions if you can store your seeds in an airtight container, at a temperature of between 80°-85° F.

For very long-term storage, it is a good idea to include some desiccating agent such as a little bag of silica gel taped to the lid of the container on the inside. This will draw off any moisture liberated by the seeds. The gel should not be in contact with the seeds. Neither should you store large quantities of seed together, because they may heat up.

Lighting Effects & Growth Patterns

There are many important differences between types of light used in cultivating plants.

Sunlight, as it comes from the sun's surface, is a continuous radiation spectrum. Sunlight appears white for the same reasons that metals glow white with a blue tinge at high temperatures, and only red-yellow at lower temperatures (the higher an object's temperature, the further its light emission moves toward the short wavelength, very high energy end of the spectrum).

When sunlight hits the outer atmosphere of earth, the random oxygen & ozone molecules floating around up there absorb most of its high-energy ultra-violet light. If too much of this energy light fell on earth, all unprotected life would blow itself apart cell by cell.

Of the sunlight which reaches earth's surface, about half is visible light, and half is infra-red. The infra-red light is not continuous because water vapor & carbon dioxide absorb certain bands.

The processes of photosynthesis require a certain energy level to start them and keep them going. The molecules involved in photosynthesis must absorb enough energy to excite them and loosen them up so that they can enter into reactions with other molecules. This process is the same one which takes place in our eyes, and explains why we have a visible range of light. Too high-energy light (ultra-violet) freaks out the molecules in the eye, gets them so excited that they can't go through their reactions in an orderly fashion; and too low-energy light (infra-red) isn't heavy enough to get the molecules up for interaction. Photosynthesis in plants requires that the plants have energy levels which they can 'see' — what is light to our eyes is life to a plant. This is the reason that infra-red light produces such odd changes in plants — they aren't getting enough energy to go through with their normal processes, so they have to come up with some abnormal processes, and thus some abnormal growth patterns, in order to draw enough energy from the environment to survive. The phenomenon seems analogous to an organism such as man, who, when deprived of life-giving or life-sustaining substances such as air & heat, stretches out toward life in an agony of death, distending the normal limits of his physical being, his muscles & internal organs all reacting violently to the low energy input.

There are two principal areas of interest in relation to lighting, both relating on a higher level to the amount of energy which light imparts to living, growing plants. The first of these areas is concerned with the profound effects which variation in the exposure period has on plants. The second concern is the varying energy levels available through different light sources.

Photoperiodicity

The number of hours of light which Cannabis receives each day has direct & dramatic bearing on the size & complexity which it will attain in its life, how long it will take to reach maturity, how healthy it will be and how well it can withstand environmental variation, and the quality and configuration of its sexual expression.

These considerations are further broken down into two fundamentally distinct growing states — indoor & outdoor cultivation. We'll deal with some general lighting period principles and then go into the differences between the two types of cultivation.

Light Sources

Cannabis reacts to the visible spectrum of light, and certain parts of this spectrum are more active than others. To get the concept of spectrum clear, because we'll be dealing with it a lot, the diagram may be helpful.

It may be helpful to keep this spectrum-energy chart in mind throughout this chapter. The normal light-bulb which is used to provide indoor illumination emits light predominantly in the red to infra-red range. Thus, such light is very low energy with well over half of the emissions being in the almost worthless invisible infra-red part of the spectrum. Many plants have been ruined by people who in good faith have believed that putting a blue filter in front of such incandescent bulbs pro-

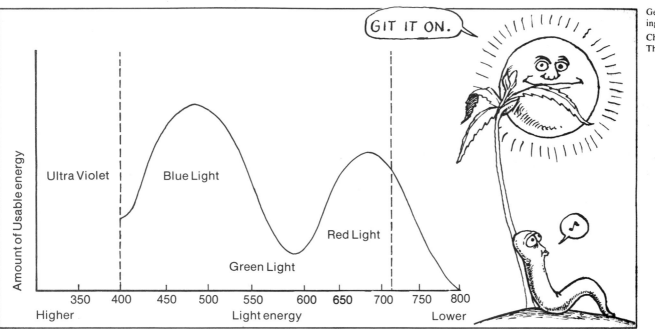

GIT IT ON.

Amount of Usable energy

Ultra Violet   Blue Light

Green Light   Red Light

350 400 450 500 550 600 650 700 750 800
Higher   Light energy   Lower

duces blue light, which they have been told is bene-ficial to plants. Blue light is high energy light, — plants do need a certain amount of this to go through their photosynthetic processes efficiently — what you get when you put a blue filter in front of a source which is emitting primarily red light is *not* blue light. The filter will not generate light, it only passes the remnants of what is being generated. Thus you will have a very small amount of predominantly *green* light being passed, the least active part of the spectrum in support-ing photosynthesis. If, because of cost, you want to use regular light bulbs in your growing situation, you should make sure that you have at least one 75 watt bulb, or its equivalent, per plant, and should put some sort of filter between it and the plant which limits the infra-red emissions reaching the plant. This filter will aid in keeping your plants sexually stable.

An additional caution — overexposure to infra-red light at the earliest stages of seedling life will prevent the plant from standing erect. In order to raise itself & spread its embryo leaves, the plant must absorb red light at about 660 on the spectrum. This promotes the growth of longer cells on the inside of the curved por-tion than on the outsides, pushing erect as though there were extensor muscles at work. Exposure to far-red & infra-red light, however, cancels this effect and the seedling will remain bent over.

Infra-red limits the energy available to the plant producing, in effect, a paroxysm resulting in elongation. If you are worried that your plants are being deprived of infra-red, and not certain that it doesn't have some beneficial effects (some research would tentatively support your viewpoint) then you can supplement your incandescent lighting with short bursts from a flood designed to emit high intensity infra-red, and note the results. In some cases, this may be beneficial, though no one has yet established precisely why it should be. At any rate, this additional trouble & expense is your decision.

Mercury fluorescent lamps are a considerable improvement over the usual light bulbs we've been discussing, though they burn out quickly and are more

191

expensive. Mercury emits a very high energy spectrum, and limits the amount of red & infra-red your plants will receive. An additional advantage is that mercury fluorescent lamps operate at very high intensity, which will give you a long-day effect without the necessity of burning them for sixteen or twenty hours at a clip. We'll get into the details of long-day effects in the indoor growing section later on.

The most useful artificial light source which is readily available for indoor cultivation is the wide-spectrum, gas-discharge lamp, many varieties of which are marketed under various trade names. Perhaps the best known is the Gro-Lux lamp, which, though it is pretty expensive does a good job of providing plants with the energy they need.

Let's take a little side trip into the whole relationship between wavelength & photosynthesis which may be helpful in understanding what the plants, all green plants, but particularly Cannabis, are doing with the energy they draw from the sun.

The controlling processes in photosynthesis begin at the atomic level, with the nucleus of the atom & its electron ring. Each orbit around the nucleus of an atom has a variety of potential energy levels at which electrons can move and still remain in orbit. If the electrons exceed the energy limits of their orbits they are forced to leave — to move into an orbit further from the nucleus and therefore an orbit which requires more energy to complete. This movement is the famous quantum leap which we have been using for years to describe an exponential increase in energy required to move from one plane to another. Knowledge, among other things, seems to operate according to this principle — you can acquire vast amounts of knowledge and still remain on the same plane, but there comes a point where the cumulative knowledge in your head — the cumulative creative energy you're trying to deal with — requires a leap into another plane. Once you've made that first leap, you realize that, while knowledge is a cumulative process, it is *not a progressive phenomenon*. You do not move from plane to plane in a smooth, harmonious progression merely by storing up knowledge. You

move from level to level, but always within the same orbit or plane, until you reach a point where you can no longer contain the creative energy you have been accumulating & remain within the same plane. So you make the quantum leap. And find yourself starting all over again, gathering energy on another level, always with successive levels above you, levels which are accessible only through the accumulation of vast amounts of knowledge, until once again the leap is within your ability.

The life process of photosynthesis in plants proceeds in this way, by quantum leaps of the atomic particles into a higher, more energetic plane. Following this leap, the electrons lose energy, their orbits decay, and the quantum leap occurs in reverse, liberating energy as the fall from the outer orbits to the inner orbits occurs. It is this energy, made possible by decay in the orbits of the excited electrons back to their original plane, which drives the engines of life. This is the conversion process which is essential to all life on earth. Without the ability to perform this leap, and the subsequent energy-liberating decay of electron orbits, all life would disappear and the earth would be stone & sand.

So you are very close to some very essential things when you are manipulating the light your plants receive, and there is no replacement for knowledge & understanding in dealing with these processes. You are moving close to life itself, to the process if not the meaning, so watch your step!

Without adequate light, | seedling can't muster energy to stand erect

For Outdoor Cultivation

We'll use, as a reference point, a line drawn between Washington, DC, Louisville, Kansas City, Colorado Springs and San Francisco. Along this line the hours of sunlight available throughout the year break down approximately as follows:

June:	Sunrise 4:30-5:00 am Sunset 7:00-7:30 pm Hours of Sunlight=approx 14
September:	Sunrise 6:00-6:30 am Sunset 5:45-6:15 pm Hours of Sunlight=approx 12
December:	Sunrise 7:00-7:30 am Sunset 4:30-5:00 pm Hours of Sunlight=approx 9
March:	Sunrise 5:45-6:15 am Sunset 5:45-6:15 pm Hours of Sunlight=approx 12

This breakdown is deliberately very loose, and does not take cloud cover into account. Therefore, the amount of effective sunlight will vary considerably. Nevertheless, some generalizations are possible which help greatly in determining the optimum planting times for Cannabis along this line, and if you are located either far north or far south of this line you will be able to adjust to fit your own seasonal picture.

As was pointed out in an earlier section, Cannabis has the potential to become either male, female, or hermaphroditic in response to threats from the environment. In this case, the chart (7) represents the plant's response to the energy levels available from the environment. It becomes immediately clear, upon inspection of the chart, that the ideal times for planting along the Washington-San Francisco axis, fall between early May & early August. This takes into account only day length, of course, and when other factors are figured in, it becomes clear that May is the best planting month for all-around good performance of the plants.

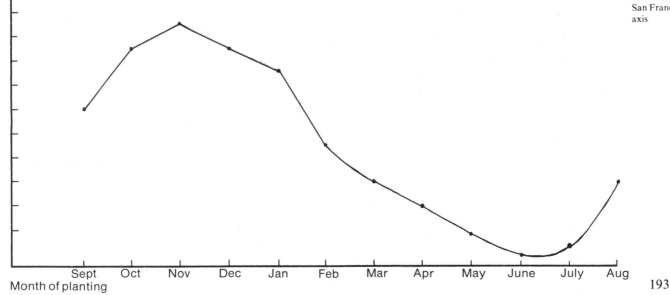

Chart 7: ideal planting along the Washington-San Francisco axis

% of plants showing sex abnormalities

Month of planting

Sept Oct Nov Dec Jan Feb Mar Apr May June July Aug

'Some guys,' said
a Berkeley
dealer, 'wouldn't
deal with an
Aries, say, if he
were giving away
Panama Red by
the ton. Every-
body's a little
paranoid in the
dope business!'

194

195

This condition will hold, incidentally, in any situation where you depend only on sunlight for energy for your plants, whether they are growing in a field or under greenhouse glass.

There are other effects of outdoor sunlight day-length which are worth noting briefly. If, in place of the curve on the sex-reversal chart (7), you substituted a chart showing size at maturity, you would find the relationship looks like chart 8.

Indoor Cultivation

We'll assume that you have chosen an appropriate light source for indoor cultivation based on the information presented earlier and that you are now ready to make a decision about how much light you can afford to give your plants. This decision will be based on cost — how much the bulbs cost, what size electric bill you can afford, the life-span of the source you're using, & so forth.

A lot of research has been done on modification of the growth cycle of Cannabis through alterations in the amount of light it receives in the indoor situation. One early experimentor (McPhee) was interested in the relative effects of day-length on growth rate in Cannabis. He set up his experiment so that he could control for the variables of temperature, soil quality, growing space per plant, soil moisture, light intensity & action spectrum. By controlling for all of these factors, he came up with a pretty close to ideal experimental situation, one where he could attribute difference in growth rate

Chart 8:
You will radically increase the mature height of your plants if you plant them at the appropriate times.
Another curve which you can superimpose on the height curve is a vegetation mass curve — you get equal returns in leaf mass and height in response to day-length in the outdoors situation.

Chart 9:
Indoor light/
growth rate

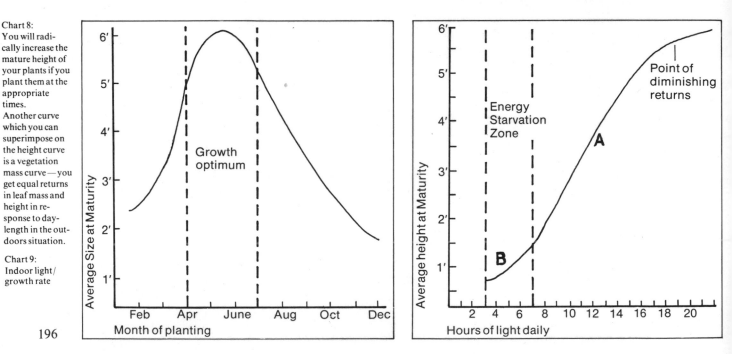

to duration of light alone, with pretty good confidence levels.

Chart 9 is based on the principal relationship which McPhee discovered, one which has been confirmed by many people since then. We can derive a couple of interesting principles from this chart.

First, it is clear that after you pass the seven hour daily exposure period, you begin to see a substantial increase in the growth & development of Cannabis for every unit of light increase provided. This relationship holds up to, and including, the 16-hour day, when the point of diminishing returns is reached. Most of your attention will probably be focused in that area of the curve labelled 'A', and the decision as to how much daylight you are going to give your plants will have a lot to do with the kind of results you're willing to accept. The part of the curve marked (B) represents an interesting example of energy starvation — the plants aren't getting enough energy, but they are growing at a fairly good rate anyway. This doesn't last, and is not a sign of vigor; rather, it is a sign of impending disaster just as is the elongation that occurs under infra-red light.

Accompanying the growth curve under increasing amounts of light are significant changes in the amount & quality of leaves produced by Cannabis. One of the best ways of judging the overall quality of your growing plant is to calculate the leaf index. This is done by taking the average number of leaves to a cluster — either 5, 7, 9, or 11 leaves to a cluster — and multiply this number by the average number of serrations per leaf. The higher the leaf index in Cannabis, the greater will be the leaf mass at maturity. This calculation is a good device for a number of purposes. First, it allows you to decide in about the fifth week which plants are going to have the greatest leaf mass at maturity. (This will be important if you anticipate thinning out your crop, particularly if you want to pull most of the males, leaving only the best.) Second, it gives you a check as to the uniformity of the growing conditions the plants are experiencing. It also gives you a good device for deciding which females you want to let go to full maturity as seed producers, and which you want to harvest before they bear fertilized seed.

Effects of Lighting Time	
Daylength	*Effects*
2-3 hours	Very poor chances for survival; radically stunted growth; very little vegetation; weakness; seeds are worthless even if produced; death can be expected within a few weeks.
4-5 hours	Rapid initial growth for some plants; growth tapers off after a few weeks; large portion of seeds sterile; very little vegetation; mature height is stunted; plants are weak and pale; resin production is low; sexual character confused; leaf index low; leaf mass light; branches opposite and alternating; low female survival rate.
6-10 hours	Growth period lengthened, especially in artificial light; good vegetative development of most plants; sex ratios exceed 1:1 female, with 15-100% more females than males; sexual expression less confused, but flowering somewhat inhibited; seeds are viable; stem elongates and thickens; internodes spaced out; branches predominantly opposite; resin production increases.
11-15 hours	Height at maturity increases; flowering is delayed considerably; seeds are viable; resin production is high; stem is strong; sex ratio dips a bit; sex expression is clear; growth period may be shorter than 6-10 hours in some strains; branches usually alternate; leaf index increases.
16+ hours	Height not increased further; excellent flower and leaf mass; strong production of resin; female survivorship lowered a bit, and sex ratio appears at 1.5:1 female; seeds have slightly lowered vitality; internodes occur between 7-10" along stem; leaf index high.

At any rate, some of the interesting effects of providing increasing light energy for the plants include greater leaf weight, higher leaf index, increased number of flowers, changes in rate of growth & shortening or lengthening of the time required to reach maturity, and the occurrence of branches opposite each other on the stem vs. the occurence of branches on alternating sides of the stem, which means more branches per unit of light.

Most of these variations can be adequately represented in tabular form. It is important to keep in mind that while this chart may appear to give you the ability to control certain factors in your plants, and you will in fact be able to manipulate these factors, the key to understanding does not lie in an ability to control. To reach a level of understanding which will put you into a harmonious relationship with the natural order requires that you analyze your plants with an appreciation of the ecological relationship which exists between the plant, with its hereditary potential on the one hand, and the environment, internal & external, on the other hand. What you will gain by manipulating environment will be a function of the interaction of the plant with the environment, not a simple, passive response. You cannot expect, therefore, that each plant will respond equally to specified changes you make in the environment; neither can you expect to be able to predict exactly how each change you make will affect all plants. You will be dealing with a range of potential responses, and must be prepared for variation.

As was mentioned earlier, a great many of the effects of altering the energy input will be regulated by the nature of the plant's hereditary character. This character is in part determined by the origin of the particular strain which you are using for seed. If your seed is first generation, that is, if it has come from somewhere else, you will find a good deal of variation in its responses to photo-period. After three generations under your care, you will be able to predict, rather accurately, how your plants will react to photoperiod.

The major source of hereditary variation in its response to photoperiod is whether the seed comes from a long-day strain or a short-day strain of Cannabis.

The only concern that will affect most cultivators is that the point of diminishing return for increased hours of light per day is reached sooner with short-day strains than with the long-day varieties. This shows up clearly in the growth cycles of the two types of plants illustrated in chart 11.

As you will see, the break-even point for the two strains occurs at about 7 hours of light per day, with increasing differences after this point showing less return per hour of light expended for the short-day than for the long-day plant. One could draw similar charts for each of the variable illustrated in the table detailing the effects of day length, but this variation just isn't that critical. The only time you would have to worry about short vs. long day differences is if you were going to have to limit the light your plants were getting. In that case, you would be far better off using seeds which came from an area where short days were the rule rather than the exception. Luckily, most of us won't have to hassle with this problem.

Another remote possibility for problems which might arise involves the use of growth stimulants such as gibberellins in combination with long exposure periods. The rule here is that long-day strains will benefit from the combination of stimulants and long exposure, but the effect with short-day strains seems to be a mutual cancellation of the effects, leaving you right back with the same growth pattern you would have had without the use of either. If you plan to use gibberellins, then make sure you have a long-day plant strain first; otherwise, there will be very little gained.

The last important relationship between growth activity in Cannabis and the amount of light which it receives is shown in chart 12. Keep in mind that blooming marks sexual maturity, and that height has very little to do with maturity. Thus, you will see in comparing this chart with others, that while you can get a mature plant relatively quickly by using short photoperiods, it will be very short of stature & with sparse leaves.

With these charts, graphs & tables, hopefully we have clarified some complex relationships. It is important to remember that a graph or chart represents a pretty ideal state, and it further assumes that all other conditions are being held constant. In real life, of course, this will not be the case — conditions will vary simultaneously with one another, and the effects of this variation on the growing plant will be difficult to predict from any one table or chart.

So, it is helpful if you approach cultivation of grass in a frame of mind where you are able to see and deal with the necessary tradeoff situations you will encounter. Keep flexible in your interpretation of the charts, using them as guides and not as absolute predictors of the results you are going to get.

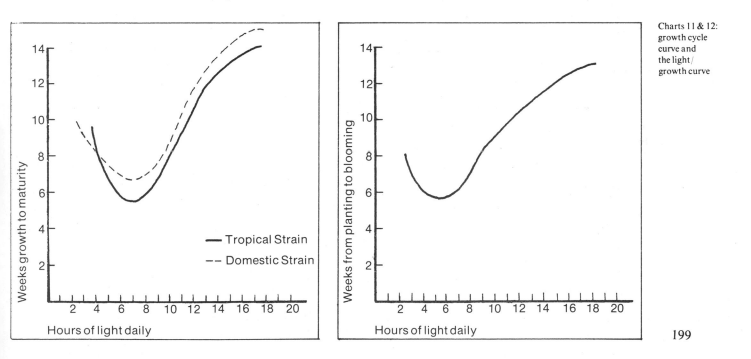

199

Harvesting & Drying

If you've given normal care to your crop of Cannabis, by the time harvest comes you will have put a lot of thought & energy into the plants, and they will be ready to give back what has been invested.

A little care in drying your plants will assure that they will retain the potency and vigor which is present at the moment that they are severed from their roots.

It almost seems too elementary to point this out, but the object of drying is to remove enough moisture from the leaves so that molds can't survive, enzymes can't go to work, and the processes of organic decay, which thrive on water, cannot set in as far as the resin is concerned.

The two factors over which you will want to have some control during drying are (1) the flow of air around the drying plants, and (2) the temperature & moisture content of that air.

Moisture being removed from the plant tissues must be converted to water vapor and then pass from the interior cells of the leaf on through the skin and the stomata and out into the air. The air which is to take up this water vapor should be circulating freely so that it doesn't get saturated and thus resist further uptake. If this happens, the leaves will not dry evenly & thoroughly. A second thing to watch for is that the temperature isn't too high in the drying chamber.

If it is, the water vapor near the surface will boil off quickly, creating a dry gap between the surface of the leaf and the moist interior, causing the skin tissues to shrivel up & resist any further water passage. The water will then be trapped permanently in the interior of the leaf, and the resin content will deteriorate far more rapidly than if it were not exposed to moisture.

When you have decided to build a dryer, there are a few basic sorts of computations it will be helpful to make.

Under normal atmospheric pressure, a drying room with 200 cubic feet of air at 32° F can only hold about an ounce of water vapor. Raise the temperature and you raise the water carrying capacity of the air. For a 200 cubic foot room, the temperature/water curve will look like chart 13.

Temp.	Water	Temp.	Water
32 F	1 oz	150 F	33 oz
70 F	3½ oz	200 F	95 oz
100 F	9 oz	212 F	120 oz

For a 100 cubic foot drying room, divide by half; for a 400 cubic foot room, multiply by two, & so on. This chart assumes that the air will be perfectly dry to begin with, which except in special cases will probably not be true. You can expect your grass to contain about 25-35% water by weight when it is harvested, so this should form a pretty good basis for estimating how much water you are going to have to draw off. You can figure on about double the capacity of the room's air at one of the above temperatures if you replace the air in the room twice an hour, three times its capacity at temperature if the air flow is 600 cubic feet per hour, and beyond that the air will be passing through too quickly to absorb what is coming off the plants, so the calculations get screwed up a bit. But since we are building a dryer and not a wind tunnel, there isn't much need to worry about replacing air that fast.

While you probably won't be passing more than 600 cubic feet per hour through a 200 cubic foot capacity room, it is important to get good air circulation within the room, so that all the leaves have an equal chance to discharge moisture. This means distributing the air and keeping it moving. If it gets saturated passing through the first few trays, it will probably cool & precipitate out some of its moisture on those trays near the vent ducts; and you'll wind up with soggy trays on top, and dry trays on bottom.

You will probably want to base your calculations on how much time to allow your plants for drying on a drying temperature of between 120° and 140° F. Stick with temperatures near the 120° F level in the beginning of the process. If your vents, both intake & exhaust, are big enough to give good circulation without losing temperature too rapidly, you won't have to worry about saturation problems. In the drying chamber we'll look at shortly, the 200 cubic foot model, two square feet of vent space at either end should be plenty, but since conditions like humidity will vary from place to place, it is a good idea to plan on experimenting a little with vent size. There will also be substantial differences in things like leaf thickness and surface area between crops, and these will help in making each drying box an individualized contraption. You can do test runs in your dryer with any green leafy material, checking the trays for uniform drying & changing the vents around to suit your requirements.

Your calculations will look something like this:

I have 100 pounds of grass, good heavy leaves and they look pretty thick, so figure closer to 35% water content. This gives me approximately 35 pounds of water to be drawn off. Setting the temperature in my 200 cubic foot dryer at 120° F, I can run 600 cubic feet of air an hour through and expect to draw off maybe 45-50 ounces of water an hour, figuring for a fair amount of humidity in the air already. That means about three pounds of water an hour, so along about the tenth I better start checking to see how they're coming. Probably it will take closer to fifteen hours, though, because of leaves' thickness.

Anyway, that's one way of gauging your time in drying, and gives you a rough estimate of how long you should leave your plants in the dryer to get them dry enough for storage.

All this assumes that you are not going to hang your crop out in the sunshine to dry, which probably won't happen unless you are really far out in the country, over the river & through the woods. One other consideration, before we run down the dryer plans—if you put the whole plant in the dryer at first, after the leaves begin to show surface dryness, you should sever the leaves from the branches, or at least cut the branches off of the stem. There is a lot of moisture in the stem of the plant, and if it remains attached it will delay the drying process a very long time. Conversely, if you're drying only the leaves, cut your time estimates by about 40% from the examples given above, to compensate for the water which is isolated in the stem and thus irrelevant to the drying process.

Construction of the Drying Box

The Department of Agriculture is a true friend, particularly when it comes to giving really helpful advice on how to do some very groovy things with very little bread. In Farmers' Bulletin No. 1231, *Drying Crude Drugs,* we are given details for construction of a shed which is designed for drying drugs, and it works particularly well for Cannabis, though USDA didn't point that out specifically. Somewhere in pentagonland, however, there is at least one head on the side of the angels.

There are, of course, multiple uses for this little shed, and no herb gatherer should be without one. In the same bulletin we are given plans for a thousand pound capacity dryer, but we'll go on the assumption that very few Cannabis cultivators are going to be this ambitious.

The first step in construction is to lay out & nail together an upright rectangular frame of two by fours. The base of the box should be square so that the trays, also square, will get equal air flow over all surface areas. If the box were deeper than wide, uneven drying would probably develop near the back. USDA recommends trays which measure 3' x 3', so the inside dimensions of the box would have to be about 3' 1" x 3' 1". The upright frame should then be covered inside & out with an insulating material, so that you have smooth walls with an insulating space between. You can fill this space or not, depending on what can be salvaged or bought in your area.

Cleats of wood or aluminum are then nailed on the inside walls to serve as runners for the trays. The positioning of these runners will depend on how many trays you want to have in the box, but the bottom tray shouldn't be too close to the heat source on the floor.

On one side of the box you should have a hinged, sealing door which can be opened to slide the trays in and out for inspection without opening up a whole side. You can install a plastic panel in one of the sides if you are fussy, but it will probably fog up in the drying process.

The trays should be made out of strip lumber

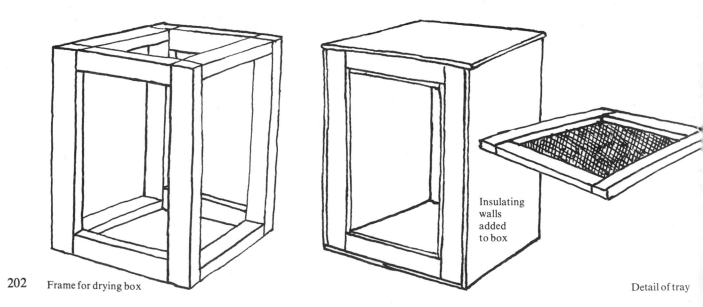

Insulating
walls
added
to box

Frame for drying box

Detail of tray

approximately 1″ x 2″ which is nailed together in a frame with outside dimensions of 3′ x 3′ as mentioned. To this frame you then staple a wire mesh, one-quarter inch mesh is recommended. After the mesh is in place, you will want to attach strips of lathe across the bottom of the tray, front to back, to help the mesh support the weight of the drugs.

The vents will be located at floor level & in the roof of the box, and they should be adjustable. Putting louvered windows in would be a gas, but pretty expensive. A simple adjustable trap door arrangement will work just as well.

The heat source will sit on the floor, and can be anything you want, from a wood stove to an electric heater. If you can use a heat source which operates on a thermostat, so much the better for control of the drying process. You should place a baffle between the heat source and the first tray so that direct heat doesn't reach the drugs.

This dryer should be used indoors in cold and/or damp weather, unless it is adequately insulated.

The drying trays can also be used as sorting & cleaning trays, and you will find that placing a sheet on the floor under the dried leaves and giving each tray a good jostling, starting with the bottom tray, will separate almost all of the seeds & small twiggy stuff.

No herb gatherer should be without one

The government's idea of what a drug dryer should look like

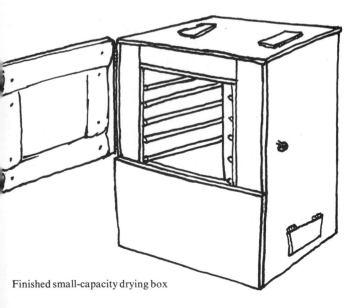

Finished small-capacity drying box

203

Making a Good Plant Better, or
How to Grow Supergrass

We've run down a great many factors having to do
with health & vitality of Cannabis, and we've been
pointing out various ways you can stimulate your plants
to produce maximum leaf mass & resin production. The
issue of real interest, once you have the ability to grow
tall, leafy & healthy grass, becomes how to assure that
the plant will produce a drug of uniform quality and
high potency. There's an awful lot of pure bullshit associated with this problem. Many people believe that drug
potency has something to do with climate, soil, harvesting technique and the like. The real dope, as far as a
scientific explanation is concerned, is that drug potency
in Cannabis Sativa is directly related to the genetic
properties of the plant. These genetic properties can be
easily manipulated, and there is no reason on earth
why the very best grass can't be grown as easily in
Anchorage as in Guererro, nor is there any reason that
Missouri mediocre can't become Ozark outasight.

Changes in the genetic makeup of a living organism can, under positive conditions, be transmitted to its
surviving offspring. One of the many simple changes
which can be transmitted in the plant kingdom is an
alteration in the number of chromosomes in the cells.
Doubling or tripling the numbers of chromosome sets
in a cell induces a change known as polyploidy. Plants
with two complete sets of chromosomes are known as
diploid strains, with three sets as triploid strains, with
four sets as tetraploid strains, and so on. One of the
most dramatic changes which takes place as a plant
moves from the normal diploid state to the polyploid
state is an increase in the plant's overall strength & vitality. Associated with this change is an increase in the
quality of foliage, a richer color, better leaves, fruits,
flowers, and all around good looks.

Under normal conditions, Cannabis is a diploid
plant. This may be thought of as an equilibrium state in
a large population of plants growing in the wild, with
ready access to the genetic materials of many other
normal plants. Occasionally, under certain conditions,
a strain of Cannabis develops which is polyploid. This

is the reason that exceptionally potent grass is associated with these places—areas like the State of Guererro in Mexico, the hills of Panama, parts of the Middle East, and so on. This fact has led, in turn, to the
erroneous conclusion that there are certain factors—
soil, climate, etc—associated with these places which
cause the superior potency, and has caused a lot of
people to despair of growing superior grass because
they couldn't duplicate these growing conditions. *It is
time that this mistaken notion was laid to rest.*

In the early Forties this country was hard at work
trying to produce a Cannabis strain which would yield
a superior quality fiber without any of that 'undesirable
drug, Marijuana.' The Axis powers had cut off our
supply of hemp from overseas, and our Navy didn't
have anything to pull on while chanting yo-heave-ho,
which left a lot of sailors feeling pretty silly. The chemical companies hadn't come up with their miracle fibers
yet, and so mankind was still dependent upon the
natural order for the war effort.

In Washington, a man named HE Warmke was
hard at work under Government contract trying to produce a plant which would tie up ships without turning
on the troops, and he kept reporting failure. He was
messing around with the genetic makeup of a diploid
strain of Cannabis, trying to make rope, and he kept
increasing the potency of the stuff. Poor Government,
what to do?

HE Warmke disappeared from the hemp scene
after his last report in 1943, leaving cultivators a legacy
which, until now, has been buried in an obscure & unlikely little place. He should now become a folk hero,
because HE Warmke has given us a method of inducing
chromosome alterations in Cannabis which will lift the
normal diploid out of its genetic rut and into the rare-
fied state of polyploidy.

In the third & fourth decades of this century, rather
extensive work was done here and in Europe on the alkaloid Colchicine, which is found in the seeds & corms
of saffron. It is a toxic substance often used for treatment of the gout. The use of Colchicine to induce polyploidy has become standard practice in the plant breeding industry, and many of the contempory ornamental

plants owe their luxuriousness & vitality to the presence of double sets of chromosomes induced through Colchicine treatment.

Colchicine acts only on plant cells which are in the process of division, so to be effective, it must be applied to those regions where there is a high proportion of dividing cells. There are three areas of interest to cultivators of Cannabis — the germinating seed, the rapidly sprouting seedling, and the growing tip of branches & stems. HE Warmke reported failure — he grew very potent Cannabis, potent far beyond the range of the normal diploid female, with the use of Colchicine to induce a polyploid state.

But let's put in a warning right here:

Colchicine is a highly poisonous substance. It can kill you. No research is available on the effects of smoking or ingesting first generation Cannabis which has become polyploid through colchicine treatment. It is not known whether colchicine is metabolized or not. So only successive generations of Cannabis — generations number two on out — should be considered safe.

In addition, great care should be exercised in handling Colchicine. It should not come in contact with the skin, the eyes, or anything else!

You will probably need a prescription to obtain Colchicine, unless you have a pipeline to a biology lab.

One way of treating Cannabis with Colchicine is to add Colchicine to the starting solution in which you soak your seeds before putting them in the germination beds. Use a strength between 0.05 & 0.15% Colchicine in distilled water. Many of the plants will fail to germinate. This is the effect of Colchicine. Those plants which do germinate & survive will be polyploid Cannabis. The problem with using Colchicine at this period of the plant's life is that the embryo is going to have a very tenuous grasp on life anyway, and the jolt from this poison will finish off an inordinate number of them.

A second, somewhat more satisfactory, but more complicated method of treatment involves plants which are two to three weeks old. Plants chosen for the treatment should be very healthy. If you plan to give the treatment at this stage, it will be best if you combine the treatment with transplantation. This means that the plants will have to stay in their germinating beds longer than usual, and so the beds should be large enough to handle the root systems which will be developing.

Proceed with transplantation in the normal manner; but, because the transplant won't be finished as quickly as usual, the roots & ball of soil should be protected from light, heat & drying out. Holding the ball of soil gently, invert the plant and immerse the growing tips & topmost sets of leaves in a solution of .05-.15% Colchicine. Hold the plant in the solution for a minute or less, and then proceed with the transplant. Make sure that none of the solution dribbles down to get onto the roots. This will kill the plant for sure. Many of the seedlings will die anyway, but those which survive will be polyploid. So will their offspring.

There is a third method for treating Cannabis which involves waiting until the plants are at least 10″ high, but anytime after that is all right, too. The only thing with this method is that the whole plant won't be

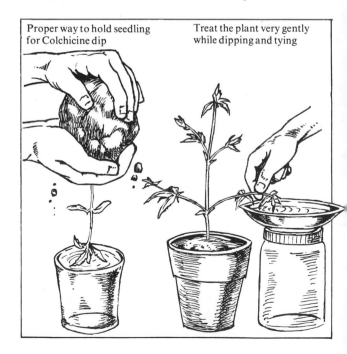

Proper way to hold seedling for Colchicine dip

Treat the plant very gently while dipping and tying

polyploid, only the treated portions. The benefit derived is that the plant as a whole has a good chance of survival.

Treating the plant with this approach can involve several alternative operations. The easiest is to place a little container of the .05-.15% Colchicine solution next to the plant, bend the growing tip or the tip of one of the little branches over and tie it down gently so that it is immersed in the solution. An hour or so at a time is adequate, but plants are going to vary in their health and so there are no absolute limits. Be prepared to lose a few plants, and experiment a little. This operation should be repeated several times, leaving a couple of hours for recovery between dips, and then discontinue to allow the plant to recover. Those parts which have been immersed will wither & appear to die, but some will regenerate and will have become polyploid.

Another way of going about essentially the same thing is to lodge little balls of cotton between the youngest leaves at the growing tip and at the nodes and moisten the cotton occasionally with some of the Colchi-

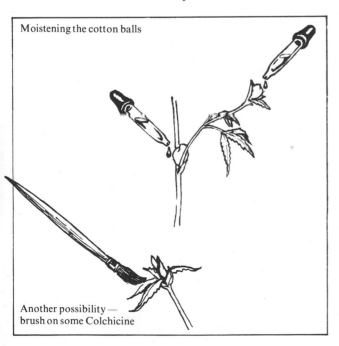

Moistening the cotton balls

Another possibility — brush on some Colchicine

cine solution. This operation can be kept going for several days, after which the cotton should be removed and treatment discontinued.

The first noticeable results of Colchicine treatment will be, as mentioned, immediate growth retardation lasting anywhere from days to weeks. The higher the strength of the solution and the lower the overall health of the plants, the higher an attrition rate can be expected. No matter what, some of the plants will not make it. As the survivors recover & grow, the parts which develop will usually be disfigured and abnormal in appearance. As growth continues, however, the defective tissue is sloughed off or left behind and the new branch & leaf tissues will become relatively homogeneous, and some should have become polyploid.

You will be able to distinguish polyploid areas from diploid because they will be thicker with more, darker green leaves, larger flowers & seeds (ultimately) and they are more hairy (though hemp does not exhibit markedly increased hairiness as a rule).

There is a relatively simple plant breeding technique which might be used by serious cultivators of Cannabis in establishing a polyploid variety. After Cannabis treated with Colchicine has resumed growth and polyploid stems become distinguished from diploid, buds which are in the axils of polyploid leaves can be forced into growth and will produce an entire branch with polyploid characteristics.

The suggested procedure would be to take a treated & fully recovered immature female Cannabis plant, locate the buds in question and cut off the end of the shoot from that leaf outward. The bud will then be forced into growth, and flowers & seeds produced by that shoot upon maturity of the plant will be polyploid in character. Offspring produced from those seeds will, then, be largely or wholly polyploid and therefore higher in drug content & potency.

But please remember, **only second and subsequent generation plants are safe to use, because first generation may contain enough lethal Colchicine to kill! Plants treated with this stuff also should not be grown where any person or animal can get to them! Please be careful!**

Only second and subsequent generation plants are safe to use

207

Producing an Unrecognizable Hybrid

In the course of its investigations in the early 40's, which we've just mentioned, aimed at producing a hemp plant which was long on fiber and short on the active drug principle in marijuana, the US Government also sponsored extensive research into methods of altering the vegetative characteristics of Cannabis Sativa. This research effort covered much old ground, in most cases repeating the genetic manipulation experiments of the twenties, but there was a good deal of original & innovative work done as well.

Perhaps the most significant work done on alteration of appearance was sponsored jointly by a private foundation in Washington and a major eastern university, in work done for the government as part of the war effort in searching for the strong fiber/no drug hemp plant strain. These research efforts resulted in some spectacularly unsuccessful plants, which were hybrids as potent as 'good drug quality Cannabis Sativa but which were botanically of an altogether different genus. The report states that 'Reciprocal grafts were made, at ground level, between . . . hemp and hops, (Humulus Lupulus). Those combinations in which hemp stems were grafted onto hops roots failed, but the combination of hops stems on hemp roots were successful & permitted assays to be made. Hops leaves from these unions were found to contain as much drug as leaves from intact hemp plants, even though leaves from intact hops plants were completely nontoxic.' HE Warmke was right in there once again.

There are many reasons why cultivators might wish to grow hybrid hops/hemp, and we won't indulge in speculation on these reasons. If you hanker to grow some of these freaky plants, however, there are a series of relatively simple steps which may be undertaken with good chances of success in creating the hemp/hops hybrid.

Grafting is not a fundamentally difficult operation in most cases, though certain conditions should prevail to assure success. The primary consideration is whether or not the scion (the plant part to be grafted) and the stock (the plant part to receive the graft) are closely related, preferably within the same botanical family. Hops & Cannabis are closely related plants, though in appearance they are quite distinct, and so there are no problems with this form of incompatability. This botanical similarity is not in itself enough to assure success, however, because botanical classifications are based largely on the reproductive characteristics of plants, and not on the total range of compatible conditions needed for solid & viable grafts.

A second potential hangup in grafting plants is the biochemical similarity or dissimilarity of the scion and stock donors. Again, Cannabis & Hops share quite similar biochemical constituents, particularly those of the tissue fluids and the organic composition of the mature plant.

A final requisite pre-condition to successful grafting is that the fluid-carrying tissues achieve close, uniform contact at the graft, or at least that they can be locked in close enough contact in the graft that the essential plant fluids can circulate. So not only should the gross structures match up, but the fluid-carrying tissues should be closely related in structure, and this condition is adequately met in the hemp/hops graft union, provided the graft takes place at certain points in the growth cycle of scion & stock. These points will be covered further on.

Grafters attempting the hops/hemp union should attempt to get shoots from polyploid hops — the same rationale applies for the hybrid plants as applied for potency in grass. Two polyploid strains of hops available commercially are *Brewer's Gold* and *Bullion Hop*.

Cannabis & Hops share similar biochemical constituents Illustration: Handbook of Plant and Floral Ornament by Richard Hatton

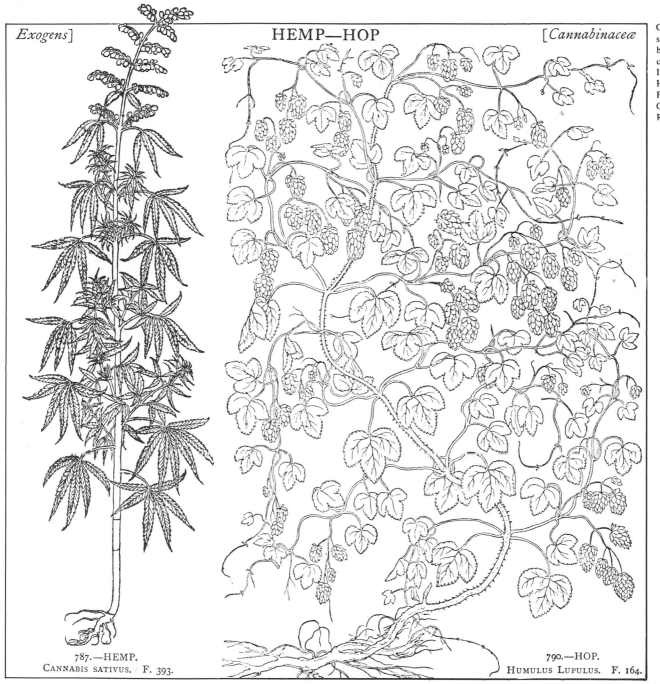

787.—HEMP.
CANNABIS SATIVUS. / F. 393.

790.—HOP.
HUMULUS LUPULUS. F. 164.

Preparation of the Scion and Stock

The graft which is suggested to cultivators by the experimental results described earlier is between the roots of Cannabis Sativa and the stem or shoot of Humulus Lupulus. As is the case with many drug plants, the active principle in grass seems to be manufactured in or controlled by mechanisms found in the root. The method commonly known as *wedge grafting* seems to be most suitable for this particular combination of plants, and several methods will be dealt with so that cultivators will have a choice of approaches to their task. These variations are known, respectively, as the *straight wedge, or cleft, graft; the wedge graft in the cotyledon stage; and the growing point wedge graft*. These methods and others are thoroughly & competently discussed in many books on the subject, and perhaps the best of the lot is the book by Garner (1958) which is cited in the bibliography and which should be reviewed if available.

Wedge Graft

Simple wedge-grafting is the most straightforward approach available to those who want to perform the hops/hemp operation. The scion of hops is prepared by selecting a shoot which is vigorous, polyploid if possible, and which is the same diameter at its base as the Cannabis stock is at the point where the stem is to be severed. The Cannabis stock would be, for this method, about five to six weeks old and it should be a well-established and healthy plant. Cultivators who have been supplementing their young Cannabis plants with stimulants or powerful organic or synthetic nutrient solutions should be especially careful that the root system of the plants chosen for stock are strong & well-founded in the soil. The hops scion may be obtained either by growing hops plants from seed; or cutting; or may, in some cases, be purchased from a reputable nursery.

The Cannabis stock is prepared by splitting it at the top, where the plant has been severed about an inch and a half above ground level, lengthwise for about one-half to three-quarters of an inch, using a thin, sharp blade.

After the Cannabis stock has been prepared as shown, the scion of hops is inserted so that there is a good match between the fluid-carrying tissues. The scion is then tied in place with raffia, a thick, flat rubber band, or any similar *flat* tying material. Flatness is desirable because it distributes the binding force equally over the union, encouraging circulation of fluids & uniform healing of the wound. There should be a minute portion of the raw tissue of the scion hops protruding just above the top of the stock when the graft is tied off.

This graft requires the use of a sealing agent. Commercial graft sealing agents should be totally satisfactory, or the really purist cultivator can concoct his own from any one of several recipes available at nurseries where the waxes, tallows and pitches are sold. Many cultivators find that crude petroleum jelly works very well as a graft sealing agent, but this should be used only when the tying material is not rubber, because rubber deteriorates and will break before the union is strong if it is exposed to crude petroleum jelly. Jelly,

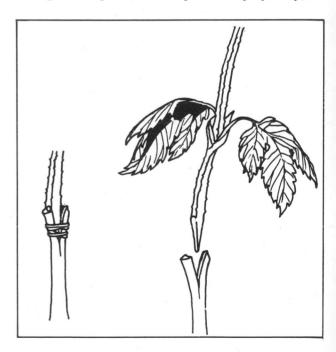

however, has the advantage of being cheap, plentiful & easily available.

Cotyledon Wedge Graft

The second grafting method we'll cover is the wedge graft at the cotyledon stage, which has several advantages over the method just outlined, and which may appeal to some cultivators. This graft is normally successful over a wider range of plants than the simple wedge, and has shown good experimental results when used with a hemp stock & hops scion.

When the Cannabis seedling has developed its first pair of true leaves, sometime during the second week under normal conditions, the cultivator may initiate grafting procedures or may wait until the second pair of leaves develops a few days later. For the cotyledon wedge graft, one should wait no longer than this point.

Preparation of the Cannabis seedling stock consists of severing the stem just above the first pair of true leaves. The stem is then split, using a thin, sharp blade, down between these leaves about one quarter to three-eighths of an inch. The split should be made so that each leaf is attached to one half of the stem (A).

The hops scion should come from a plant or a sprout of approximately the same age as the Cannabis stock. The scion should be cut off at the ground and shaped into a wedge just below the cotyledons (B). The prepared scion is then inserted into the split Cannabis stock and tied with raffia, a thin rubber strip, or sterile surgical cotton.

If the scion hops plant is not readily available in an early enough stage, and it becomes necessary to use a more mature seedling, the scion leaves should be trimmed to prevent as much water loss as possible (C). Care should also be taken that the grafted plants are not overexposed to nitrogen at this point under these conditions, as excess nitrogen promotes water loss, particularly in the early growth stages of both hops & hemp. The trimmed scion should then be shaped into a wedge (D), tied with any of the materials already discussed or, better yet in this instance, secured with self-sealing rubber (E) available through all nursery supply outlets.

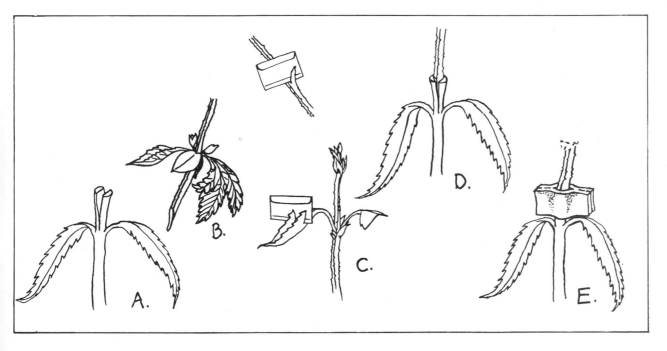

Whichever scion/stock combination is used for the cotyledon graft, the plant should be placed in some sort of a glass or plastic case which protects it from exposure to over-dryness, temperature changes and fungal or bacterial infestation until the union has healed, which should take about a week to set firmly. This protection is much more vital if the cotyledon graft approach is used than if the simple wedge graft is employed.

Growing Point Wedge Graft

This is the third successful approach which can be used in making the hemp/hops combination plant. The method is very similar to the cotyledon wedge graft in many respects. The hops scion should be as young as possible, as in cotyledon grafting, and preparation of the scion is exactly the same. The Cannabis stock, which should be in its fifth to seventh week of life, healthy & well-rooted, should be cut off at the growing tip and cleared of all but the first and second sets of leaves (A). The severed end of the Cannabis stock should then be split about a half-inch, and the formed hops scion inserted and fixed in the same fashion as the cotyledon wedge graft (B). A sleeve of very thin plastic is then fitted as in (C) and the grafted plant allowed to recover for a week, after which the plastic can be removed.

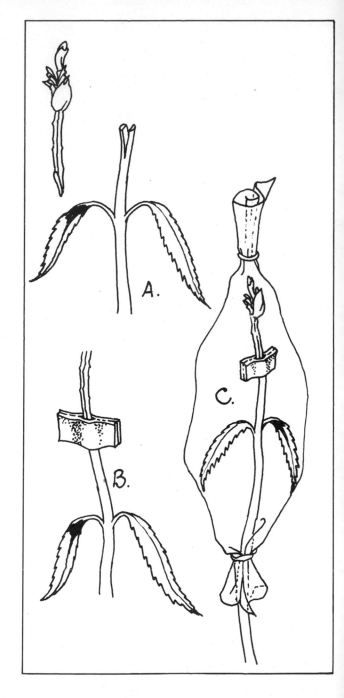

'It was the 8.29 every morning until I discovered Cannabis'

The effect is shattering

CANNABIS

Botany & cultivation. With apologies to Smirnoff Vodka, an advertisement from *Friends,* November, 1970 Photograph: Phil Franks

213

All of these grafting operations will, if successful, produce a plant which will look like hops, which in fact it will be. The leaves, however, will have taken up the active principle manufactured by the Cannabis root stock and the hops resin will be as potent as that of high quality grass.

Rather than go into a whole dissertation on the cultivation of hops, we'll just make some brief comments. Hops is very similar to Cannabis in its soil requirements, water needs, response to photoperiod and in almost all other aspects of cultivation technique. Because of this fortunate coincidence, you may treat secretgrass just as you would Cannabis, with one significant exception.

Hops is a vine-like climbing plant which reaches lengths of twenty to thirty feet as a matter of course. It needs supports on which to climb, and there are a variety of arbor arrangements which hops growers use. There are as many designs for stringing an arbor as there are hops growers, and design is not an essential concern for those of you planning to experiment with the grafting plants. The only real guideline to keep in mind is that the higher the arbor, and the less crowded the hops vines, the more leaves they will want to produce.

There are some very good descriptions and layouts of various sorts of arbor-arrangements for growing hops in the Garner book noted in the bibliography, a book that should be available through any decent library.

A 7'6" hashish pipe/totem, Berkeley, 1971 Photograph: Annie Leibovitz

The government relies heavily on a procedure called the Duquesnois test to establish the presence of the active principle of grass in vegetable matter suspected of being marijuana. This test was first reported in the Journal of the Egyptian Medical Society in 1938 and is used pretty much cookbook fashion in most places. It is basically a color-change test, and the presence of Cannabinol and/or Cannabidiol reacts with the test solution of acetalehyde, vanillin-HC1 to change the liquid from a clear solution to a clear blue which becomes somewhat opaque and darker on standing. Since secret-grass will contain these active principles, the Duquenois test will react to it as if it were grass. That's not the whole issue, however, because the government often uses other tests to establish whether or not grass is grass, and these won't work with secretgrass. For one thing, Cannabis Sativa has some characteristic leaf structures which can be readily identified through a microscope. Structures such as the tiny hairs on the underside of the leaves, and the characteristic resin ducts of Cannabis show up clearly in these examinations. These structures will not be present in the hops/ hemp plant, which will be vegetatively indistinguishable from Humulus Lupulus. The only structures on the original grafted plant identifiable as Cannabis Sativa would be the root. It is very difficult to establish beyond reasonable doubt that grass is grass by the root alone, because its structure and appearance is by no means unique. Needless to say, second generation hybrid secretgrass will be impossible to identify on the basis of vegetative structures alone. Which brings us back around to the infamous test of one Duquesnois, lately of Cairo & points west.

The test is considered positive — the killer weed is present — when the solution turns blue after the suspect material has been added. Any prosecuting agency must specify the material it is getting hysterical about, and it would seem that the wide range of stuff that reacts with the Duquesnois solution would make this job very difficult. The test shouldn't be able to discriminate effectively between high grade hash & low grade canary food containing sterilized hemp seed, because it is used to confirm or deny the presence of the active principle, not its concentration, and hemp seed does contain resin — 1.6% by weight. It would be interesting to see whether the government was able to prove in certain cases that the substance some free soul was busted for possessing was *not* concentrated bird food for his far out parakeet.

The Duquesnois test does not appear to discriminate between Cannabinol & Cannabidiol, the one containing the active principle of marijuana and the other containing no such thing. Structures very similar to each substance, however, occur widely in the vegetable world, partially hydrogenated cannabinols, isomers of cannabidiol, or unsaturated molecules resembling cannabidiol.

Other speculative trips: Who says what blue is, and how blue is blue?

What if other plants or substances turn the Duquesnois solution a pretty shade of blue?

The Duquesnois test.

215

One of the flowers the flower people have been growing this year is the towering cannabis sativa, with its fronds of pretty saw-toothed leaves which Queen Mary used to admire so much. The male plant used to be harvested for hemp for the rope industry, but it is the female plant with its flowering tops which has been attracting the amateur gardener. When dried and smoked like tobacco it releases the drug tetrahydrocannabinol, whose effects many young people apparently prefer to those of alcohol.

Word leaking through from the Underground suggests that this year's sunny summer and late autumn sunshine has enabled this sub-tropical plant to grow on unlikely English sites, railway cuttings, canal banks, country farms, and remote greenhouses from Kent to Cornwall. But as Section 16 of the Dangerous Drugs Act provides for fines up to £1,000 and imprisonment up to ten years, it's hard to get a cannabis grower to talk. In view of this we are extremely grateful to gardeners Fred Digme and Percy High.

Percy: First thing we ought to make clear, Fred, is if you know enough to grow the plant you probably wouldn't; you'd get some decent stuff from a dealer.

Fred: That's right, Perce, as highs go, English grass gives you a pretty low high. You need a climate like Mexico, Abyssinia, Brazil for good grass.

Percy: You've got to have it growing under proper greenhouse conditions; humidity 65 per cent, steady temperature of 70° F. I don't believe all this nonsense about growing it out on railway cuttings.

Fred: Unless you're lucky and find some hemp seeds in a packet of budgie food, you'll have to get some seed from a consignment of commercial grass. The stuff at the moment isn't very good, because it was picked too early, and you'll have germination trouble.

Percy: Put the seeds in a pot, water with water at 70° F., and if everything's OK there should be a sign of growth in ten days.

Fred: Within two months it'll grow to the height of six feet or more, so you'll have to transplant to make room for the root growth.

Percy: Oh-aah. Now you should bring on the flowering by gradually decreasing the amount of light. When they start to flower you can recognise the female plant by the different kind of stamens.

Fred: I take it that it's not illegal to grow the male plant, Perce?

Percy: You have me there, Fred. Now you dry the flowery tops gently, put them in your pipe and smoke them. If you're greedy you might use some of the coarser leaves. A good plant will yield about four ounces of the stuff.

Fred: Is there anything you should specially look out for, Perce?

Percy: An early frost, or much worse, a late police raid, Fred.

Atticus, *The Sunday Times* (UK), November, 1970.

Professions of the 70's Cannabis grower from the *Sunday Times,* © November, 1970. Drawn by Michael Heath.

**Appendix three:
Detecting Opiate Adulteration**

While this chapter contains most, if not all, of the technical knowledge which anyone would need to grow grass, a considerable number of people who will read it do not intend to join the ranks of cultivators of the killer weed. It's probably fair to say, however, that most such non-agrarian folks have & do, from time to time, indulge in just a teeny toke. Among friends.

For these gentle protestors, with only a battered constitution between them and the long arms, this next section is specifically intended. Just as in the supermarket vegetable section, you can never tell where your grass is coming from, what it's been through, and what's been added unless you grow your own.

People who can't or won't sow a seed can still take a few precautions to guard against adulteration of their grass — an increasingly serious problem. The most common adulterants are the opiates, and there are some very simple tests — using inexpensive chemicals and very few implements — with which one can test grass for specific kinds of opiate adulterations. Before running through the tests, let's distinguish among the many varieties of the opiate family.

Collection and Preparation of Crude Opium

Opium varies considerably in quality & physical/chemical properties with the climate in which it is grown and the methods used in its preparation. Methods of collection of the raw material for the drug do not vary much from country to country.

After the heat of the day is past, around 3 or 4 pm, the plant's seed capsules are incised using a three or four-bladed knife. Cuts are made to a depth of precisely 1/12″. This incision in the outer skin is enough to start the milky latex flowing. Each plant undergoes several incisings at intervals of two or three days; extremely fruitful plants can be milked up to ten times before they are drained of their juices & die.

During the temperate nights, the milky juice coagulates on the sides of the seed capsule and on the upper parts of the stem, from which it is scraped each morning and placed into pottery vessels. Upon settling in these vessels, the coagulated material separates into two parts. The upper portion of the mass becomes a wet, somewhat granular pinkish tapioca-like substance

OPIUM POPPY

PAPAVER SOMNIFERUM

and the lower portion becomes a dark brown fluid called passewa. The firm upper mass is separated & placed in the shade, where it air-cures for from three to four weeks. During the curing the mass sets & changes color gradually to a soft dark brown, deepening in color with age & temperature/humidity conditions until it finally becomes raw opium of commerce.

Opiates are a valuable medicinal drug series, and opium itself is used mainly for its sedative, pain-suppressant qualities. When taken internally in medicinal doses, opium acts first as a stimulant, then successively as a narcotic, pain-reliever & antispasmodic. In small dosages, it is primarily a stimulant, whereas in large dosages its effects are blended and it is a powerful, occasionally lethal poison. Opium is most useful in combatting various forms of mucous inflammation & irritation — catarrh, bronchorrhea, diarrhea, etc. It is also frequently prescribed in diabetes, fevers, colic, vomiting, dysentery and other amoebic & organic disorders.

Crude or raw opium comes in the form of a thick, soft but firm, chestnut to dark brown mass which may be cut into angular chunks with a knife, but which is also pliable enough to be molded with the fingers. It is very malleable & plastic when fresh, becoming brittle with age. It has a characteristic narcotic, but pleasant odor and a persistent, bitter & acrid taste. It normally feels greasy to the touch, and globules of oil usually form on a cut surface, particularly where the raw opium has been oil-processed. Raw opium is graded by aroma, color, touch, texture, specific gravity, consistency & degree of adulteration. The grading scale corresponds with that of gold, with 24 carat opium being pure, raw, first-class drug.

Opium can be tested for quality either by the experienced estimator or by the scientific analyst. The experienced estimator has several reliable methods of gauging the quality of opium after determining that the material offered for sale is in fact opium.

Consistency of the drug can be fairly accurately determined by feel, but some of the more subtle adulterants can only be detected through measurements of specific gravity. The color of a sample is tested by

Opium valuable medicinal drug, and dangerous poison

219

pressing a small piece between two pieces of glass and looking at a powerful light source. The texture of high quality opium is waxy, and a smooth shiny surface can be produced by rubbing. This texture can be either granular or homogeneous, however, depending on how the drug has been processed; but normally the darker varieties are more granular. When a piece of raw opium is drawn out between the fingers, the granular variety should break, leaving an angular surface long before the strand becomes thin; while the homogeneous varieties should draw out into long, thin strings without breaking. Actual morphia content analysis requires fairly rigorous scientific testing, and normally only those engaged in the legal market where the drug is being purchased for medicines are concerned about the morphia content. There are, however, several general principles which govern probable morphia content which enter into the consideration of the price of the raw drug regardless of its intended ultimate destination.

Morphia content varies widely from one point of origin to another. Opium from poppies grown in hill country normally contains more morphia than opium from poppies grown on the plains. Opium which is fresh contains more morphia than opium which is old, other things being equal. Opium which has been quickly dried has more morphia than opium which has taken a long time drying.

Photograph:
Hank Lebo,
Good Times,
November, 1970

While this section will be concerned primarily with the use of the opiates in adulterating grass, the opiates themselves often undergo interesting adulterations.

The relatively high price for illicit opium, coupled with a consistently strong & increasing demand based on the needs of millions of addicts, has resulted in a widespread practice of adulterating the drug as it passes through the hands of middlemen. The chief adulterants are powdered poppy trash, dried fruits, turpentine, gums, ground stone, lead oxides, clay, sand, soot, manure, grain flours, betel nut, butter, fruit and milk sugars, charcoal, a paste of sesame seed & beans, licorice, mucilage, and various other vegetable pulps, pastes, & extracts. The grosser adulterants can be detected by smell, feel, and sight; but many of the more subtle adulterants are undetectable without resort to

elaborate tests.

Testing for Opium-Adulteration

While grass is adulterated with many grades of opium, the most commonly used is the low-grade Passewa, the dregs of the manufacturing of raw opium. Both grass & tobacco are adulterated with Passewa in many countries, but in America only the grass freak needs to get uptight about opiates, if he chooses to.

The symptoms of an opiate hit are somewhat different from those of organic grass — a feeling of heavy lassitude, a warmth & tingling in the extremities, a giddy feeling verging on nausea when you move up & around which disappears if you sit or lie down, a fullness in the head & particularly the ears, and a dull hangoverish feeling for the next day or so. Symptoms such as these are pretty idiosyncratic, but anyone experiencing them when smoking unfamiliar grass might realistically become suspicious. In that case, there are several tests for opium he might want to perform.

One useful & easily performed test consists of washing the suspected grass thoroughly in a bowl of water. The resin won't go into the solution, but after vigorous rubbing & pounding & splashing about in the bowl the opium or Passewa, if any, will dissolve in water.

A small amount of this solution is then placed in a test tube and a few drops of a ferric chloride are added. If solution opium is present a red color will appear, and the depth of the red will give a rough indication of the proportion of opium present in the material — the deeper the color, the more opium.

This red color can be produced by other adulterants, however, and further confirmatory tests are required. Using the same test tube of solution as before, add one drop of hydrochloric acid to the already red solution. Upon heating over a low flame, if the red color disappears, the substance either was not opium or there is very little opium present. If the red color holds, the assurance that the substance is opium grows stronger. A further test is necessary, however, because adulterants could still be affecting the solution.

Taking another test tube of original, clear solu-

tion, a little lead acetate is added. If the test solution contains opium, a white precipitate will appear. This precipitate will, however, disappear readily if a few drops of nitric acid are added to the test solution.

If positive reactions are experienced in the above series of tests, the substance may be assured to be opium. Several other tests are available, and are regularly used by both police & dealers.

To a solution of .5% selenious acid in sulphuric acid, add a crushed sample of the material suspected of containing opium. If opium is present, the solution will turn blue, gradually changing through green to an organic brown.

Taking a dry crushed sample of the suspected substance, stir in a few drops of potassium hydroxide. Then add a few drops of ether. Moisten a strip of untreated fiber paper with the ether-potassium hydroxide solution and let it dry. Repeat several times. After three cycles, expose the paper to steam. If it turns red, opium is present.

Adulteration of grass with the more sophisticated, complex & more highly toxic forms of opiate drugs is not too common, primarily because the economics of such a practice are prohibitive. While Passewa is a cheap by-product of processing crude opium, the opiate drugs further down the line are expensive & relatively scarce. Only under special conditions would anyone have to be concerned that grass was adulterated with morphine, codeine, or heroin.

The tests for the presence of these drugs, and a brief description of their properties, are included in this book because knowing how to test for the opiates may, in some cases, come in handy as a survival skill in a society & subculture where survival is often severely threatened.

Opium Derivatives — Morphine

Morphine is probably the most important alkaloid of opium, though the negative sides of its sister alkaloid heroin are more widely felt. It was the first alkaloid isolated from opium, and is a widely used medicine. It is administered both by ingestion & hypodermic, and acts as an anodyne, sedative, hypnotic & diaphoretic. It is extremely poisonous. For non-addicts, swallowing two to three grains is usually fatal. For non-addicts, hypodermic injections of 1/6 grain pure morphine for adult males and 1/10 grain for adult females are the maximum safe dosages. People addicted to opiates can, of course, tolerate amounts far in excess of these dosages, but that doesn't mean that such amounts represent safe limits, only that under special conditions — addiction — the limits are moved outward a bit.

Pure morphine appears in the form of small, white to clear, odorless shining rhombic crystals; in fine, needle-like prisms; or as a crystalline powder. It will not deteriorate when exposed to air under normal room conditions. It has a specific gravity of 1.32, an alkaline ph reaction, and a very bitter taste. It unites readily with acids to form salts, most of which dissolve easily in water. Morphine is soluble in fixed as well as volatile oils; in fixed caustic alkali solutions; in lime water; and is somewhat soluble in caustic ammonia. It is very slightly soluble in cold water; more soluble in boiling water; quite soluble in cold alcohol; and very soluble in boiling alcohol. One gram of pure morphine needs 3340 cc of cold water to go completely into solution; 1220 cc of chloroform; 1075 cc of boiling water; 210 cc of cold alcohol; and 98 cc of boiling alcohol. A saturated water solution of morphine will test very slightly acid with litmus paper. Morphine is insoluble in benzine and almost insoluble in ether. It commonly appears as a hydrochloride, a sulphate, and an acetate.

Morphine hydrochloride is prepared by dissolving morphine in water with a little bit of hydrochloric acid, then evaporating the solution until crystals of morphine appear. Morphine hydrochloride is quite odorless, will not dissolve in chloroform or ether. One gram of morphine hydrochloride will dissolve in 17.55 cc of water or 52 cc of alcohol at 25° C, or .5 cc of boiling water or

Laboratory Room No 3; Bulgarian heroin & morphine processing factory, 1930's.

223

46 cc of alcohol at 60° C. Morphine hydrochloride is sold as a white to colorless microcrystalline powder, in white shining needle-like crystals, or as a packed, crystalline cube. It has a very bitter taste verging on horrible.

Morphine sulphate is perhaps the most common form of the drug. Its preparation is similar to that of morphine hydrochloride except that sulphuric acid is substituted for hydrochloric. Morphine sulphate is insoluble in ether & chloroform, but one gram dissolves readily in 15.5 cc of water or 565 cc of alcohol at 25° C; or in .7 cc water at 80° C; or 240 cc alcohol at 60° C. Morphine sulphate sold in solution normally has a strength of one grain to one fluid ounce.

Acetate of Morphia is prepared by treating an aqueous solution of morphine with acetic acid. It is distinguished from the other morphine preparations by a faint odor of acetone — like nail polish remover.

There are many tests for the presence of morphine compounds, but they share a common fault in that the substance being tested should be as close to pure morphine as possible in order for the tests to be fully reliable. In cases where grass is suspect, the testing will be complicated by the presence of many of the organic compounds which are integral to grass. Some of the more reliable tests which would be of some use in such cases are:

Mix the suspected material with approximately six times its weight of pure sugar, then add a few drops of concentrated sulphuric acid. If the substance is morphine, the mixture will show a red color at once, the color gradually changing to green and finally to a brownish yellow. If the suspected substance is already in solution, dissolve as much white sugar as possible in a test tube of the solution, then add a few drops of sulphuric acid, plus a drop or two of bromine water. The solution will turn red, then green, then brown-yellow if morphine is present.

A confirming test involves sulphuric acid mixed with a solution of selenious acid in a ratio of .005 grams of selenious acid per mil of sulphuric acid. This test applied to suspected substances will yield the following color changes:

Morphine: blue to green & then to brown.
Codeine: green to blue & then to organic green.

If the color changes do not occur, or occur out of sequence, it is fairly certain that the substance either is not morphine or a closely related alkaloid; or is morphine, but heavily adulterated with another similar-appearing and tasting substance such as quinine, a common adulterant.

Opium Derivatives — Heroin

Heroin is diacetyl-morphine, $C_{21}H_{23}O_3N$. It is a white crystalline alkaloid, an acetyl derivative of morphine. It is used medicinally as an anodyne & sedative in the treatment of coughs, bronchitis, bronchial asthma and pneumonia. It is one of the most toxic of the addictive opiates.

Heroin is prepared by heating morphine with an acetyl chloride solution, washing the product with cold water & a diluted solution of sodium carbonate, then crystallizing out the heroin by treatment with boiling alcohol which evaporates quickly, taking the water with it.

Heroin appears on the market as a white crystalline, odorless powder which is soluble in chloroform and alcohol, less soluble in ether and still less in pure water. It melts between 171.5° & 173° C.

Heroin possesses the therapeutic properties of morphine, but requires smaller doses to be equally as effective. Because of this property, it can be used medically with less risk of addiction. On the illicit drug market, however, this same property becomes a liability because of the increased chance of addiction when compared to the addictive potential of the same quantities of similar opiate derivatives.

Tests for heroin are relatively straightforward. If grass suspected of being dusted with heroin is dissolved in a few drops of nitric acid, and a yellow is produced which changes gradually to a green-blue, the presence of heroin is confirmed. An equally simple test involves mixing the suspect grass with a little alcohol and an equal amount of sulphuric acid. If the smell of fingernail polish remover is strongly in evidence, there is a very strong likelihood that diacetyl-morphine (or pure heroin) is present.

Another common form which heroin can take is heroin-hydrochloride (diacetyl-morphine hydrochloride and diamorphine hydrochloride), prepared by treating heroin with hydrochloric acid. The powder obtained from the process is a white, odorless, crystalline substance which has a bitter taste; is soluble in water or alcohol, but not in ether or chloroform. It has a melting point of 230° C. The addition of silver nitrate to an aqueous solution of diacetylmorphine hydrochloride will cause the formation of a white precipitate which is insoluble in nitric acid. Heroin hydrochloride dissolves in nitric acid, producing a yellow which changes gradually to a green-blue, then back to yellow once again.

Opium Derivatives — Codeine

Codeine is a narcotic alkaloid derived from opium with a chemical formula $C_{12}H_{21}O_3N \bullet H_2O$. It is obtained by heating morphine which has been placed in solution with methyl iodide and soda or potassium salt. Pure codeine is colorless & translucent, appearing either in rhombic crystals or as a white crystalline powder. Codeine is colorless, but gives a stinging taste. It is a highly soluble alkaloid, dissolving readily in ether, water, chloroform or alcohol. Its medicinal value lies in its sedative effects, and it is widely used in treatment of diabetes, mellitus, and bronchial irritations & infections.

If codeine were dusted on grass it would be quite difficult to test for its presence with a high degree of reliability. The most accurate tests under these circumstances would be:

One mil of sulphuric acid with .005 gram of selenious acid produces a green changing rapidly to blue, then slowly to a dark, organic green in the presence of codeine.

Codeine can be distinguished from morphine as follows: blend .05 gram of the suspected material with 2 cc of nitric acid. If the liquid becomes yellow & the yellow holds, it is codeine; if the yellow goes to red, it is morphine.

More common than pure codeine are its two salts — codeine phosphate & codeine sulphate. Codeine sulphate is more heavily narcotic than codeine phosphate,

though both are widely used in medicine.

To recapitulate briefly: adulteration of grass with some form of opiate is not widespread in the sense that everyone ought to get paranoid, but it is common enough to merit caution when you have not grown your own and do not know the ultimate source. Of the opiate adulterants, the process by-product Passewa is most common, constituting probably 95% of the opiate adulteration which takes place. The tests for the other, more toxic opiate drugs are included here, then, as pieces of potentially useful information for a small group of people who might be unknowingly & unwillingly exposed to morphine, codeine, & heroin in the process of seeking out a little grass. As for people who are either willingly or knowingly involved with such drugs, there's not much this book can say or offer except to say good luck and I hope you make it.

Opiate adulteration is common enough . . .

Portions of this chapter have appeared in a different form in The Cultivator's Handbook of Marijuana © 1970 by Bill Drake.

A Fable (No 3) — *Smokestack El Ropo*

He made a
pleasant living
from his trade . .
Illustration by
Bob Kingsbury

Once upon a time, there lived a trafficker in contraband whose name was Zig, and he was very quick. Seven seventh sons of seventh sons might have more magic, but Zig would surpass them in wits.

He made a pleasant living from his trade, for he never had to hoe a furrow or lift an axe to his shoulders. Instead, he had a little house, some space from town in the wild, and thence from time to time by devious routes he would undertake to exchange goods for goods.

Now one time two officers had suspicions of him and determined to put him in jail. So they went to his house early in the morning and surrounded it. The first of them was skinny and slow-witted, and the second was fat and mean. The skinny one came in through the front door and the fat one through the back; and there was Zig, in the middle of his wares, lighting a pipe. What could he do? He gave up.

They ransacked his house, pulling contraband from every corner (but they were not as clever as Zig, and there was a lot they didn't find). At length they had a pile as tall as a man in the center of Zig's floor. Now Zig had noticed that they had come on horseback, without a cart, so he said this:

"Officers, I observe you have no provision for taking this contraband back to town. May I suggest that it all be piled up outside, to make it easier for you to collect when you come back?"

"He's right," said the skinny one, "that would make it easier to collect." But the fat one, observing Zig's many smiles and ingratiating gestures, scratched his chin and said, "Why should we?"

At this, Zig said, "You're probably right, leave it inside. After all, it looks like rain."

"Looks like rain, he's right," said the skinny one, nodding. But the fat one was now very suspicious. He said, "Listen to him, he wants us to make it easy for his accomplices to steal it away while we're gone. The wickedness will spread through the community, and probably they will raise money by selling it and spring him from jail."

Just at that moment, Zig kicked something under the table. The skinny officer got on hands and knees to see what it was, and behold, it was equipment for making fire.

"Aha!" cried the fat one. "You have not succeeded in hiding this from us. We shall burn this store of contraband into nothingness, first saving out enough evidence to put you in jail to rot forever." And they moved the whole pile out to a clearing, so as not to burn the trees, and set fire to it.

Now Zig engaged them in light conversation and gradually the three of them were moving further and further toward the downwind side of the fire. As it was a cold day, the officers made no objection to the warm smoke. When they began laughing and pointing at one another, Zig stole their horses and made good his escape.

He turned his trail to the south, until he came to a town where he was not known. There he sold the two horses to raise some money, and he walked through the streets wondering what to do next. As he was a stranger, some local officers stopped him to ask questions, and soon they found contraband in his pockets. He was taken to court.

When Zig appeared before the judge, he was wringing his hands and making many contrite glances heavenwards. This is what he said to the judge:

"Your honor, I am glad I was caught. I had always known it would happen. Indeed, the sinner knows a thousand deaths of fear each day, and there is no one more debased than I. But let me tell my story before you pass sentence; sordid though it may be, perhaps it will save some other from my wretched fate.

"Until a short time ago, I was a student. At school, I fell in with a questionable crowd, and soon my studies lost interest for me; I became aimless, confused. From a bad crowd I fell in with a worse, and these were people who would not shrink

Zig stole their horses and made good his escape.

from the most degraded of vices — and soon enough, I became one of them! Just last night, I bought this sack of contraband" — and here Zig dabbed at his eyes — "for 25 pieces of money."

At this the judge picked up his ears, for it was common knowledge that such a sack was worth no more than ten pieces of money, and even the highest quality could only fetch 15. The judge smiled to himself, and said:

"My son, I see that your contrition is sincere: Take heed that you learn these lessons well. The court finds itself willing to overlook your crime, if you will tell us who sold you this bag."

"I do not know their names," said Zig, "but nothing would make me happier than to lead you to where they made their sale." And they rode forth in the direction of Zig's house.

When they came to a clearing in the woods, they found the two officers, fast asleep beside the remains of a fire. Zig rose in his stirrups and cried out:

"O shame! O horror! This morning they appear in the uniforms of officers! Must this age continually surpass itself in vileness? See how they lie in a stupor after their corrupt indulgence!" And indeed, the smell of smoke hung heavy in the woods.

The sleeping officers were searched, and behold, their pockets contained enough contraband to put them in jail to rot forever. When the officials of the town heard of Zig's help in making the arrest, they were moved to settle a huge reward upon him. But what he did with that reward is another story.

Illustration by Dian Aziza Ooka

—*from Rolling Stone, May 28, 1970.* 227

Fly Free — *George Andrews*

Drugs are like rocket fuel. If you use them right, you can travel very far very fast. But if you make a mistake in handling these highly explosive substances, they blow up in your face. I can't lay down any rules. I can say how I've stayed high night and day for over 22 years, out of my skull around the clock on the strongest charge in town, and am in better health now than when I started.

The high is much more complete if one is in good health. When the body's tensions are in balance because you are living out your impulses, the whole system resonates in tune and then this is amplified to infinity. Any lack of balance to start with is reflected back at one as a wrathful deity at the level when one is high enough to hallucinate and unconscious internal states are being projected on the screen of consciousness as waking dream visions which are hieroglyphic symbols with specific meanings to be deciphered.

If the system is not in balance to start with, so much rocket fuel must be spent balancing out tensions that you don't travel very far and the experience is less complete. Be aware of body signals. Recognise intuitive signs to stop or go when they first appear. Signals become confused when repeated. Don't overload the system. I never inject anything, never use leapers or sleepers. I've seen speed kill. Once a year I spend a night sniffing cocaine or smoking opium or drinking alcohol. Opium is the friendly tiger. Keep in mind that if you make the mistake of visiting him too often you are going to be eaten alive. Opium is a substance to be approached rarely and with reverence or not at all. I've seen too many of my friends

The good high and good health

Pan is Alive

228

eaten slowly from within by the friendly tiger to want to make the trip more often than once a year myself. Cocaine is so concentrated that it is a shock for the nervous system to absorb, and repeated shocks may shatter it altogether. I should like to try chewing coca leaf as the Indians do, perhaps that way it could be absorbed without damaging the health. I find it useful sometimes for precision work when I want to get everything very clearly into focus, but don't like feeling as if someone had punched me in the face all the next day, so hardly ever use it. I drop acid or one of the other hallucinogens about every ten days.

When smoking hash and grass my sign to stop is when a heavy dull feeling replaces the light elated feeling. Then I go to sleep for a while before smoking again. Much of the mediocre quality stuff being sold only gives the heavy dull feeling without the euphoria: it doesn't really get you high, it just stones you out. So don't accept mediocre merchandise, keep looking until you find the real thing. The best quality gets you very much higher with a smaller quantity. You know that this is what you have been looking for when you take three puffs and the joint goes out and you forget to re-light it. Such quality is so rare as to be practically priceless. Operating within the range of qualities normally available, if one whole cigarette doesn't get me high, I figure it's not worth smoking. Smoke only good quality if you want to smoke a lot for a long time without trouble. It is better to go without a smoke than to smoke something that doesn't really get you high. Take care of your lungs, you only have one pair, so offer them the best available and let them tell you when they've had enough for the time being.

I prefer to smoke it pure. Mixing it with tobacco dilutes and coarsens the effect. People say that a joint made out of pure hash won't burn, but here is how I do it. Heating the hash reduces it to powder, and a cigarette made of powder is difficult to draw on. Tiny chunks and thin shavings are what is required, so patiently break it up with finger-nails or a knife. Then put a thin trickle of it into a single cigarette paper, roll it up, and light it. It is sometimes difficult to get going, but once it gets going it really works. If the joint keeps going out too often, a little basil or sage or peppermint or any aromatic herb can be added to the cigarette, just enough to make it burn but not so much as to drown out the hashish.

Of course the best way is to have both very good hash and very good grass, clean the grass carefully removing all seeds, break up the hash, mix them in equal quantities, and roll into thin joints. It is interesting to make marriages between different parts of the world this way: mix some Acapulco gold with some hash from the Himalayas, or some Congo bush with some hash that grew under the cedars of Lebanon. The varieties and combinations are endless as are the states of mind to be explored. It is up to us to imagine ideal reality into being.

—from *Friends*, November, 1970

229

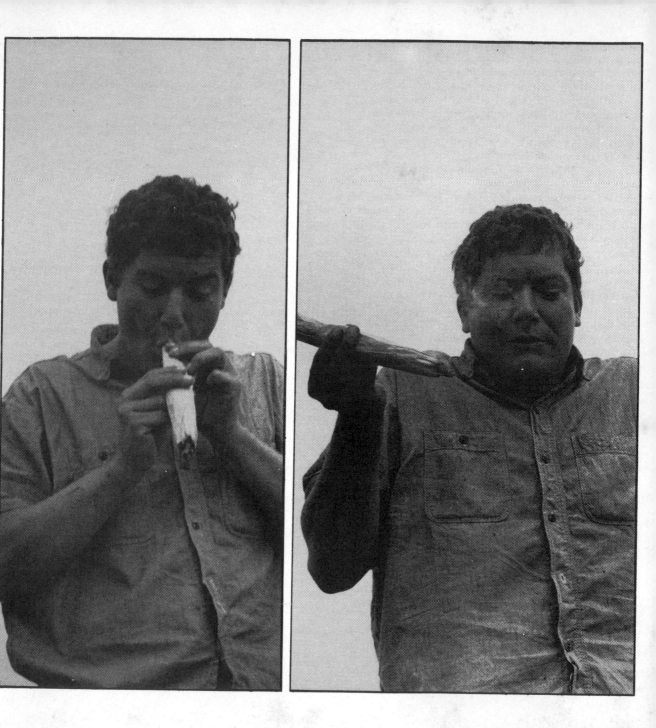

Photographs:
Bill Brach

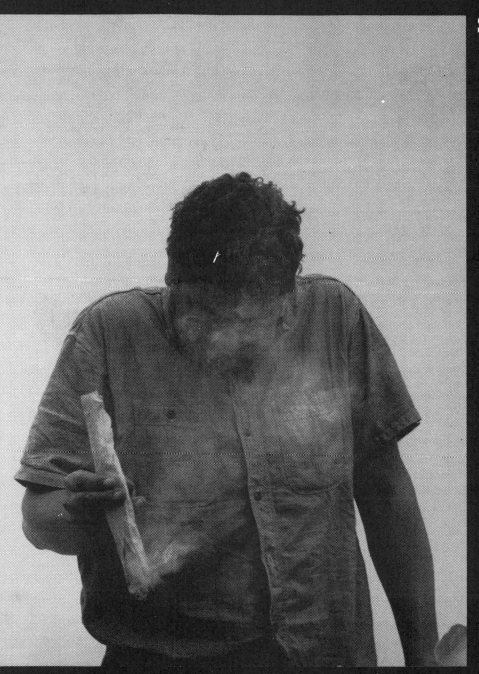

Cooking with grass is a time-honored culinary endeavor which permits the unimaginative cook to reach heights of achievement undreamed of with parsley, sage, rosemary or thyme. Cannabis should not be thought of as a spice or, even, as an herb in the sense of garnishment. More properly, Cannabis Sativa is a versatile essence which properly belongs with the aromatic oils & resins of your condiment repertoire, along with the spice extracts, the essences of fruit rinds and the bruised fresh flowering plants which impart distinctive, yet complimentary auras to your preparations.

Since Cannabis is never available in prepared form for the gourmet cooks of America & Europe, some of the elementary principles of Cannabis cuisine want explication.

Of primary importance is the medium. The sad fact of life is that the resin which carries the active & inert principles of Cannabis is not water-soluble in the slightest. This means that if your recipe anticipates penetration of the essence of Cannabis into the body of the dish, you must first place the resin into solution. Fortunately, Cannabis resin & oil is eminently soluble in alcohol & the great variety of fats which share a similarity of molecular structure with alcohol, fats such as butter & vegetable oils in general. Animal fats may also be utilized from the dripping pan to produce an exquisite gravy. Avoid water at all costs, however, unless you are not interested in permeating your dish with the essence, but rather with simply dispersing the particles over the superficial surfaces. This would imply, of course, that the beverages which are mostly water — wines, beer and so forth, are very inefficient solutes for Cannabis. The ideal is grain alcohol, and once you have achieved a solution with the grain, the liquid may then be added to any other medium you desire — wines, beers, sauces.

A second principle which the careful cook will do well to note is the temperature at which the potency of Cannabis begins to deteriorate. It should come as no great surprise that the critical temperature is 98.6° Fahrenheit & that prolonged exposure to greater degrees of heat will bring about expiration of the active principle. This doesn't mean that all recipes calling for greater heat must be rejected, merely that caution & a small, simple formula should be observed. Temperatures up to 150° Farenheit which last no longer than 30 minutes may be employed with impunity. Beyond that, you should increase your original measure of Cannabis by 10% for each 15 minutes or 50° F, or both, in excess of this demarcation. This general rule will allow your potage to retain its original zing even after attrition of the active principles from heat or exposure.

A third principle which one would do well to observe really has little to do with preparation, but rather with effect. Recall that ingestion of Cannabis by way of the stomach has a remarkably and, often, horrifically different impact on the mental & physical processes than that produced by smoking the killer weed. Use judgment. There's no percentage in getting your guests so stoned on the hors d'oeuvres that they can't appreciate the piece de resistance.

The basic recipes for Cannabis cookery come to us from Mother India. These recipes, while delicious & different, are not so much cuisine as an admirable series of disguises for what some consider to be the disagreeable taste & odor of grass. There are many variations on each of these preparations, so the adventurous may feel free to experiment.

Cannabis Sativa —
a versatile
essence of
distinction

233

Bhang:

a refreshing drink for hot summer days

Ganja	½ ounce
Poppy seeds	¼ ounce
Pepper	¼ ounce
Dry Ginger	⅛ ounce
Caraway seeds	pinch
Cloves	pinch
Cinnamon	pinch
Cucumber seeds	¼ ounce
Cardamom	pinch
Almonds	6 medium
Nutmeg	pinch
Rose	1 fully developed including hip*
Sugar	8 ounces
Milk	20 ounces

Begin by bringing ten ounces of water to a rolling boil and remove from heat. Add the ganja to the water after removal and let soak for five minutes. The ganja should then be kneaded vigorously in the still-hot water for several minutes to transfer some of the flavor to the liquid — the ganja is then taken out, drained and the water set aside. Remove any stalks or seeds at this point. Place the ganja on a grinding board or pestle and reduce to a pulp, adding milk gradually along with the mixture of all other ingredients, except the poppy seeds, cucumber seeds & sugar which are kept separate. When all of the ingredients are mixed into the paste, set aside. Repeat the process with the poppy & cucumber seeds, adding milk as needed. When all the seeds have been ground to a paste, set aside. You should still have most of your milk left. Add the two paste balls to the remaining milk, mix well, and strain through fine muslin. Throw away the filtered substance. Add the sugar, stirring until it is dissolved. Strain again through fine muslin, throwing away the residue. Add milk to obtain a consistency which suits your taste, flavoring with the original water if desired. Place the mixture in a cool place and, when chilled, serve in 4 ounce portions preferably before meals. You may if you wish substitute water for milk in the final solution, but must still grind with milk. Buttermilk makes for a heavier but more sensuous drink. In some circles a strong, moist cheese is ground into the first paste for additional body.

Rose: Wild Briar; under Jupiter. Strengthens the heart, the stomach and liver; Stays the running of the reins (gonorrhoea); cleanses the body from choler and phlegm.

*When cooking with roses it is a good idea to pluck the petals and snip off the white areas at their base. This part of the petal contains a very bitter subtance, but hips are an excellent source of vitamin C.

Majun:

a delicacy often served as a dessert or eaten in much the same way as you would snack on cake or candy

Ganja	2 ounces
Cloves	2 pinches
Caraway seeds	¾ ounce
Poppy seeds	1¼ ounce
Cinnamon	½ ounce
Crude Brown Sugar	1 pound
Butter	1 ounce

Blend ganja & butter and let stand for several hours. Place the crude sugar in a skillet and stir in water slowly until the sugar is dissolved in its thickest form. Place the skillet on heat and cook slowly to the thread stage, about 230° F. Add all ingredients except ganja & butter, and continue to cook to the hard crack stage, about 300° F. Remove from heat and blend in ganja-butter along with 1 teaspoon soda. You may add your favorite nutmeats at this point. Pour the rapidly cooling mixture on to a greased surface, preferably marble, and begin turning and stretching it at once until it forms a thin sheet. Allow to cool thoroughly and break into chunks. Peanut brittle was never like this!

Poppy: Red Horned; under the Sun. An aperitif and cleanser; for jaundice, scurvy and sore eyes.

235

Alwa:

a sweet-spice confection which is a favorite of children.
It will keep for a long time, so the portions are rather large. Modify for your own purposes.

Ganja	½ ounce
Nutmeg	1 ounce
Cardamom	¼ ounce
Cloves	¼ ounce
Caraway seeds	½ ounce
Cinnamon	½ ounce
Sandal	½ ounce
Anise seed	½ ounce
Rose Petals	1½ ounces
Honey	1½ ounces
Dry Figs	½ ounce
Sugar	12 ounces
Almond	12 ounces
Saffron	pinch
Butter	1 ounce

To prepare, place the ganja in 5 ounces of cold water and heat over high flame for 15 minutes. Strain out the ganja and squeeze out excess water. Set water aside. Remove seeds & stalks from the ganja. Place ganja in the butter & a pan and heat over low flame for 30 minutes. Strain and throw away the vegetable residue. Add the sugar to the 5 ounces water and boil until it becomes a thick syrup. Grind the poppy seeds, figs, almonds & rose petals and place in the syrup mixing well. Grind all other ingredients except honey and bring all ingredients together in a bowl. Mix well. Add honey and mix again. Chill until firm. Serve in small portions the size of a marble.

Fig: under
Jupiter.
For coughs,
hoarseness,
shortness of
breath, all dis-
eases of breast &
lungs, dropsy and
falling sickness.

Churun:

more of a meal than a confection

Ganja	1½ ounces
Graham crackers (crushed fine)	3 ounces
Poppy Seed	¼ ounce
Cinnamon	¼ ounce
Clove	¼ ounce
Pepper	¼ ounce
Almond	¼ ounce
Ginger	¼ ounce
Dry Coconut	1½ ounces
Fried Brown Rice	1½ ounces
Cooked Brown Rice	1½ ounces
Caraway seed	¼ ounce
Sugar	3 ounces
Butter	3 ounces

Mix ganja & butter in a pan, heat slowly for thirty minutes. Strain and reject the sediment. Set aside coconut & sugar and mix all other ingredients together in a skillet, frying them until crisp. Remove from skillet, and grind to a fine powder. Add the butter-ganja sauce to the sugar and mix well. Chop the coconut very fine and add to the sauce. Stir all ingredients together in a bowl. Chill and serve.

Curry Powder:

I'll presume that you enjoy hot curries, and offer this recipe for your experiment with pleasure.

Ganja	1 ounce (cleaned)
Coriander	2 ounces
Tumeric	2 ounces
Fenugreek	2 ounces
Black Pepper	2 ounces
Dill	1 ounce
Cumin seed	2 ounces
Poppy seeds	1½ ounces
Cardamom seed	1½ ounces
Mustard seed	½ ounce
Ginger	½ ounce
Chile peppers (dry, red)	2 ounces
Cinnamon	1 ounce
Cloves	½ ounce
Butter	4 ounces

Many people think of curry as a ready-made spice which sits on the shelf until it is called for in a recipe. In fact the best curry cooking is done with a freshly made curry powder, ground the day of its intended use.

Place the seeds and the powders in separate bowls holding ganja aside. Grind the seeds to a fine powder and strain to remove husks. Add to the rest of the powders. Heat butter until melted, grind and add ganja. Cook over low heat for a half an hour. Strain & reject residue. Add other ingredients and cook over low heat for several hours. Be sure to experiment with other ingredients if your palate isn't fully satisfied with this particular combination.

Fenugreek: under Mercury. Softens the wastes and hardness of the spleen and bowels

Rather than going on and on with some of my own favorite recipes which include Cannabis, I'll simply leave it at this collection of genuine Indian preparations. Cannabis, very simply, can be used in any dish where it happens to suit your taste. Merely keep in mind the principles of such cooking, which are important to your successful use of Cannabis in any dish, and let your imagination wing it.

Poisonous Water Hemlock, *Cicuta Virosa*, and Thick Water Hemlock, are but accidental variations which situation and soil naturally produce, they are thought to be poisonous, but there is nothing certain on this head.

HEMP.—(*Cannabis Sativa.*)

Descrip.—The stalks grow to five or six feet high, angular, covered with a strong tough bark : and clothed with many digitated or fingered leaves, each leaf composed of five, six, or seven parts, long and narrow, sharp-pointed, and serrated about the edges, the middlemost being longest, set together upon one long footstalk ; they are green above, hoary underneath, and rough in handling. The flowers grow toward the tops of the stalks, in that they call the male, in small and staminous bunches, which perish without bringing any seed ; that being produced by the female only, without any previous flowers.

Place.—It is cultivated in many counties.

Time.—It is sown at the end of March, or beginning of April ; and is ripe in August or September.

Government and Virtues.—It is a plant of Saturn. The seed expels wind, and too much use of it dries up the seed for procreation ; yet being boiled in milk, and taken, helps such as have a hot or dry cough. The emulsion of the seed is good for the jaundice, if there be ague accompanying it, for it opens obstructions of the gall, and causes digestion of choler. The emulsion or decoction of the seed stays the lax and continual fluxes, eases the colic, and allays the troublesome humours of the bowels, it also stays bleeding at the mouth, nose, or other places. It is good to kill worms in man or beast ; and the juice dropped into the ears kills worms in them, and draws forth earwigs or other living creatures. The decoction of the root allays inflammations of the head, or any other parts ; the herb or the distilled water of it, does the same. The decoction of the root eases the pains of the gout, the hard humours of knots in the joints, the pains and shrinkings of the sinews, and the pains of the hips. The fresh root mixed with a little oil and butter, is good for burns.

HENBANE (COMMON.)—(*Hyoscyamus Niger.*)

Descrip.—Our Common Henbane has very large, thick, soft, woolly leaves, lying on the ground, much cut in, or torn on the edges, of a dark, ill greyish green colour ;

WAIT!

YOU'LL GET NO MORE SPIRITUAL ADVICE FROM DIS HOLYMAN! AS A GURU I'M THROUGH! GOOM BYE!

R. Crumb

Smoking marihuana can ruin mental health and soundness of mind. Is that what you want?

Seven: Further reading

indications are the official probe will barely touch the surface of the deeply rooted involvement of many Detroit policemen of virtually every rank. The investigation is being conducted by the Wayne County prosecutor and he, after all, is part of an administration that to date has passed the buck or dismissed the allegations as trivial.

Yet, interviews with heroin pushers in the ghetto tell a different story.

"The vice squad," one 18-year-old pusher told this reporter, "knocked on the door and I had to let them in. I had a houseful of people and they were shootin' up, snortin'. They (the police) took me into the back room and said if I didn't pay them off they would bust me."

Another young heroin dealer told this story:

"The police kicked my door down and a lot of people were sitting around using and I was using also. So they asked who was the owner of the house. To keep everyone else out of trouble, I spoke up and said I was the owner. They called me into a room and asked me how much business I was doing. I told him I was only doing a small business, enough to support my own habit and (the habits of) my two girls. He (the lead cop) informed me that if I didn't pay him $200 they haven't been heard about in the newspapers at all. But I read in the newspapers about one white guy overdosing out in Grosse Pointe (a well-to-do lily white suburb) and dig, they're willing to stop all drugs. "I mean, why don't they do it when all these black people are down here in the morgue from overdoses of drugs? Why?"

In the past, Detroit's top public officials denied that heroin ever touched the hands of their police. But, today, Mayor Roman Gribbs seems to be passing the buck and Police Commissioner John Nichols appears to be preparing the city for a predictable blow to its image.

Gribbs: "I suppose when you have 5,000 men (on the police force) one or two or whatever number may succumb to a temptation from time to time. There are great profits in the trafficking of drugs and it requires great vigilance on the part of everyone and vigilance on the part of the police to clean their own house."

Nichols: "We would all be naive and somewhat unrealistic if we did not recognize the possibility of internal involvement.

"As honey attracts the insects who feast upon honey, so money attracts those people who feast upon money.

"I don't think we can say without fear of contradiction that because an individual puts on a badge he automatically ascribes to all the puritanical attributes that we hope he would."

A former pusher was asked, "Could you have operated without police help?"

"Man," said the ex-dealer. "Are you serious?"

This bibliography is intended to serve as a guide for more detailed reading in the subjects discussed in this book. Readers who are mainly interested in reading on the contemporary drug scene won't find much, but those turned on to a historic view will probably find many of the references cited pretty interesting.

Code for the bibliography:

* * - not reviewed
* ** - reviewed and found wanting
* *** - of interest and value
* **** - essential for cultivators and grass freaks

AMERIKA'S ONLY HOPE IS FACED WITH A DECISION!!

(1) Annual Report; Central Narcotics Intelligence Bureau, Government Press, Cairo, years 1929, 1930, 1931, 1932, 1933, 1934, 1935, 1936, 1937.***

(2) E Anson; (in) *Journal of the Dublany Agricultural Experimental Station*, Vol II, No 2, 1913; pp 50-68.**

(3) Attice, J; *A Case of Poisoning by Cannabis Indica*, British Medical Journal, London, 1896; p 948.**

(4) Arutinyantz, SM; *Chemical Investigation of Indian Hemp*, St. Petersburg, 1881.*

(5) Auide, J; *Studies in Therapeutics; Cannabis Indica*, Therapeutics Gazette, Detroit, 1890; Vol 6, pp 523-526.***

(6) George Avery and Elizabeth Johnson; *Hormones and Horticulture*, New York, 1947; pp 282-300.****

(7) LH Bailey; *Cyclopedia of American Agriculture*, Vol II, London, 1907; pp 377-380.***

(8) Banal; *Note Sur Les Extraits de Cannabis Indica*, Montpelier Med, 1890; Vol 15, pp 461-465.***

(9) Battaglia, B; *Sul hascisch etsua azione nell' organismo umano*, Psichiatria, 1887; Naples, No 5, pp 1-38.****

(10) Beane, FD; *An experience with Cannabis Indica,* Buffalo Medicine and Science Journal, 1883-84; Vol 23, pp 445-451.***

(11) Benson, C MRAC; *Bulletin on the Cultivation and Manufacture of Ganja*, Madras, 1893.***

(12) Bentlif, PB; *A Case of Poisoning by Extract of Cannabis Indica*, Clinical Sketches, London, 1896.*

(13) Bertherand, E; *A propos de la prohibition due haschisch en Turquie*, Journal of Medicine and Pharmacy of Algeria, Algiers 1896.*

(14) Berthier; *Le Haschisch Administre comme hypnotique* Bulletin of the Society of Medical Practicioners, Paris, 1867.*

(15) Birch, E; *The Use of Indian Hemp in the Treatment of Chronic Chloral and Chronic Opium Poisoning*, Lancet, London, 1889.***

(16) Borthwick & Scolly; *Photoperiodic Responses in Hemp*; Botannical Gazette, 1954; Vol 116, p 14.***

(17) Brockman, HV Drake, Officiating Commissioner of Excise, Central Provinces; *On the Cultivation and Manufacture of Ganja in the Khandwa Tahsil of the Nimar District,* 1894.***

(18) Browne, EG; *A Chapter from the History of Cannabis Indica*, St Bartholomews Hospital Journal, London, 1896-97; Vol IV, pp 81-86.***

(19) Buchwald, A; *Veber Cannabis Praparate*, Breslau 1885.*

(20) Bureau of Plant Industry; *The Cultivation of Hemp in*

the United States, Cir No 57, 1910.***

(21) Burgess, AH; *Hops-Botany, Cultivation and Utilization*, New York, 1964.****

(22) Burroughs, H; *Le Chanvre Indien (Cannabis Indica)*, Lyons, St Etienne, 1896.*

(23) Campbell, JM, CIE; *On the Religion of Hemp*, Bombay, 1893.***

(24) Vera Charles and A Jenkins; *A Fungous Disease of Hemp*, USDA, Vol III, No 1, Oct, 1914; pp 81-85.***

(25) Christison, A; *On the Natural History, Action, and Uses of Indian Hemp*, Monthly Journal of the Medical Society, London & Edinburgh; 1851, Vol 13.***

(26) Comfort, L; *An Overdose of Cannabis Indica*, Milwaukee Journal 1895; Vol III, p 370.*

(27) Cook, AB; *Poisoning by Cannabis Indica; Two Drams of Herrings English Extract of Indian Hemp being taken without Suicidal Intent*, The American Practitioner, Louisville, Ky; 1884, Vol XXX, pp 25-30.**

(28) Cunningham, DD, FRS, CIE, Brigade-Surgeon-Lieutenant Colonel, *On the Nature of the Effects Accompanying the Continued Treatment of Animals with Hemp Drugs and with Dhatura*, Calcutta, 1893.***

(29) DeCourtive, E; *Haschish - Etude Historique et Physiologique* Paris, 1848.****

(30) Dewey, Lyster; *The Hemp Industry in the United States*, (in) USDA Yearbook, Vol 118, 1901, pp 541-555, illus.**

(31) Charles Dodge; *Cultivation of Hemp and Jute*, (in) Fiber Investigations No 8, USDA, 1898, pp 5-23.**

(32) Charles Dodge; *Culture of Hemp in Europe*, (in) Fiber Investigation No 11, USDA, 1898; pp 5-28.**

(33) Charles Dodge; *Fiber Investigations* No 9, USDA, 1897, pp 106-110.***

(34) Charles Dodge; *Hemp Culture* (in) USDA Yearbook, 1895, Vol 74, pp 215-22.***

(35) Charles Dodge; *The Hemp Industry in France* (in) Fiber Investigations No 1, USDA, 1892, pp 27-31; 64-74.**

(36) G D'Ippolito; (in) *State Agricultural Bulletin of Italy*, Vol 45, No 4, 1912; pp 302-320.***

(37) C D'Lima; *Indian Hemp Fiber* (in) Agricultural Journal of India, Vol II, No 1, 1916; pp 31-41.**

(38) Dudgeon, Dr HW, Director, Lunacy Provision; Staff Memo, Abbassia, Egypt, 1928.***

(39) JWT Duvel, *The Vitality and Germination of Seeds*, PhD Dissertation, Univ of Michigan, 1902.****

(40) Edes, RT; *Cannabis Indica*, Boston Medical & Scientific Journal, 1893.*

(41) Evans, JF, Surgeon-Captain; *Regarding Physiological Investigations Concerning Hemp Drugs*, Bengal 1894.***

(42) JV Eyre et al; (in) *Journal of the Royal Agricultural Society of England*, Vol 74, 1913; pp 127-172.**

(43) Fisher, H; *Case of Cannabis Poisoning*, Cincinnati Lancet-Clinic, 1896, Vol 37, p 405.**

(44) Fishlowitz, GG; *Poisoning by Cannabis Indica*, Medical Record, New York, 1896, Vol 50, p 280.**

(45) Fristedt, RF; *Hemp from a Medical View*, Upsala, 1869-70.*

(46) Robert Garner, *The Grafters Handbook*, New York, 1958.****

(47) W Garner and H Allard; *Effect of the Relative Length of Day and Night and Other Factors of the Environment of Growth and Reproduction in Plants* (in) Journal of Agricultural Research, USDA, Vol 18, 1928, pp 553-606.****

(48) W Garner and H Allard, *Flowering and Fruiting of Plants as Controlled by the Length of Day*, (in) USDA Yearbook, 1920, pp 377-400.****

(49) W Garner and H Allard, *Further Studies in Photoperiodism*, (in) Journal of Agricultural Research, USDA, 1923, pp 871-920, illustrated.****

(50) Geiser, M; *Poisoning by Cannabis Indica*, Medical Record, New York, 1896, Vol 50, p 519.*

(51) N Gill and K Vear, *Agricultural Botany*, London, 1958, pp 204-205.***

(52) Giraud, J; *L'art de faire varier les effects due hachich*, Encephale, Paris, 1881, pp 418-425.*

(53) Thomas Githens, *Drug Plants of Africa*, Philadelphia, 1949.***

(54) Gley, E, & Richet, C; *Notes Sur le hachich*, Bulletin of the Society of Psychology and Physiology, Paris, 1886, pp 1-13.**

(55) Godard, E; *Egypte et Palestine*, Paris, 1867, pp 343-357.***

(56) Robert Gould (ed); *Symposium of Gibberellins*, No 28, Advances in Chemistry Series, Washington, DC, 1961.***

(57) Grierson, GA, CIE; *References to the Hemp Plant in Sanskrit and Hindi Literature*, Howra, India, 1892.***

(58) Grimaux, E, *Du hachisch, ou chanvre indien*, Paris, 1865.*

(59) Hamaker, W; *A Case of Overdose of Cannabis Indica*,

"The effects of hemp drugs in this respect (increasing appetite and aiding digestion) may be to a certain extent comparable with those of tea. The most recent experiments [on the action of tea] is thus described by Dr Edward Smith: 'It increases the assimilation of food of both the flesh and heat-forming kind, and with abundance of food most promote nutrition, whilst in the absence of sufficient food it increases the waste of the body.'" — *Indian Hemp Drugs Commission Report*, Ch. X

Illustration:
Carl Lundgren,
*Tales from
the Ozone*,©
No 2, 1970

Therapeutics Gazette, Detroit, 1891, Vol 7, p 808.**

(60) Hare, H; *Clinical and Physiological Notes on the Action of Cannabis Indica*, Therapeutics Gazette, Detroit, 1887, Vol 3, pp 225-228.***

(61) G Havas, (cited in) *Agricultural Botany*, USDA, Vol 36, 1917.***

(62) Herman Hayward, *The Structure of Economic Plants*, New York, 1938, pp 214-245.****

(63) Alice Henkel, *Weeds Used in Medicine*, Bureau of Plant Industry, USDA, 1904, Farmers Bulletin No 188.***

(64) Alice Henkel, *Wild Medicinal Plants of the United Sates*, Bureau of Plant Industry, USDA, 1906, Bulletin No 89.**

(65) Heslop-Harrison; *Auxin and Sexuality in Cannabis Sativa*, 1956, Physiology of Plants, Vol 9, p 588.***

(66) Heslop-Harrison; *The Experimental Modification of Sex Expression in Flowering Plants*, Biological Reviews, 1957, Vol 32, p 38.***

(67) Heslop-Harrison; *The Sexuality of Flowers*, 1957, New Biology, Vol 23, p 9.****

(68) Heslop-Harrison; *Growth Substances and Flower Morphogenesis*, 1959, Journal of the Linnaen Society, London; Vol 56, p 269.*

(69) Heslop-Harrison; *The Modification of Sex Expression in Cannabis Sativa by Carbon Monoxide*; 1957, Proceedings of the Royal Society of Edinburgh (Sec B) Vol 66, p 424.****

(70) Heslop-Harrison; *Leaf-shape Changes Associated with Flowering and Sex Differentiation in Cannabis Sativa*; 1958, Proceedings of the Royal Irish Academy (Sec B) Vol 59, p 257.*

(71) Heslop-Harrison; *Effects of Gibberellic Acid on Flowering and the Secondary Sexual Difference in Stature in Cannabis Sativa*, 1961; Proc. of the Royal Academy (Sec B), Vol 61, p 219.*

(72) Heslop-Harrison & Woods; *Temperature - Induced Meristic and other Variation in Cannabis Sativa*; 1959; Journal of the Linnaen Society of London, Vol 55, p 290.*

(73) Heslop-Harrison; *Cannabis Sativa*; 1969 (in) Evan's *The Induction of Flowering*, Cornell Univ Press, pp 205-226.****

(74) Hirata, K, *Sex Determination in Hemp*, Journal of Genetics, Vol XIX, 1927-28, pp 65-79.***

(75) Hooper, David, Government Quinologist; *On the Results of Analysis of Hemp Drugs*, Madras, 1893.***

(76) Hungerford, M, *An Overdose of Haseesh*, Popular Science Monthly, New York, 1883-84, Vol 24, pp 509-515.**

(77) Ireland, T, *Insanity from the Abuse of Indian Hemp*, Alienist and Neurologist, St Louis, Mo., 1893, Vol XIV, pp 622-630.***

(78) L Johnson, *A Manual of the Medical Botany of North America*, New York, 1884, pp 245-46.***

(79) Jones, HL, *Note on Cannabis Indica as a Narcotic*, Practitioner, London, 1885, Vol XXXV; p 251.*

(80) LF Kebler, *Habit Forming Agents*, Farmers Bulletin No 393, Bureau of Plant Industry, USDA, pp 3-19.***

(81) Kelly, W, *Cannabis Indica*, British Medical Journal, London, 1883, p 1281.**

(82) RH Kirby, *Vegetable Fibers*, New York, 1963, pp 46-61.****

(83) Henry Kraemer, *Botany and Pharmacognesy*, Philadelphia, 1902, pp 226-227; 275; 351-353.***

(84) Lailler, A, *Therapeutique: du chanure indien*, Ann. Med.-Psychologie, Paris, 1890, Vol XII, pp 78-83.*

(85) Lallemand, CF, *Le Hachych*, Paris, 1843.****

(86) Lapin, L, *Ein Beitrag zur Kenntniss der Cannabis Indica*, 8, Jurjew, 1894.*

(87) Lees, MC, *Cannabis Sativa sen Indica: Indian Hemp*, British Medical Journal, London, 1888, Vol XI; pp 95-98.***

(88) MacKensie, S, *On Some Classes of Cases in which Indian Hemp is of Special Service*, Med. Weekly, Paris, 1894, Vol II p 457.***

(89) Marshall, CR, *The Active Principle of Indian Hemp*, Lancet, London, 1897, pp 235-239.***

(90) MaHinson, JB, *Cannabis Indica as an Anodyne and Hypnotic*, St Louis Medical and Scientific Journal, 1891, LXI, pp 265-71.*

(91) McPhee, Hugh, *The Influence of Environment on Sex in Hemp, Cannabis Sativa L*, (in) Journal of Agricultural Research, Vol XXVIII, No 11, USDA, 1924, pp 1067-1083.****

(92) Nelson, Clarence, *Growth Responses of Hemp to Differential Soil and Air Temperatures*, (in) Journal of Plant Physiology, 1936, pp 294-309, illustrated.****

(93) Oertel, TE, *Observations on the Effect of Cannabis Indica in Large Doses*, American Medical-Surgical Bulletin, New York, 1895, Vol 8, pp 365-68.***

(94) Oliver, J, *On the Action of Cannabis Indica*, British

Medical Journal, London, 1883.*

(95) O'Shaughnessy, WB, *On the Preparations of the Indian Hemp, Gunjah (Cannabis Indica), Their effects on the animal system in health, and their utility in treatment of tetanus and other convulsive disorders.* Calcutta, 1839*

(96) *Pot Art & Marijuana Reading Matter*; Stone Mountain, Apocrypha Press, Tucson, Arizona, 1971.***

(97) Prentiss, DW, *Case of intoxication from a comparatively small dose of Cannabis Indica*, Therapeutic Gazette, Detroit, 1892, Vol VIII, p 104.**

(98) Pritchard, F, *Change of Sex in Hemp*, (in) Journal of Heredity, Vol 7, 1916, pp 325-29.***

(99) Ramnek, G, (in) *Journal of Experimental Agronomy*, (USSR), Vol II, No 6, 1910, pp 865-66.*

(100) Renz, GA, *My Experiment with Cannabis Indica*, Northwestern Lancet, St Paul, Minn, 1885-86, Vol V, p 203.*

(101) Report of the Advisory Committee on Traffic in Opium and Dangerous Drugs; League of Nations, Geneva, January 1930.***

(102) Report of the Anti-Opium Advisory Commission; League of Nations, Geneva, 1928.***

(103) Report of the Conference for Limitation of Manufacture of Narcotics; League of Nations, Geneva, May 1931.***

(104) Report of the Indian Hemp Drugs Commission; Vols 1-7, Simla, 1894.***

(105) Report of the Indian Hemp Drugs Commission; Government Central Printing Office, Simla, 1893-4.***

(106) Report of the Indian Hemp Drugs Commission; John Kaplan ed, Thos Jefferson Publishing Company, Silver Springs, Mo, 1969.***

(107) Report of the Permanent Central Opium Board; League of Nations, August 1931.***

(108) Resolution of the People's Party of Turkey; (printed in) Hakimiyeti Milliye, December 26, 1932.***

(109) Reynolds, JR, *On the therapeutic uses and toxic effects of Cannabis Indica*, Lancet, London, 1890, p 637.**

(110) Richet, C, *Poisons of the intelligence: Hasheesh*, Popular Science Monthly, NY, 1878, pp 482-86.***

(111) Robertson, R, *Toxic symptoms from the Tincture of Indian Hemp in Official Doses*, Medical Times and Gazette, London, p 817-19.***

(112) Rochebrune, A, *Toxicologie Africaine*, Paris, 1897.**

(113) Rosevear, John, *Pot, A Handbook of Marijuana*, New York, 1967.**

(114) Ochse, Soule and Dijkman, *Tropical and Sub-Tropical Agriculture*, Vol 2, 1966, pp 1161-65.**

(115) Schaffner, J, *Complete Reversal of Sex in Hemp*, Science, Vol 50, 1919, pp 311-13.****

(116) Schaffner, J, *The Influence of Environment on Sexual Expression in Hemp*, (in) Botanical Gazette, 1921, pp 197-219.****

(117) Schaffner, J, *Influence of the relative length of daylight on the reversal of sex in hemp*, Ecology, 1923, Vol IV, pp 323-34.****

(118) Schaffner, J, *Rejuvenations in Hemp*, Ecology, 1927, pp 315-25.****

(119) Schaffner, J, *Further Experiments in Rejuvenation*, American Journal of Botany, Jan, 1928, pp 77-85.****

(120) Schaffner, J, *Sex Reversal and Photoperiodivity*, American Journal of Botany, June, 1931, pp 424-30.****

(121) Sinnott, Edmund, *Plant Morphogenesis*, New York, 1960, pp 221; 317; 399; 430.***

(122) Stockberger, WW, *Drug Plants Under Cultivation*, Farmers Bulletin No 663, Bureau of Plant Industry, USDA, 1915.***

(123) Stockberger, WW, (in) *Production of Drug-Plant Crops in the United States*, Bureau of Plant Industry, USDA Yearbook, 1917, pp 169-176.**

(124) Suckling, W, *On the Therapeutic Value of Indian Hemp*, British Medical Journal, London, 1891, p 12.**

(125) Talley, Paul, *Carbohydrate-Nitrogen Ratios with Respect to the Sexual Expression of Hemp*, (in) Journal of Plant Physiology, 1934, pp 731-748.****

(126) Sister Mary Etienne Tibeau, *Time Factor in Utilization of Mineral Nutrients by Hemp*, (in) Journal of Plant Physiology, 1933, pp 731-747.****

(127) Toth, L, *Grimault et Compagnie cigarettes indiennes au Cannabis Indica*, Budapest, 1881.*

(128) Tukey, HB, *Plant Regulators in Agriculture*, New York, 1954.***

(129) Van Der Veen, R, and Meijer, G, *Light and Plant Growth*, London, 1959, pp 41, 52, 65, 78-9, 83-92, 119-154.****

(130) Walsh, JHT, *Hemp Drugs and Insanity*, Journal of Mental Science, London, 1894, Vol XL, pp 21-36.*

(131) Warden and Waddeil, *The Active Principle of Indian Hemp*, Indian Medical Gazette, Calcutta, 1884, Vol XIX, pp 259, 354.**

Some
Ephemera

247

'Advertising
contributed for
the public good!
Why do *you* think
they call it dope?

(132) Warmke, H and H Davidson, *Polyploidy Investigations*
(in) Carnegie Institute of Washington Yearbook, No 41, 1941-
43.******

(133) Warmke, H, and H Davidson, *Polyploidy Investigations*
(in) Carnegie Institute of Washington Yearbook, No 42, 1941-
43.******

(134) Warmke, H and H Davidson, *Polyploidy Investigations,*
(in) Carnegie Institute of Washington Yearbook, No 43, 1943-
44.******

(135) Wood, HC, *On the Medical Activity of the Hemp Plant
as Grown in North America*, Proceedings of the American
Philosophical Society, Philadelphia, 1869, Vol XI, pp 227-
33.***

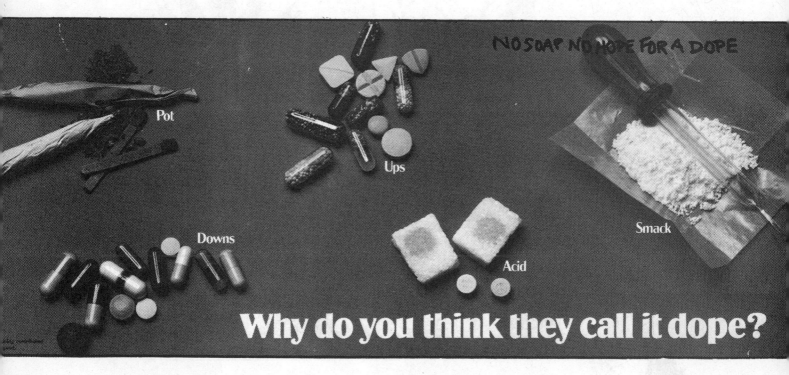

THE WHITE HOUSE   Dec.14,1970
(L-R) John INGERSOLL, Director Federal Bureau of Narcotics & Dangerous Drugs
PRESIDENT RICHARD M.NIXON   Matthew M.O'CONNOR   John BELLIZZI,Exec.Sec.INEOA

'I don't think we can say, without fear of contradiction, that because an individual puts on a badge he automatically ascribes to all the puritanical attributes that we hope he would.'

Report by the Advisory Committee on Drug Dependence

Dear Home Secretary,

I have much pleasure in sending you and your colleagues, the Secretary of State for Social Services and the Secretary of State for Scotland, the Report on Cannabis prepared by the Hallucinogens Sub-Committee of the Advisory Committee on Drug Dependence. The Report is submitted for consideration, with the complete endorsement of the Advisory Committee, subject to the minor reservations mentioned below.

Experience of cannabis within the United Kingdom has hitherto been too limited for comprehensive assessment. The Committee wish to pay tribute to the authors of the report for the many hours and painstaking study each contributed.

We think that the adverse effects which the consumption of cannabis in even small amounts may produce in some people should not be dismissed as insignificant. We have no doubt that the wider use of cannabis should not be encouraged. On the other hand, we think that the dangers of its use as commonly accepted in the past and the risk of progression to opiates have been overstated, and that the existing criminal sanctions intended to curb its use are unjustifiably severe.

The Sub-Committee's recommendations are clearly stated in paragraph 101 of the Report and fall into five main groups—research (recommendations (1) and (2)); recasting of the general drugs legislation (recommendation 3)); amendment of the existing law relating to cannabis (recommendations (4)–(9), (12)); synthetic cannabinols (recommendation (11)); and a review of police powers of search and arrest in relation to drug offences generally (recommendation 10)). In sum they represent a plea for the use of cannabis to be judged more realistically in our codes of law and social behaviour, in the light of our present understanding and pending the further studies that are necessary. These recommendations do not in any way run counter to the obligations to control cannabis assumed by H.M. Government as a Party to the Single Convention on Narcotic Drugs 1961.

The Advisory Committee has accepted recommendation (10) and intends to undertake as soon as possible a review of the present powers of arrest and search in relation to drug offences. We hope that you and your colleagues will feel able to accept the remaining recommendations and to initiate the appropriate legislative and other action that their implementation demands.

I should now mention reservations to the Report. Those made by individual members of the Sub-Committee need no elaboration on my part. Miss Murphy sympathises with the reservation made by Mr. Schofield to paragraphs 85 to 90 and regrets the proposal to retain imprisonment as a possible penalty for minor first offences. She suggests that on summary conviction unlawful possession, sale or supply of cannabis should be punishable in the case of a first offence with a fine not exceeding £100; and for any subsequent such conviction or any conviction on indictment the penalties should be those recommended by the Sub-Committee. The Committee is generally of the view that imprisonment is no longer an appropriate punishment for those who are unlawfully in possession of a small amount.

The Committee has carefully reviewed the problem of trafficking in the light of the reservations expressed by Mr. Brodie and Mr. Schofield. The dilemma is that a maximum penalty on indictment for unlawful possession which might be expected to deter a large-scale trafficker would have to be inordinately larger than the harmfulness of the drug itself would justify. The Sub-Committee felt that if possession with intent to use and possession with intent to supply could not be distinguished in law, the penalties for unlawful possession should be matched more obviously to the known harmfulness of the drug than to the potential profitability of large-scale professional trafficking. Dr. Bannister, Miss Hobkirk and Dr. Gibson wish fully to associate themselves with Mr. Brodie. Other members of the Advisory Committee would be disposed to favour a somewhat higher penalty on indictment than that proposed in paragraph 89 but do not consider that the matter can be determined without review of the corresponding penalties for other drugs; the majority of us endorse the recommendation of the Sub-Committee.

In conclusion, may I add that in the Advisory Committee's view general publication of the Sub-Committee's Report would make a valuable contribution towards a more informed understanding of the problem of cannabis. We earnestly recommend to you and your colleagues that the Report should be published as soon as possible.

Sir Edward Wayne,
M.D., Ph.D., D.Sc., F.R.C.P., F.R.C.P.(G.))
Chairman

The Rt. Hon. James Callaghan, M.P.

'Government reports may be the prelude to legal reform, but they are not a particularly good way of enlightening the judiciary,'— Mr Michael Schofield, member of the Advisory Committee on Drug Dependence, HM Government, UK.

'The leaves make a good snuff for deterging the brain; the juice of the leaves applied to the head as a wash removes dandruff and vermin; drops of the juice thrown into the ear allay pain and destroys worms and insects. It checks diarrhea, is useful in gonorrhea, restrains the seminal emissions, and is diuretic. The powder is recommended as an external application to fresh wounds and sores, and for causing granulations, a poultice of the boiled roots and leaves for dressing inflammations and cure of erysipelas, and for allaying neuralgic pains. The dried leaves, bruised and spread on a castor-oil leaf, cure hydrocele and swollen testes.'—"On the medical qualities of hemp," from the Makhzan-El-Adwiya, a Muslim medical source book of the 16th century.

Opposite: Photograph: Ted Benhari, *Good Times*, March 1971.

BOOK DESIGN JON GOODCHILD

Editorial Assistant: Micky Lapenta. Production:
Vickie Jackson, Dian Aziza Ooka, Marilyn
Gross, Tom Hardy, Kathy Burlingham,
Carol Wolleson, Brec Brown
Cosmic Giggle:
Alan Rinzler